COOKING WITH
CLYDE

FABULOUS FOOD WITH MY FELINE FRIEND

SUE CASSIDY

www.singingsuechef.com

www.singingsuechef.wordpress.com

Copyright © 2009 by Susan Welsh Cassidy | ISBN: 978-0-615-52961-5

Book & Cover Design by: www.sixhalfdozen.com

Testimonial - from Pat Cassidy

On our first date, when an event we had planned to attend was cancelled, I offered to take Sue out to dinner. Instead she volunteered to cook for us. I protested (mildly I confess) saying it would be too much work for her, after laboring all day at her extremely demanding job. Sue insisted that cooking for her was not work, but fun and relaxing.

That night I witnessed first-hand the joy that can be found when cooking is viewed as a fun activity rather than a chore. I sat in Sue's kitchen, a place filled with conversation, laughter, and scintillating aromas. Sue chopped, simmered and sautéed fresh ingredients in a seemingly effortless manner, paying equal attention to me and the meal preparation.

Sue had assured that she was aware of any strong food dislikes I had, and also things I especially enjoyed eating, and had prepared a menu using these guidelines. These actions alone made me feel special and appreciated.

After over 20 years of spending time with Sue in the kitchen, I have learned that the food experience is much more than just cooking and eating. If you are lucky enough to have Sue prepare a meal for you, you know that you are special. Countless times I have watched the appreciative faces of our friends as Sue served a delicious meal tailored especially for them. I continue to be amazed at how effortless it seems for Sue, even when she was working full time.

I have heard it said that the "joy of life lies in the journey and not the destination." This has always been true for Sue. Further, Sue has always believed one of the best ways she can show her caring for people is to cook for them. How lucky for me and for us that she feels this way!

table of contents

Love Italian Style

My Italian mother, Toni, taught me by her example from a very early age that "food is love." Toni always felt one of the best ways she could show how much she cared for her husband and children was to ensure they were fed meals that were nutritious as well as delicious. Feeding people gave my mother as much pleasure as it gave to those being fed, and the act of sharing food had a significance and expression way beyond just the serving of a simple meal.

It is no wonder that I became interested in cooking when I was quite young because my mother always made it look like fun to be in the kitchen preparing meals. She taught me many things about cooking procedures, but aside from the "how to" aspects of preparing food, I learned l'arte d'arrangiarsi – Italian for the ability to make something special and wonderful out of a few simple ingredients. This phrase can also refer to social gatherings, meaning the ability to get a few friends together and make it seem like a party. This was Toni's forte.

Boun Appetito & Mangia, Mangia!! Grazie mille, Toni – Ti amo always

Mamma Mia Toni

I mention in other sections of this book my mother's fanaticism for ingredients being very fresh and of the highest quality. Toni was also fanatical about one other thing related to food, specifically: its consumption. Toni's attitude about food has served me well all my life in terms of weight control, which is to eat anything you want, just not a lot of it. One of her most common expressions to me as I was growing up was, in different variations, "Go ahead, have another bowl of ice cream, if you don't care about being big as a house." Now I ask you, what is the reality of a person becoming as big as a house?

My mother's attitude about not overeating served her very well. In short, she was a knockout. She had a figure when she was in her 60s most women in their 30s would envy. Have you ever heard the saying if you are dating a woman and want to have an idea what she'll look like as she ages, take a look at her mother? If guys I dated in high school had really taken this to heart, I would have had to hire a social secretary to fit everyone into my schedule.

I said before that Toni knew how to make a very small gathering of people feel like a fête. She also entertained on a large scale, and those parties evoke some of my fondest childhood memories. At the beginning of the afternoon, marvelous aromas would begin to emanate from the kitchen. My mother and I are very much alike in that we both love company with us in the kitchen, but are not prone to allowing people to help much. I loved to sit and converse with her, and, as a bonus, witness her superior cooking techniques. My father would arrive home from his afternoon golf game, sniff appreciatively at the fabulous fragrances, and do his part -- which was to set up the bar. His contribution was significant, because he made terrific cocktails. His whiskey sour formula is a family favorite that we always serve over the Christmas holiday season. At some point my mother would go upstairs to get dressed, and my favorite part of the evening was to see her descending the staircase in her elegant cocktail dress, with the aroma of her perfume wafting delicately in her wake, portraying a physical exquisiteness that was almost, but not quite, matched by her inner beauty.

Having dedicated this cookbook to my mother, I naturally wanted to include a lot of recipes from "La Cucina de Toni." I did my best to provide a good representative sample of our family favorites, and they are as follows:

Cheesy Chicken	Eggplant Gratin	Potatoes Twice-Baked with Parmesan
Corn Pudding	Flank Steak, Marinated	Snickerdoodles
Crab Delight Dip	Green Beans Oriental	Stuffing for Poultry
Cranberry Waldorf Salad	Lemon Cheese Cake Pie	Tomatoes Provençal
Deviled Eggs with Olives	Pecan Cookies	Toni's Famous Spare Ribs

Much of my mother's cooking did not involve recipes. My mother had mastered making simple meals that only required extremely high quality ingredients, a sense of timing and a sense of how ingredients work well together. These ingredients frequently included butter and garlic. We were very big on butter and garlic in my home.

We live in a hurly-burly modern world, and sometimes we are moving so quickly that we do not take time to stop and enjoy the celebration of food. In my mother's memory and honor I have aspired to provide you with recipes that will ensure your table will be endowed with wonderful food. I hope you share your meals with people you love.

Mamma Mia – Sue

You may be wondering why Sue named her cookbook "Cooking with Clyde" when the dedication is to her mother. Well, the theme of her cookbook is really all about love – love of family, friends, and great food. Since this book is about love, naturally I would be featured prominently.

When you look at our relationship, I had Sue at "meow." When I went to live with Sue and Pat it was supposed to be a temporary arrangement (not worth going into the details as to why). After a couple days of me being in residence at Sue and Pat's home, I heard Sue sobbing to Pat that there was no way she was going to be able to give me up, and she convinced my caretaker (who traveled a great deal for his job) that I would be better off with her. Her powers of persuasion were phenomenal, because no one could relinquish me without some serious soul-searching and heart-wrenching second thoughts.

It was clear to me from the start that Sue gave to me the true definition of unconditional love. She is such an easy mark. When early on I scratched off the expensive wallpaper in her foyer, she said, "Well, I never liked that wallpaper much anyway." When I ripped through the upholstery on her modular sofa, she said, "I've been looking for an excuse to buy a new sofa." When I wake her up at 5AM out of a sound sleep, she says, "Are you hungry, my little angel?" You get the drift.

Toni, on the other hand, was a different story. Shortly after Sue adopted me, she took me to Toni's home for a weekend. I was a lot younger then with much more energy to burn; plus, I was a few pounds lighter – oh OK, more than a few. When I decided that one of the most fun things to do at Toni's home was to climb up her raw silk custom-made drapes, she had nowhere near the accepting attitude that Sue would have had. The bottom line is that I unfortunately never got to know Toni very well, because Sue decided that leaving me at home was preferable to her mother having a nervous breakdown.

I have digressed from where I started: to explain why this cookbook is appropriately named "Cooking with Clyde." Sue used to have a demanding job that kept her away from home from approximately 8AM until 7 or 8PM at night. But I have to hand it to her – she always made up for her absences by showering me with unremitting and constant love and attention the second she walked in the door. I know that some of my feline brothers and sisters think it's cool to punish their caretakers by being aloof when they have been left alone for a long period. I don't play those games. My attitude is, why waste time and energy copping an attitude when all I really want is to bask in the glow of that unadulterated and blissful affection?

When Sue decided to semi-retire about five years ago, one of the main reasons was so she would have more free time to spend with friends and family and, of course, with me. Also, for many years she had a goal and desire to write a cookbook, and now she finally had the time to do it. So why do I deserve to have the cookbook named after me? I'll tell you. Because I'm the one who has been by her side every step of the way. I'm the one who is in the kitchen with her every time she cooks, who plays with her and makes her laugh and dances with her, and assures that she does not get worn out with the major consumption of time it takes to test and re-test recipes.

OK, but to really get to the point – you have seen my picture, right? I mean, Toni is cool and beautiful and all that, but seriously: When it comes down to whether it's a better marketing strategy to have my picture on the cover versus Toni's picture, frankly it's no contest.

Clyde's Clips:

There are two kinds of people in the world: cat people and numbskulls.

"I definitely believe in the mystical, magical, healing power of a good home-cooked meal."

Oprah Winfrey, "The Oprah Magazine Cookbook"

Author's Note

I have been cooking for more than 40 years, and I have been reading *Gourmet* magazine during all the years I have been experimenting in the kitchen. So it is no surprise many of the recipes in my cookbook have been adapted from *Gourmet*. I have attempted to give credit for the origination of the recipes in my book where and when possible.

However, the majority of the recipes have been modified from the original version to the point that it would be difficult and often not possible to pinpoint exactly where I obtained the original source, usually many years ago. Also, many of the recipes are my own, and were not adapted from another source.

One of the many joys of spending time in the kitchen is the opportunity presented to be creative. This means that instead of robotically following recipes (including mine!), never be intimidated, and know that you may have a better idea. Have confidence your cooking skills are not necessarily inferior to those of a good cook who was motivated to write a cookbook.

Often people change recipes simply to suit tastes, dietary habits, or allergies. For examples, I have a friend who dislikes cilantro, and not being aware of this fact, once I made a dish that included cilantro as a main ingredient. As I noted her stealthily trying to eat around the cilantro leaves, she admitted she was not fond of this herb. She told me whenever she comes across a recipe containing cilantro, she substitutes fresh basil, and the result is always successful. The point of this anecdote is if you see a recipe and you find it appealing except for one or two ingredients, be creative and see what happens when you substitute an ingredient you prefer.

There is immense satisfaction when you experiment with recipes and make changes to put your own personal flourish on them. Being creative is one of the many things that will help to assure you will have fun, rather than equating time spent in the kitchen as a chore.

CATNIP – There is no substitute.

Appetizers

By definition, an appetizer is a beverage or food served prior to a meal to stimulate the appetite. Therefore, appetizers should not be so copious and filling that by the time the main event is served your guests are bursting at the seams, and appetites have not been stimulated but expunged.

I will freely admit that many times I have been guilty of overdoing it with appetizers, and have been saddened to find my guests too full to totally enjoy their meal. This has also happened to me frequently as a guest in the home of someone who is an excellent cook, when the appetizers are so scrumptious that I talk myself into believing that having one or two more bites/portions won't spoil my appetite.

If you don't have time to make an appetizer, there is nothing wrong, and a lot right, with the tried and true "cheese and crackers" routine, especially if you assure that the cheese is of especially high quality. When I go the cheese-and-crackers route, I frequently serve a bowl of assorted brine-cured olives on the side. Serving fresh vegetables with a dip is always a good option.

The bottom line is that most guests expect and desire some kind of appetizer prior to the meal, especially when cocktails are being served. A good rule of thumb is that if you are having a light meal, you can comfortably serve heartier appetizers, and conversely, a heavier meal would dictate less and lighter appetizers (that sentence may evoke a "duh" response).

The devil made me do it.

Testimonial

I am blessed to have a circle of supportive girlfriends who are beautiful - inside and out. As a bonus, many are wonderful cooks. We are so fortunate to be able to spend time together and share the events of our busy and full lives. Our get-togethers allow us to highlight our love for food, which often include picking a theme and each person brings a dish to share. Over the many years we've known each other, Sue has honed her already considerable cooking and entertaining skills on us. We've been both her "guinea pigs" and the biggest fans of every dish she prepares for us, always made with our individual tastes and likes/dislikes in mind. I will remember forever the fun evenings with Sue and my circle of girlfriends – eating, sharing, laughing, dancing, singing, crying, drinking, more eating, and enjoying every moment together.

Sue is the consummate hostess and an amazing cook. An invitation to her home is a promise of a warm, wonderful evening full of camaraderie and incredible food, prepared with the freshest ingredients and yielding the most amazing flavors. Every dish she serves is selected to please her guests and assure their dining experience is without parallel. Sue is truly one of a kind as a cook, hostess and friend!

Darla Robenolt
Systems Analyst (retired) by vocation, and "Foodie" by avocation
Greensboro, NC

Prosciutto & Parmesan Stuffed Mushrooms

Adapted from The Gourmet Cookbook (2004), Condé Nast Publications

INGREDIENTS

12 very large (about 2 inches wide) mushrooms

2 tbsp. olive oil

1 large clove garlic, finely chopped

¼ cup (generous) chopped shallots

⅓ cup finely chopped prosciutto (chop in a mini food processor)

3 tbsp. fine fresh bread crumbs (preferably whole-wheat bread)

1½ tbsp. minced fresh flat-leaf (Italian) parsley

½ cup grated Parmesan cheese

¼ tsp. salt

⅛ tsp. black pepper

PREPARATION

Lightly grease with butter a shallow baking dish large enough to hold the mushroom caps in one layer.

Cut tips of stems off of mushrooms and discard. Then remove stems from mushrooms and finely chop. Note: removing a stem from a mushroom is easy if you gently cut through the middle of the stem with a sharp knife – do not pierce the mushroom cap itself, just the stem. Once this cut has been made, it is easy to lift out the stem halves.

Heat one tbsp. of oil in a 10 to 12-inch heavy skillet over moderately low heat. Add the chopped mushroom stems, garlic and shallots and cook, stirring, until the stems and shallots are softened and very tender. Transfer to a bowl and add prosciutto, bread crumbs, parsley, all but 2 tbsp. of the ½ cup Parmesan cheese, salt and pepper, and stir to combine. Add remaining 1 tbsp. of olive oil and stir gently to incorporate olive oil into mixture.

Preheat oven to 400 degrees. Divide filling evenly among mushroom caps, mounding slightly. Arrange the caps in a single layer in the prepared baking dish. Sprinkle the mushrooms with the reserved 2 tbsp. of Parmesan cheese. Bake until the mushroom caps are tender, approx. 20 minutes.

Makes 12 appetizers

Superior Shrimp Appetizer

INGREDIENTS

½ tsp. salt

¼ tsp. pepper

2 tbsp. fresh lemon juice

3 cloves garlic, finely chopped

2 tbsp. mayonnaise

1 lb. medium shrimp, shelled and deveined

1 cup fine fresh bread crumbs (preferably whole wheat)

¾ tsp. dried basil

1½ tsp. dried parsley (or 3 tsp. fresh parsley, finely chopped)

¼ tsp. (generous) dried dill weed

4 tbsp. butter

2 tbsp. extra-virgin olive oil

PREPARATION

Mix salt, pepper, lemon juice, garlic and mayonnaise in a small bowl. Add the shrimp and stir to coat evenly with the marinade. Refrigerate the shrimp covered for 2–3 hours.

Process some bread in a mini-food processor to equal 1 cup. Add basil, parsley and dill weed to the processor and pulse briefly until herbs are combined with the bread crumbs. Place bread crumbs on a plate and set aside.

Preheat oven to 400 degrees. Remove shrimp from refrigerator. Dip each shrimp lightly in the bread crumbs on each side and place shrimp in a single layer in a shallow baking dish.

Place butter and olive oil in a small saucepan and heat over low heat just until the butter is melted. Add any marinade remaining in the bowl to the butter/olive oil mixture; stir to combine and pour evenly over the shrimp. Bake in preheated oven for 15 minutes. Put shrimp on a serving dish and serve with toothpicks. Serves 3–4

Note: This is also wonderful served as a main dish with rice. The above recipe serves 2 as a main dish.

Green Olive & Almond Tapenade

Adapted from The Gourmet Cookbook (2004), Condé Nast Publications

INGREDIENTS

1½ cups brine-cured large green olives, pitted

½ cup loosely packed finely chopped fresh parsley (flat-leaf)

¼ cup slivered almonds, toasted

2 tbsp. fresh lemon juice

⅓ cup extra-virgin olive oil

3 tbsp. mayonnaise

PREPARATION

Accompaniment/s: Toasted pita chips, crackers, raw veggies

In a mini-food processor, place the olives, parsley, toasted almonds and lemon juice. Pulse scraping down the sides occasionally until the mixture is finely chopped. With the motor running, add the olive oil in a steady stream, blending to form a paste. Add the mayonnaise and pulse just until combined. With a small spatula, remove tapenade from the processor and put in a small serving dish or bowl.

Serve with your choice of one or more of the above mentioned accompaniments.

Your turn for the remote?
I don't think so.

Darla

Darla (sadly) relocated from the D.C. area to Greensboro, N.C., some years ago. We have been close friends for over 30 years, which feels like forever. We have been there for each other during some of life's most difficult times, and have shared advice, wisdom and comfort.

It is no surprise that often the "comfort" component during times of stress comes in the form of food! Over the years we have cooked for each other, critiquing our less than stellar attempts, and praising our mutual successes. One of Darla's signature dishes is the one she contributed for my book. I know you will enjoy her –

Richmond, VA, 1987
You Make Me Smile!

Alexandria, VA, 1987

Blue Cheese Tart

INGREDIENTS

6 oz. cream cheese, softened to room temperature

4 oz. blue cheese, crumbled

2 tbsp. butter, softened to room temperature

¼ cup half and half

3 eggs

⅛ tsp. cayenne pepper

¼ tsp. salt

⅛ tsp. black pepper

1 tbsp. chopped fresh chives

Assorted fresh fruits for garnish

PREPARATION

Beat cream cheese in a medium sized bowl with an electric mixer (I use an immersion blender) until softened and creamy. Add the blue cheese and beat until blended.

Add the butter, half and half, eggs, cayenne, salt and pepper. Beat until smooth. Stir in the chopped chives.

Preheat the oven to 375 degrees. Lightly butter a baking dish of choice – fluted tart pan, quiche dish, pie plate, small jelly roll pan, as examples. Pour the cheese mixture into the pan and bake for 35–40 minutes, until the tart is very puffy and brown.

Remove from the oven and cool on a wire rack for at least 5 minutes. When ready to serve, cut the tart into small appetizer size pieces and arrange decoratively on a serving platter. Garnish the platter around the edges with fresh fruit of choice (my preferences are grapes and small melon balls or slices). This recipe is great served either warm or at room temperature. Serves 10–12

Note: Darla usually made this recipe with a pie crust, and I prefer this no-crust version. If you want to bake the tart in a pie crust, follow the recipe as above, except that instead of pouring the mixture into a lightly greased baking dish, you would line the baking dish with a thin layer of pie crust.

Buffalo Grilled Shrimp with Blue Cheese Dip

Adapted from Gourmet magazine, Condé Nast Publications

Blue Cheese Dip:

¼ cup sour cream

¼ cup mayonnaise

¼ cup finely chopped shallots

½ cup crumbled blue cheese

1½ tbsp. fresh lemon juice

1 tbsp. chopped fresh parsley (flat-leaf Italian)

1 tbsp. chopped fresh chives

¼ tsp. Herbamare® or salt

¼ tsp. ground white pepper

For Shrimp:

1½ lbs. medium shrimp, peeled and deveined

2 tbsp. extra-virgin olive oil

½ tsp. salt

½ tsp. black pepper

½ stick (4 tbsp.) unsalted butter, melted

2 tbsp. bottled hot sauce

Spray cooking oil (I like Spectrum Naturals® Organic Olive Spray Oil)

To accompany: fresh celery cut into 4-inch sticks

PREPARATION

Stir together all of the dip ingredients and refrigerate, covered, until needed.

Place shrimp in a bowl and toss with the olive oil, salt and pepper (better distribution if you do this with your hands).

Place the melted butter and hot sauce in a separate large bowl, mix together and set aside.

Place a large ridged grill frying pan on the stove over medium-high heat and spray generously with the cooking oil. Add the shrimp in a single layer and grill until just cooked through, which should take about 3–4 minutes per side. When shrimp are cooked, place in the bowl containing the butter and hot sauce. You should be able to cook all the shrimp in 2 batches. Stir shrimp with the butter mixture until evenly coated.

Serve shrimp warm with the blue cheese dip and celery sticks on the side. Serves 3–4

Pico De Gallo Dip

INGREDIENTS

1 cup coarsely chopped fresh tomato

¾ cup coarsely chopped fresh cilantro

⅓ cup finely chopped red onion

2 tbsp. canned diced green chiles, drained

1 generous tsp. white wine vinegar

8 oz. cream cheese, softened

1 tsp. salt

PREPARATION

Pulse all ingredients in a food processor until smooth. Scrape contents with a spatula into a serving bowl and chill covered for at least an hour before serving. Serve with tortilla chips and/or fresh vegetables. Makes approx. 2 cups

Warm Blue Cheese Dip

Every time I make this dish I am asked to fork over the recipe

INGREDIENTS

7 bacon slices

2 large garlic cloves, minced

8 oz. cream cheese, softened in a medium bowl

¼ cup milk

4 oz. blue cheese, crumbled

2 tbsp. (generous) chopped fresh chives

PREPARATION

Cook bacon in skillet over medium heat until crisp. Remove from skillet and remove as much fat as possible (see p. 153). Drain excess fat from skillet and return skillet to stove (there should be a very small residual amount of bacon fat remaining in the skillet – about 1 tsp.). Add minced garlic to skillet, and sauté over very low heat for about a minute and remove from heat.

Preheat oven to 350 degrees. With a small electric hand mixer, beat cream cheese until smooth. Add milk and beat until milk is all combined and incorporated into the cream cheese. Add blue cheese and beat about 5–10 seconds. The blue cheese should be not fully incorporated, meaning that before you added the blue cheese the mixture was perfectly smooth, and now it should look a bit lumpy. Remove as much of the mixture as possible from the mixer blades. Then stir in the bacon (crumbled), sautéed garlic, and chives.

Transfer the mixture to a small ovenproof baking dish and cover with foil. (Note: this can be prepared ahead. After covering with foil, refrigerate; before baking, bring to room temperature). Bake until thoroughly heated, approx. 30 minutes. Serve with crackers and/or assorted cut up fresh vegetables.

"There is no such thing as a little garlic"

Arthur Baer

Sausage-Stuffed Mushrooms

Adapted from The Silver Palate Cookbook, published by Workman Publishing Co., Inc.

INGREDIENTS

2 Italian sweet sausages (approx. ⅓ lb.)

¼ tsp. fennel seeds

⅛ tsp. red pepper flakes

½ cup chopped shallots

1 large garlic clove, minced

¼ cup chopped fresh parsley

¼ cup chopped black olives

⅓ cup Béchamel Sauce (see p. 165)

12 large white mushrooms

Salt for sprinkling on tops of mushrooms

Shaved Parmigiano Reggiano cheese for sprinkling on top

PREPARATION

Remove sausage meat from casings and crumble into a small skillet. Cook over moderate heat, stirring often and breaking up further, until meat is thoroughly done and in very small pieces. Stir in fennel and pepper flakes and with a slotted spoon, remove sausage to a plate lined with paper towels and set aside. Leave any rendered fat in the skillet.

Reduce the heat to low and add the shallots to the skillet. Cook the shallots, stirring frequently until softened and golden. Stir in the garlic and chopped parsley. Return the sausage meat to the skillet and mix to combine. Stir the olives and Béchamel into the sausage mixture and combine thoroughly. Remove from heat and set aside.

Clean mushrooms and pull off the stems gently. Arrange caps in a lightly oiled baking dish. Fill each cap generously with the sausage stuffing. Sprinkle the tops lightly with salt, and then sprinkle generously with shaved Parmigiano Reggiano cheese.

Preheat the oven to 450 degrees and bake the mushrooms in the middle of the oven for approx. 15 minutes, or until they are bubbling and well browned. Cool for 5 minutes before serving. Makes 12 appetizers

Tex-Mex Creamy Black Bean Dip

INGREDIENTS

1 can (14–15 oz.) black beans, rinsed and drained

1 cup sour cream

1 14½ oz. can diced tomatoes, drained

1 medium jalapeno chili pepper, seeded and finely chopped

1 tsp. cumin

1 tbsp. fresh lime juice

½ tsp. chili powder

1 tsp. Herbamare® or salt

1 tsp. black pepper

2 cups shredded Mexican Blend cheeses (e.g., a combination of Cheddar, Monterey Jack, Asadero and Queso Blanco) – if not available, you can use any one or more of these cheeses in any combination to equal 2 cups

Tortilla chips to accompany

PREPARATION

Preheat the oven to 325 degrees. Place the beans in a large bowl and process with a hand-held immersion blender until smooth but still lumpy. Stir in the sour cream, tomatoes, jalapeno, cumin, lime juice, chili powder, Herbamare® and pepper. Finally stir in 1 cup of the cheese.

Place the mixture in a shallow baking dish and top with the remaining cup of cheese. Bake the dip for 10–15 minutes, or until hot. Makes approx. 3 cups of dip

---

Salt & Herbamare®

(A. Vogel Herbamare® Original Organic Herb Seasoning Salt)

A lot of my recipes specify Herbamare® as an ingredient. I have used Herbamare® for a long time, and love it immensely as a salt alternative. Herbamare® has sea salt as an ingredient, and is not always acceptable in recipes as a substitute for salt and therefore if the recipe specifies salt, that's what should be used. If you choose not to use Herbamare® for whatever reason, then simply use salt (in the same proportionate amount) when making any recipe that specifies Herbamare®.

When using salt, I always use Kosher or Sea Salt. Normal salt is fine for any recipe, but here's why I prefer Sea Salt: the salt is dried naturally (using the wind and the sun) in "Salinas" (salt fields). The salt is unrefined and minimally processed, thereby retaining its natural goodness and wholesomeness. After all of the water has been evaporated from drying in the sun, the magnesium and iodide content is maximized, and the salt is slightly sweet and naturally snow white.

Goat Cheese, Olives, Lemon & Thyme

Adapted from Gourmet magazine, Condé Nast Publications

INGREDIENTS

½ to ¾ lb. assorted olives (get in refrigerated section – preferably packed in olive oil, wine vinegar, and seasonings)

6–8 fresh thyme sprigs

6 tbsp. extra-virgin olive oil

2 tsp. grated fresh lemon zest

¼ tsp. black pepper

1 10-oz. log of goat cheese (not seasoned)

Crackers to accompany

PREPARATION

Drain the olives, and place them along with the thyme, olive oil, lemon zest and pepper in a medium skillet over low heat, stirring gently occasionally, just until the mixture begins to simmer. Immediately remove from the heat and cool to room temperature.

Place the goat cheese on a serving dish and pour the cooled olive mixture over top, arranging the olives and the thyme sprigs decoratively on the sides of the goat cheese. This appetizer should be served at room temperature. Serves 6–8

Oven Barbequed Chicken Wings

INGREDIENTS

1½ lbs. chicken wings

1 tbsp. grapeseed oil

Herbamare® (or salt) and black pepper for sprinkling over wings

½ cup honey

¼ cup soy sauce

¼ cup dry red wine

1 large garlic clove, minced

1 tbsp. chili sauce

PREPARATION

Cut off small wing tips of each chicken wing and discard. Cut remaining wing into two parts (one of the parts will look like a baby drumstick). Place chicken, skin side up, in a baking dish large enough so that the wings are in one layer. Rub chicken wings with the oil, then sprinkle wings with Herbamare® (or salt) and black pepper.

Preheat oven to 375 degrees. Combine the remaining ingredients thoroughly and pour over the wings. Bake the wings, basting with the sauce occasionally, for an hour to an hour and a half, or until the chicken pieces are thoroughly cooked (they should have a blackened appearance) and the sauce is caramelized and syrupy. Serves 4

Honey Ginger Meatballs

Here's a great way to cut the cost of a wedding: a friend of mine requested (selectively) that in lieu of a wedding gift, attendees would provide food to be served at the reception. I was implored to bring these meatballs, and was assured my present was superior to a toaster oven.

INGREDIENTS

1½ lb. lean ground pork	1 tsp. salt	¼ cup soy sauce
1 large egg	2 tsp. Worcestershire sauce	¼ cup honey
1¼ cup finely processed fresh bread crumbs (whole wheat or white)	2 tbsp. dry vermouth	1 tbsp. finely grated fresh gingerroot
	3 large cloves garlic, minced	½ tsp. black pepper

PREPARATION

Preheat oven to 350 degrees. Combine all ingredients in a bowl. Form mixture into small balls, approx. 1 inch in diameter. Place on a non-stick baking pan and cook for 20 minutes. Serve hot or at room temperature.

Kristine

My wonderful and unique in all ways sister Kristine (also known as Krazy Krissie) resides in our hometown York, Pa., with her husband Loony Larry.

Like me, Kris continues to make many recipes we loved growing up that recall so many fond memories of Toni in her kitchen. We both know how fortunate we were to have had a mother who showed her love consistently by preparing fabulous food, and who encouraged us to view the kitchen as a place to have fun and create magic.

The recipe contributed by Kristine is:

Toni's 60th Birthday Party
York, PA, 1977

Toni's 80th Birthday Party
York, PA, 1997

Hot Spinach Dip
(Almost every time Kris makes this dip for company she is asked to fork over the recipe – truly a crowd pleaser!)

INGREDIENTS

Half of a large red bell pepper

2 10-oz. packages frozen chopped spinach, thawed and drained

2½ cups grated Parmesan cheese

½ cup finely chopped leeks (white part only), well rinsed and cleaned before chopping

2 large garlic cloves, minced

1½ cups mayonnaise

PREPARATION

Place red bell pepper on a broiler-proof pan and broil 6–8 inches from the heat with the oven door ajar for approx. 10–15 minutes, turning occasionally, until the pepper is blackened and softened. Remove from the oven and set aside until cool enough to handle.

Meanwhile, squeeze as much moisture as possible from the spinach (I use my hands) and transfer to a mixing bowl. Add the mayonnaise, Parmesan, leeks and garlic. Stir to combine ingredients thoroughly. Place in a pie plate or quiche style baking dish.

Remove any seeds and inner membranes from the pepper and peel off the blackened skin. Cut the pepper into thin strips lengthwise. Arrange the roasted pepper strips in a pinwheel design on top of the spinach mixture.

Preheat the oven to 350 degrees and bake the dip for approx. 15–20 minutes, or until heated through. Serves 6–8

Shrimp with Zesty Creamy Sauce

This is a nice change from serving shrimp with your basic "cocktail sauce," which is normally something along the lines of ketchup with some horseradish thrown in. Unless of course you make "Orange Tomato Cocktail Sauce" – (see p. 164)

INGREDIENTS

¼ cup mayonnaise

¼ cup sour cream

¼ tsp. Tabasco or other hot sauce

4 tbsp. chili sauce

2 tbsp. lemon juice

⅛ tsp. salt

1 tbsp. chopped capers

1 lb. cooked shrimp (steamed or sautéed) (See p. 178)

PREPARATION

Blend mayonnaise and sour cream together. Stir in the Tabasco/hot sauce. Add remaining ingredients (except for the shrimp) and mix thoroughly. Refrigerate until ready to serve with well-chilled shrimp.

You can serve this either by having the sauce in a small serving bowl for dipping, and arrange the chilled shrimp on a decorative platter, or if preferred, chop some salad greens of choice and arrange on 4 small serving dishes. Place shrimp on top of the greens and spoon a generous amount of the sauce over top.

Note: If you sauté the shrimp, here's what you do: Place 1 tbsp. of light cooking oil (e.g. sunflower or safflower) in a medium non-stick skillet and heat over moderate heat until hot. Add the shrimp (shelled and deveined) and cook for approx. 1½ minutes on one side (they will be pink on the cooked side), and then turn and cook for an additional 1½ minutes on the other side. The shrimp should feel firm to the touch. Pour shrimp from skillet onto a dish that is lined with paper towels and then pat with additional paper towels to remove any excess cooking oil. Serves 4

Marinated Lime Basil Shrimp

Adapted from Gourmet magazine, Condé Nast Publications

INGREDIENTS

½ cup fresh lime juice

¼ cup (generous) apricot jam or preserves

3 large garlic cloves, minced and mashed to a paste with 1 tsp. salt

½ cup fresh basil leaves (measure leaves first to ½ cup, and then chop finely)

3 tbsp. extra-virgin olive oil (plus 1 tsp.)

1 tbsp. soy sauce

½ tsp. dried hot red pepper flakes

1 lb. large shrimp, shelled and deveined

PREPARATION

In a small bowl, whisk together the lime juice, preserves, garlic paste, chopped basil, 3 tbsp. olive oil, soy sauce, and red pepper flakes. When well combined, measure ⅓ cup of the mixture and put in a small serving bowl, to be used for dipping.

Place the shelled and deveined shrimp in a large sealable plastic bag. Pour remaining sauce mixture into the bag and marinate the shrimp, chilled, tossing occasionally, for 1 to 2 hours.

Put a very small amount of olive oil (about 1 tsp.) in a large heavy non-stick skillet and heat over moderately high heat. Remove the shrimp from the bag with your hand and place into the heated skillet (some of the sauce will also end up in the skillet that clings to the shrimp). Cook the shrimp briefly, about 1 to 1½ minutes on each side, or until JUST cooked through. Remove shrimp from the skillet with a slotted spoon and put on a serving dish. Serve with toothpicks and dipping sauce on the side. Serves 3–4 as an appetizer. *Note: If desired, fresh cilantro leaves may be substituted for the basil.*

Brie with Sun-Dried Tomatoes & Garlic

Adapted from Gourmet Magazine, Condé Nast Publications

INGREDIENTS

1 lb. Brie (preferably soft Brie with rind removed)

2 tbsp. minced fresh Italian (flat-leaf) parsley

2 tbsp. grated Parmesan cheese

¼ cup finely chopped sun-dried tomatoes (packed in oil and drained)

2 tbsp. extra-virgin olive oil (if desired, use Basil Oil (olive oil infused with fresh Basil)

1 tbsp. minced fresh garlic (use garlic press)

1 tsp. dried basil

Crackers as an accompaniment

PREPARATION

If you purchased Brie with rind, remove the rind with a sharp knife and put the Brie on a serving plate. In a small bowl combine the parsley, Parmesan, sun-dried tomatoes, olive oil, garlic, and basil. Combine the mixture well and spread evenly over the Brie.

Let the Brie stand for 1 hour before serving. Serve with crackers. Serves 4–6

I have six-pack abs...They're hiding behind a keg.

Crab Delight Dip

(Another scrumptious and very easy recipe from the kitchen of Toni – its success depends on using very fresh, best quality (lump) crabmeat.)

INGREDIENTS

1 cup mayonnaise

½ cup sour cream

1 tbsp. finely chopped fresh parsley

1 tbsp. medium-dry sherry

1 tbsp. fresh lemon juice

½ tsp. Herbamare® or salt

¼ tsp. white pepper

1 lb. fresh lump crabmeat, gently but thoroughly picked over to remove ALL shells

Crackers to accompany

PREPARATION

Place all ingredients except for the crabmeat in a bowl and stir until well combined. Gently stir in the crabmeat, taking care to not break up the crab lumps/pieces any more than is necessary to thoroughly incorporate it.

Cover, place in the refrigerator and chill for at least 2 hours before serving. Serves 6–8

Garlic

Can you get too much of a good thing? Maybe. Can you put too much garlic in a recipe? Rarely. Any time I try a new recipe, whatever the amount of garlic indicated, my rule of thumb is normally to double it (at a minimum).

When I was a youngster and was just starting to get really interested in cooking, I made Eggplant Parmigiana for my parents and my aunt and uncle. I am half Italian, and my family never met a garlic clove they didn't love. The recipe called for one clove of garlic. Being very much of an apprentice cook, I thought that a clove meant a bulb. Consequently, I used a whole bulb of garlic (approx. 10 large cloves) instead of the one clove specified. Everyone raved about my meal except my Uncle Bob commented, "Honey, this is fabulous, but next time you may want to back off just a bit on the garlic." (Uncle Bob wasn't Italian). I retorted, "How can I back off? I only used one clove." It soon became clear that my knowledge of garlic terminology was faulty.

Other important tips when cooking with garlic:

1) Always use fresh garlic.

2) The garlic flavor will not be as pronounced when you use a garlic press as opposed to finely chopping the garlic with a sharp knife. However, there are some recipes that specify minced garlic instead of chopped garlic, which means using a garlic press, or in some cases a mini-food processor, as the preferred method.

3) Store garlic at room temperature in a container especially designed to hold garlic (there will be holes for adequate ventilation). Attractive garlic holders are available in kitchen specialty shops and can enhance your kitchen ambiance.

4) Don't use garlic past its prime – for example, if you cut into a clove and there are brown spots, or if the bulb starts to grow sprouts out of the top. If sprouts develop the garlic is still usable, but it will not have the desired pungency.

Deviled Eggs with Olives

(Toni's deviled eggs were always a hit – the only change I made to her recipe was adding some green olives, so consider them optional)

INGREDIENTS

6 hard-boiled eggs

2 tbsp. mayonnaise

1 tbsp. white wine vinegar

1 tsp. spicy brown mustard

½ tsp. Worcestershire sauce

⅛ tsp. salt

Several shakes of ground black pepper

2 tbsp. finely chopped green olives with pimentos

Paprika for sprinkling on top of eggs

PREPARATION

To make hard-boiled eggs: Place eggs gently in a saucepan large enough to hold them in a single layer and cover completely with cold water (the water should come to about an inch above the eggs). Bring to a boil over medium high heat. As soon as the water comes to a full boil, completely remove the pan from the heat and cover. Let the eggs sit, covered, for 15 minutes, then drain immediately, plunge into ice water and allow to sit for a couple minutes, then peel.

Christmas, York, PA
Mamma Bear Hug!

Halve peeled eggs lengthwise. Add all remaining ingredients to yolks (except paprika) and mix with a fork until the mixture is very smooth and fluffy. Lightly mound yolks in egg white halves, evenly distributed. Sprinkle tops of eggs lightly with paprika. Makes 12 deviled eggs

Chicken-Cheese Puffs

INGREDIENTS

¾ lb. boneless skinless chicken breasts (cooked)

1 cup mayonnaise

2 large shallots, minced (should equal at least ½ cup of minced shallots)

½ tsp. dried basil

½ tsp. dried oregano

½ tsp. Herbamare® or salt

⅛ tsp. white pepper

⅔ cup grated Asiago cheese

¼ cup grated Parmesan cheese (plus additional for sprinkling on top)

Whole wheat pita bread (8 inches in diameter)

PREPARATION

Place cooked chicken in a mini-food processor and process until it is finely chopped. Place 2 generous cups of the chopped chicken in a large bowl, and stir in the mayonnaise and shallots. Blend in the basil, oregano, Herbamare® or salt and white pepper. Add the Asiago and Parmesan cheeses and stir until well combined.

Preheat the oven to 350 degrees. Slice pita bread in half, and then slice each half into 4 equal triangular-shaped pieces. Gently separate each piece at the seam (one 8" pita pocket should produce after cut 16 pita triangles). Slice 2 8-inch pita pockets so there will be 32 pita triangles.

Spread a generous amount of the chicken mixture on each pita triangle using all of the chicken mixture, and place them on ungreased cookie sheets (or jelly roll pans). Sprinkle each triangle with Parmesan cheese and bake in the preheated oven for 15 minutes. The cheese mixture should be bubbling and have a slightly puffed appearance, and the pita bread should be nicely browned and crispy. Allow to cool on the baking pan for several minutes before serving. Makes 32 appetizers

Joyce

You may have heard the joke about what people make for dinner when they don't like to cook? Answer: Reservations. My friend Joyce resembles this axiom totally. Joyce lives in the Capitol Hill area of Washington, D.C., and always has a pulse on the latest and greatest restaurants there.

When my husband Pat and I joined her and Floyd at their home for pre-dinner beverages one evening, I was surprised and delighted when Joyce said she had "thrown together a little something as an appetizer." These small gems couldn't be easier to prepare, and as another friend of Joyce's emoted when he tasted them, "These things taste like you're having a party in your mouth!"

Party In Your Mouth Canapés

INGREDIENTS

1 block of good quality extra-sharp white cheddar cheese

Crystallized gingerroot

Dried cranberries

PREPARATION

Cut small (bite-size) pieces of cheese and place a small piece of crystallized gingerroot on top. Put one or two dried cranberries on top of the gingerroot and secure the gingerroot and cranberries to the cheese with a decorative toothpick.

Make a lot or a small amount, depending on the number of guests. Not only delicious, these canapés are very pretty and decorative when arranged on an attractive serving plate.

Washington, DC, Dec. 1983
Holiday Party
Sue's Boss Showing Her Who's Boss

Arlington, VA, 1992, Halloween
Party 'til the cows come home.

Hot Crab & Artichoke Dip

Adapted from Gourmet magazine, Condé Nast Publications

INGREDIENTS

Juice of one lemon

2 14-oz. cans artichoke hearts

1 tbsp. grapeseed oil

1 large green bell pepper, chopped

2 cups mayonnaise

½ cup thinly sliced scallions (white part only)

1 large red bell pepper, roasted and chopped (See p. 213)

1 generous cup grated Parmesan cheese

2 tbsp. fresh lemon juice

4 tsp. Worcestershire sauce

2 tbsp. finely chopped jalapeño peppers (seeded and inner membranes removed)

1 tsp. celery salt

1 lb. lump crab meat, picked over very well to remove all shell fragments

⅓ cup sliced almonds, lightly toasted

Pita chips for dipping (preferably whole wheat or multi-grain, baked)

PREPARATION

Fill a medium bowl half full of water and add the juice from one lemon. Trim the end off of each artichoke heart (should only remove about ¼ inch) and cut each one in half. Add the artichokes to the lemon water and set aside. Allow to sit in the lemon water for at least 15 minutes. Drain in a colander and chop very finely (this is easiest to do in a mini-food processor).

In a small heavy skillet heat the oil over moderate heat and add the green bell pepper. Cook, stirring occasionally, until softened. Remove from heat and let it cool.

In a large bowl combine the artichokes, green bell pepper, mayonnaise, scallions, roasted red pepper, Parmesan, lemon juice, Worcestershire sauce, jalapeno peppers, and the celery salt. Stir until the mixture is combined well, and then gently stir in the crab meat. Transfer the mixture to an ovenproof chafing or baking dish and sprinkle the top with the almonds. Bake in a preheated 375 degree oven for 25 to 30 minutes, or until the top is golden and the mixture is bubbly. Serve with pita chips. Serves 10–12

Note: You can make this dip one day ahead and refrigerate, covered, until ready to bake.

Baked Italian-Style Chicken Wings

INGREDIENTS

1½ cup fresh bread crumbs (whole-wheat bread preferred, or white bread)

1 generous cup grated Parmesan cheese (or grated/shaved Parmigiano Reggiano cheese)

¼ cup minced fresh parsley (flat-leaf, Italian)

1 tsp. salt

¼ tsp. black pepper

⅛ tsp. red pepper flakes

¼ lb. (8 tbsp.) unsalted butter, melted and cooled

3 minced garlic cloves

2 lbs. chicken wings

PREPARATION

In a mini-food processor combine the bread crumbs, cheese, parsley, salt, black pepper and red pepper flakes and pulse until well combined. Put mixture on a plate.

Melt butter in a pan large enough to roll the wings in. As soon as the butter is melted, remove from heat and add minced garlic and stir to combine.

Remove the tips from the chicken wings and halve the chicken wings. Dip the wings in the melted butter, letting the excess drip off, and coat them with the crumb mixture. Arrange wings in a baking pan big enough to hold them in a single layer. Spoon any remaining garlic butter over the wings and bake in a preheated 350 degree oven, basting several times, for 45 minutes, or until a deep golden brown on top.

Marinated Korean-Style Pork Tenderloin Strips

INGREDIENTS

1 lb. boneless lean pork tenderloin

½ cup soy sauce

3 tbsp. dark brown sugar, firmly packed

2 tbsp. minced shallots

1 generous tbsp. finely chopped fresh gingerroot

3 cloves garlic

⅓ cup toasted sesame seeds

2 tbsp. safflower oil

PREPARATION

Trim any excess fat from the tenderloin. If it is thick, split lengthwise in half.

Combine the soy sauce, sugar, and shallots in a bowl and stir until the sugar is dissolved. In a mini-food processor, grate enough fresh gingerroot to equal 1 generous tbsp. Add the garlic cloves and process to chop the garlic and combine it with the gingerroot. Add this combination along with the sesame seeds to the bowl. Add the pork, turn to coat all sides, and refrigerate, turning and basting occasionally, for 2 ½ hours. Remove from the refrigerator and let marinate an additional ½ hour at room temperature. Reserve the marinade after removing the pork.

Preheat the oven to 375 degrees. Grease the bottom of a small roasting dish with 1 tbsp. of the oil. Place the pork in the baking dish and rub the remaining tbsp. of oil on the pork. Then rub a generous amount of the sesame seeds from the marinade onto all sides of the pork. Roast until tender, which should take approx. 45 minutes.

Place the reserved marinade in a small saucepan and simmer for 10 minutes. Put in a small serving bowl. Cut the pork into thin bite-size strips and serve with cocktail picks and the marinade to dip. Serves 4–6

Warm Artichoke Dip

INGREDIENTS

1 lemon

1 14-oz. can artichoke hearts, well drained

1 8-oz. package cream cheese, softened to room temperature in a medium bowl

½ cup mayonnaise

1 package (4-oz.) crumbled Feta cheese

½ cup grated Parmesan cheese

2 large garlic cloves, finely chopped

1 tsp. hot pepper sauce (e.g. Tabasco)

1 tbsp. fresh lemon juice

3 tbsp. diced pimentos

PREPARATION

Fill a medium bowl half full of water and add the juice from one lemon. Trim the end off of each artichoke heart (should only remove about ¼ inch) and cut each one in half. Add the artichokes to the lemon water and set aside. Allow to sit in the lemon water for at least 15 minutes. Drain in a colander and chop very finely, preferably by hand. Note that artichokes chopped in a food processor tend to become puréed instead of chopped.

With a hand-held immersion blender, blend cream cheese, mayonnaise, Feta cheese, Parmesan cheese, garlic, pepper sauce, and lemon juice until well combined.

Stir artichokes and pimentos into cheese mixture. Spoon into a shallow baking dish (a quiche dish is especially good).

Bake in a preheated 350 degree oven for 20–25 minutes until thoroughly heated through. The top should be lightly browned. Serve with whole grain crackers.

Pesto Deviled Eggs

INGREDIENTS

6 hard-boiled eggs, peeled, cut in half, and yolks mashed in a small bowl

¼ cup sour cream

8 tbsp. prepared sun-dried tomato pesto (see p. 166)

¼ tsp. salt

⅛ tsp. black pepper

PREPARATION

To make hard-boiled eggs: Place eggs gently in a saucepan large enough to hold them in a single layer and cover completely with cold water (the water should come to about an inch above the eggs). Bring to a boil over medium high heat. As soon as the water comes to a full boil, completely remove the pan from the heat and cover. Let the eggs sit, covered, for 15 minutes, then drain immediately, plunge into ice water and allow to sit for a couple minutes, then peel.

Combine the thoroughly mashed yolks with the sour cream and pesto. Stir in the salt and pepper. Fill the whites evenly with the mixture.

Note: If you refrigerate the eggs after they are prepared, they should sit at room temperature for at least 15 minutes before serving. Makes 12 stuffed eggs

Reuben Dip
Adapted from Gourmet magazine, Condé Nast Publications

INGREDIENTS

8 oz. cream cheese, softened to room temperature in a large bowl

½ cup sour cream

1 cup chopped drained sauerkraut (not canned)

½ lb. very lean corned beef, chopped fine (best in mini-food processor)

1 tbsp. chopped scallions, white part

2 tbsp. ketchup

2 tsp. spicy brown mustard

1½ cups grated Swiss cheese

Rye crackers to accompany

PREPARATION

Preheat the oven to 375 degrees. Add the sour cream, sauerkraut, corned beef, scallions, ketchup, mustard and Swiss cheese to the cream cheese and combine well. Transfer the dip to a small ovenproof casserole and bake, covered, for 25 minutes, or until bubbles form around the edges. Remove the cover and bake for an additional five minutes, or until it begins to turn golden.

Serve the dip warm with the rye crackers. Makes approx. 2 cups

Clyde's Song Parody – Sung to the tune of "Sunshine On My Shoulders"

Sunshine on my whiskers makes me drowsy

Sunshine on my belly makes me snooze

Sunshine on my torso looks so lovely

Wake me up and you will pay some dues

Bread & Muffins

The majority of the recipes in this section are "quick breads," e.g. muffins, coffeecake, etc. as opposed to actual bread recipes where you use yeast, knead the dough, and so on. I don't make bread in this manner for two reasons. First of all I own a bread machine, and it makes absolutely marvelous bread. The second reason is that I live in an area that abounds with wonderful bakeries that produce bread at least as good, probably better, than what I would make.

It is well known among my friends and family that when they come for a visit, my signature tradition is to always make fresh muffins in the morning. Consequently, there is an abundance of muffin recipes included.

As an aside, the first time I made muffins for my husband, while I was in the shower and the muffins were cooling on a rack, he ate 11 out of 12 of them. Upon my return to the kitchen he said, "I saved a muffin for you" (like this was a sacrifice). We had a wonderful relationship right from the start – I love to cook, and he loves to eat.

Everybody should believe in something.
I believe I'll take another nap.

Testimonial

"Friends are Flowers in the Garden of Life" – Proverb

There is a very special garden where the flowers of friendship grow. For more than 30 years I have gone to that wonderful place where I am nurtured by Sue's friendship, through the kindness and concern that good friends show. When I need to walk through the showers of life, Sue's love and laughter always strengthen and renew the seedlings planted in this garden.

One of my favorite places to be with Sue is in her kitchen. She shares secret recipes with only one condition: that she can cook for and entertain her friends. Happiness, giggles and fabulous aromas regularly emanate from Sue's kitchen. As a regular member of her "fan club," I have savored many memorable dishes that Sue has created, tested and re-tested for perfection.

Among many of these unforgettable dishes, one has stayed in my mind and my taste buds awaken just at the thought. Sue's crab cakes, with their slightly crisp exterior and a delectable creamy inside with a velvety texture, complemented by her zesty tartar sauce infused with capers, shallots, mustard and herbs are close to heaven on earth.

The friendship garden I share with Sue blossoms in my heart, with cherished memories of good times that always include laughter, harmony and fabulous food.

Nathalie Cadot
Realtor, Long & Foster Realtors
Falls Church, VA

Pumpkin Muffins

INGREDIENTS

1 large egg

¾ cup canned pumpkin puree (plain)

½ cup milk (low-fat OK)

¾ cup well-drained canned unsweetened crushed pineapple

4 tbsp. unsalted butter, melted and cooled

1½ cups unbleached all-purpose flour

½ cup granulated sugar, preferably organic

2 tsp. double-acting baking powder

½ tsp. salt

½ tsp. cinnamon

½ tsp. nutmeg

¼ tsp. allspice

¼ tsp. ground ginger

¼ cup firmly packed light brown sugar, for sprinkling on top of muffins

PREPARATION

In a large bowl, combine the egg, pumpkin puree, milk and pineapple. Add the cooled melted butter and stir gently to incorporate with the other ingredients.

Sift together the remaining ingredients, <u>except for the brown sugar</u>. Add the flour mixture to the pumpkin mixture and stir gently just until the flour mixture is incorporated (the batter should be lumpy). Spoon the batter into buttered muffin tins, and sprinkle the tops with the brown sugar.

Preheat the oven to 425 degrees. Bake the muffins in the middle of the oven for 20–25 minutes, or until a cake tester inserted in the center comes out clean. Remove from the oven and allow the muffins to sit in the baking pan for a couple minutes before removing to a rack to cool. These muffins taste wonderful no matter what, but I prefer them warm. Makes 12 muffins

Pumpkin Cranberry Bread

INGREDIENTS

Butter for greasing the loaf pan

1 cup canned solid-pack pumpkin

1 cup sugar, preferably organic

¼ cup fresh orange juice

2 large eggs

¼ cup canola oil

2 cups unbleached all-purpose flour

2 tsp. baking powder

½ tsp. salt

¼ tsp. baking soda

¼ tsp. cinnamon

¼ tsp. ginger

¼ tsp. cloves

1½ tbsp. freshly grated orange zest

1 cup frozen cranberries, completely thawed and drained on a paper towel

PREPARATION

Generously butter a loaf pan (8 ½ by 4 ½ by 2 ¾ inches).

In a large bowl with an electric mixer beat together the pumpkin, sugar, orange juice, eggs and oil. Sift into the bowl the flour, baking powder, salt, baking soda, cinnamon, ginger, and cloves. Add the orange zest and stir just until the batter is smooth.

Place the cranberries in a mini-food processor and process until finely chopped. Stir the cranberries into the batter, and spoon the batter into the loaf pan, spreading evenly.

Preheat the oven to 350 degrees. Bake the bread in the middle of the oven for 1 hour, or until a tester comes out clean. Cool on a rack for 10 minutes, then turn the bread out onto the rack and cool completely.

Stuffing for Poultry

(Toni's recipe for poultry stuffing was simple and simply delicious. The recipe provided is almost the way my mother used to make it, except she used Pepperidge Farm® seasoned bread cubes and I use plain unseasoned cubes, with the addition of fresh sage, savory and Herbamare®).

INGREDIENTS

1 stick (8 tbsp.) butter

3 cups finely chopped onions

½ cup (generous) finely chopped celery

¼ cup chopped celery leaves

1 tbsp. finely chopped fresh parsley

2 tsp. summer savory (dried)

2 tbsp. fresh sage, finely chopped

8 cups soft bread cubes

¼ cup chicken broth

2 tsp. Herbamare® (preferably) or salt

PREPARATION

Heat butter in a large skillet over moderate heat and cook the onion until translucent and tender. Add the celery and celery leaves and cook another 5–10 minutes. Add the rest of the ingredients and combine thoroughly. Remove from heat to cool.

IMPORTANT! Allow the stuffing to cool completely before placing in poultry cavity. Stuffing should be packed loosely in the bird! If there is stuffing left over, see below.

Note: I am not big on the stuffing that comes out of the poultry because grease will usually seep into the stuffing during the cooking process. Many people prefer the stuffing from the bird because they like the flavor better with the added poultry grease and juices. If you want the option of stuffing served both in and out of the bird do the following:

Place leftover stuffing in a large casserole dish and bake at 325 degrees for approx. 15–20 minutes, or until warmed thoroughly, and very lightly browned on top.

The Forties

Banana Streusel Coffeecake

Adapted from Gourmet magazine, Condé Nast Publications

INGREDIENTS

6 tbsp. unsalted butter, softened to room temperature in a large bowl

¾ cup granulated sugar, preferably organic

1 large egg

1 generous tbsp. freshly grated lemon rind

1 tsp. vanilla

½ cup milk (2% low-fat OK)

2 cups unbleached all-purpose flour

2 tsp. double-acting baking powder

¼ tsp. salt

3 bananas sliced about ¼ inch thick (should equal approx. 3 cups)

Note: The bananas should be ripe but still firm and not yet at the mushy stage

Streusel Topping:

⅓ cup firmly packed light brown sugar

⅓ cup unbleached all-purpose flour

½ tsp. cinnamon

¼ tsp. nutmeg

4 tbsp. cold unsalted butter, cut into pieces

PREPARATION

Cream together the butter and the sugar, adding the sugar ¼ cup at a time, beating until the mixture is light and fluffy. Add the egg, lemon rind, and vanilla, beating to combine ingredients well. Stir in the milk.

Sift together the flour, baking powder and salt. Stir the flour mixture gently into the butter mixture. Fold in the bananas gently, and spoon batter into a well-buttered 8-inch square baking pan, smoothing the top with a spatula.

Preheat the oven to 375 degrees. Place all of the streusel topping ingredients into a mini-food processor and pulse quickly until the mixture resembles meal. Sprinkle the streusel evenly over the batter and bake the cake for 45 minutes, or until a cake tester inserted in the center comes out clean. Let the coffeecake cool in the baking pan on a rack for 20 minutes before cutting into squares.

Goat Cheese Croutons

(Salad Garnish)

INGREDIENTS

1 French Baguette (6–12 inches long)

Fine quality extra-virgin olive oil with herbs

4 oz. goat cheese, softened to room temperature

PREPARATION

Preheat oven to 350 degrees. Slice twelve ¼-inch thick bread rounds from the baguette. Brush each bread slice lightly with the herbed olive oil and place on a baking sheet and bake 3–4 minutes. Remove from the oven and spread each round with a generous amount of the softened goat cheese. Return to the oven and bake for several minutes longer, or until the tops are lightly browned.

Sue's Tips:

Don't judge a banana by its peel. If you leave a banana alone long enough, eventually it will ripen to the point where the skin is blackened and totally unappetizing in appearance. Also when you press gently on the banana it is clear that it is very soft. Be aware that your fruit is not fruitless! This is the perfect time to pull out your favorite recipe/s that include mashed bananas as an ingredient. Peel away the blackened softened skin, place the very ripe bananas in a small bowl, and they will easily mash with a spoon to a pulp and be recipe ready.

Banana Bread with Coconut & Nuts

Adapted from The Gourmet Cookbook (2004), Condé Nast Publications

INGREDIENTS

2¼ cups unbleached all-purpose flour

¾ tsp. baking powder

½ tsp. baking soda

1 tsp. salt

1½ sticks unsalted butter, softened to room temperature

1 cup packed light brown sugar

½ cup granulated sugar, preferably organic

3 large eggs

2 tsp. vanilla extract

2 tbsp. grated lemon zest

1⅓ to 1½ cups mashed ripe bananas (about 4 medium bananas)

¼ cup sour cream

½ cup (generous) coarsely chopped macadamia nuts

1 cup unsweetened flaked coconut, lightly toasted

PREPARATION

Sift together flour, baking powder, baking soda, and salt. Beat together butter and both sugars in a large bowl with an electric mixer at medium speed until pale and fluffy. Add eggs, one at a time, and beat well after each addition to thoroughly combine. Add vanilla, lemon zest, bananas and sour cream and beat until just combined. Reduce speed to low and add flour mixture. Beat until just combined. Stir in the nuts and toasted coconut.

Preheat oven to 350 degrees. Generously butter two 8½-by-4½-inch loaf pans. Divide batter between the pans and smooth tops. Bake until a wooden toothpick inserted in the center of the bread comes out clean, approx. 45 to 50 minutes.

Remove bread from pans and cool right side up, on rack. If not serving bread shortly after it is cooled, wrap well in plastic wrap. After one day at room temperature, the bread should be refrigerated. Makes 2 loaves

Pecan Cinnamon Sugar Muffins

INGREDIENTS

1½ cups coarsely chopped pecans

1 stick (½ cup) unsalted butter, melted and cooled

½ cup firmly packed light brown sugar

1 cup milk (reduced fat (2%) OK)

2 large eggs

2 cups unbleached all-purpose flour

½ cup granulated sugar, preferably organic

2 tsp. double-acting baking powder

2 tsp. cinnamon

¼ tsp. nutmeg

¼ tsp. salt

PREPARATION

Preheat the oven to 325 degrees. Put the chopped pecans in a pie plate and toast in the oven until fragrant and lightly browned, approx. 10 minutes. Remove from oven and set aside. Increase oven temperature to 425 degrees.

In a bowl combine the butter and the brown sugar. Stir in the milk, then stir in the eggs, one at a time. Sift together the flour, granulated sugar, baking powder, cinnamon, nutmeg and salt. Add the flour mixture and the toasted pecans to the butter mixture, and stir until it is just combined. The batter will be lumpy.

Divide the batter among 12 well buttered muffin tins, filling each one about seven-eighths full. Bake the muffins at 425 degrees for 20 minutes, or until they are golden brown. Makes 12 muffins

Banana Muffins

Adapted from Gourmet magazine, Condé Nast Publications

INGREDIENTS

1½ cups unbleached all-purpose flour

1 cup sugar, preferably organic

½ tsp. salt

½ tsp. cinnamon

½ tsp. baking soda

¼ tsp. baking powder

4 large egg whites

½ cup canola oil

1½ tsp. vanilla

2 medium bananas, very ripe, peeled and mashed (should equal about 1 cup)

¼ cup low-fat vanilla yogurt

½ cup golden raisins

PREPARATION

Preheat oven to 350 degrees and butter a 12 cup muffin tin.

Sift the dry ingredients together (flour, sugar, salt, cinnamon, baking soda and baking powder) into a large bowl. Add egg whites, oil, and vanilla and stir to combine. Stir in the mashed bananas, yogurt and raisins, stirring until just combined.

Divide the batter evenly among the muffin tin cups and bake in the middle of the oven until golden brown, about 25 minutes. Remove muffins from tin and place on a rack to cool. Serve warm or at room temperature. Makes 12 muffins

---

Mincemeat Muffins

Adapted from Gourmet magazine, Condé Nast Publications

INGREDIENTS

Butter for greasing muffin tins

1 apple

1 large egg

¾ cup unsweetened apple juice (organic if available)

⅓ cup canola oil

1 12-oz. jar (gourmet quality) bottled mincemeat (approx. 1½ cups)

2 cups unbleached all-purpose flour

1 tbsp. baking powder

1 tsp. cinnamon

⅓ cup granulated sugar, preferably organic

½ cup finely chopped pecans, lightly toasted

Glaze:

¾ cup confectioners' sugar

¼ tsp. cinnamon

1 generous tbsp. unsweetened apple juice

PREPARATION

Preheat oven to 400 degrees. Generously grease twelve muffin tin cups with butter.

Peel and core the apple and cut into ¼ inch dice. In a large bowl whisk together the egg, apple juice, and oil and stir in the mincemeat and diced apple.

In a large bowl sift together the flour, baking powder, cinnamon and sugar. Add the flour mixture to the mincemeat mixture along with the pecans and stir the batter gently just until combined.

Divide the batter evenly among the muffin cups and bake in the middle of the preheated oven for 20–25 minutes, or until a tester comes out clean. Remove the muffins from the cups and place on a rack. Cool for 5 minutes.

While the muffins are cooling make the glaze by stirring together the glaze ingredients in a small bowl until all of the confectioners' sugar is incorporated. Spoon or spread the glaze evenly over the muffins after they have cooled for 5 minutes. Do this slowly and gently. Do not be concerned if some of the glaze drips off the muffins. Serve the muffins warm or at room temperature. The muffins can be stored in an airtight container for up to 3 days at room temperature. Makes 12 muffins

Banana Bread

INGREDIENTS

1 stick (8 tbsp.) unsalted butter, softened to room temperature

1⅓ cups firmly packed dark brown sugar

2 eggs

1 tsp. vanilla

1 tsp. baking soda

⅓ cup sour cream

¾ cup whole wheat flour

¾ cup unbleached white flour

¼ tsp. salt

1 cup mashed ripe bananas (about 2 large bananas)

PREPARATION

In a large bowl cream together the butter and the brown sugar until the mixture is well blended. Add the eggs and vanilla and beat well until the mixture is light.

Dissolve the baking soda in the sour cream and stir into the butter mixture. Sift together the whole wheat flour, white flour, and the salt. Add the flour mixture to the creamed mixture alternately with the mashed bananas, combining well.

Preheat the oven to 350 degrees. Pour the batter into a buttered loaf pan and bake for 45 to 50 minutes, or until a cake tester is inserted in the middle and comes out clean. Let the bread cool in the pan on a rack and serve warm or at room temperature.

My buddy Nicky – Sue's very own Nittany lion.

Lemon Yogurt Muffins

INGREDIENTS

2 cups unbleached all-purpose flour

1 tsp. double-acting baking powder

1 tsp. baking soda

¼ tsp. salt

¼ cup sugar (preferably organic)

2 tbsp. honey

2 large eggs at room temperature

2 6-oz. containers lemon yogurt

½ stick (4 tbsp.) unsalted butter, melted and cooled

1 generous tbsp. freshly grated lemon rind

Lemon Syrup:

⅓ cup fresh lemon juice

⅓ cup sugar (preferably organic)

PREPARATION

In a small bowl stir together well the flour, baking powder, baking soda and salt with a fork. In a separate large bowl place the sugar, honey, eggs, yogurt, butter, and lemon rind and stir until the mixture is well combined. Add the flour mixture and stir the batter until it is just combined.

Preheat the oven to 375 degrees. Divide the batter equally among 12 buttered muffin tin cups and bake the muffins in the middle of the oven for 15–20 minutes, or until they are pale golden on top and a tester comes out clean.

While the muffins are baking make the syrup. In a small heavy saucepan combine the lemon juice and the sugar and bring the mixture to a boil. Boil for 1 minute.

When you remove the muffins from the oven, pierce the top of each muffin gently several times with a fork and drizzle several tsp. of the syrup over each muffin, letting the syrup run over the top and around the edges of the muffins. Allow the muffins to cool in the pan for 3 minutes, then remove from the pan and place on a rack to cool. Serve the muffins warm or at room temperature. Makes 12 muffins

Lemon Bread

INGREDIENTS

8 tbsp. (1 stick) unsalted butter, softened to room temperature in a large bowl

1 cup sugar (preferably organic)

2 eggs

1¼ cup unbleached flour

1 tsp. baking powder

¼ tsp. salt

½ cup milk (low-fat OK)

½ cup finely chopped pecans, lightly toasted

Grated rind of 1 medium lemon (should equal approx. 3 tbsp.)

Lemon Syrup:

Juice of 1 medium lemon

¼ cup sugar (preferably organic)

PREPARATION

Cream together the butter and sugar. Stir in the eggs, one at a time. Sift together the flour, baking powder and salt. Stir the flour mixture into the creamed mixture alternately with the milk. Add the nuts and lemon rind.

Preheat oven to 350 degrees. Generously grease with butter a 9 x 5 inch loaf pan and add the batter to the pan. Bake in preheated oven for one hour.

While the bread is baking, make sugar syrup, simply by combining the lemon juice and sugar well, stirring until the sugar is dissolved. Set aside. As soon as the bread is done and removed from the oven, pierce the surface all over with a fork to make small holes. Pour the lemon syrup over the hot bread very slowly until all syrup has been absorbed.

Serve bread sliced warm or at room temperature.

Linzer Muffins

Adapted from Gourmet magazine, Condé Nast Publications

INGREDIENTS

Butter for greasing muffin tin cups

1 cup whole blanched almonds (skins removed), toasted

¾ cup sugar, preferably organic

1½ tsp. finely grated fresh lemon zest

1½ cups unbleached all-purpose flour

2 tsp. baking powder

½ tsp. salt

¼ tsp. cinnamon

6 tbsp. unsalted butter, melted and cooled

1 cup whole milk

1 large egg

⅛ tsp. almond extract

⅓ cup (approx.) seedless red raspberry preserves or seedless red raspberry jam (a great choice is Dickinson's® Pure Seedless Cascade Mountain™ Red Raspberry Preserves)

Confectioners sugar for dusting

PREPARATION

Generously butter a 12-cup muffin tin. Grind the toasted almonds in a mini-food processor with the sugar and lemon zest until the mixture is finely ground and well combined. Place the almond mixture in a large bowl; add the flour, baking powder, salt and cinnamon and whisk to combine. Pour in the melted butter and stir.

In a small bowl whisk together the milk, egg and almond extract, then stir into the almond/flour mixture until combined.

Preheat oven to 400 degrees. Put a scant ¼ cup of the batter into each muffin cup, and top each with 1 rounded tsp. of the preserves. Divide the remaining batter equally among the cups, and bake in the middle of the preheated oven for approx. 20 minutes, or until the muffins are golden and pull away from the edges of the cups.

Cool the muffins on a rack for 5 minutes, then remove from the pan and place directly on the rack. Dust the muffins with confectioners sugar. Makes 12 muffins

Cooking with Clyde
— Priceless!

Garlic Bread

INGREDIENTS

¼ lb. butter (8 tbsp.), softened to room temperature

2 large cloves garlic, finely chopped

½ cup grated Parmesan cheese

1 tbsp. mayonnaise

1 tbsp. extra-virgin olive oil

2 tbsp. finely chopped fresh Italian flat-leaf parsley

½ tsp. dried oregano

1 1-lb loaf of good quality Italian bread, not sliced

PREPARATION

Thoroughly combine all ingredients (except for the bread) in a small bowl.

Preheat oven to 375 degrees. Halve bread loaf lengthwise and place each half on a large piece of aluminum foil. Spread garlic butter on cut sides of bread, dividing evenly between the two loaf halves. Fold up sides of foil so that bread is covered, but do not let the foil touch the top of the bread. Place bread halves on a baking sheet, cut side up, and bake for 20 minutes. Fold back foil to expose tops of bread and continue to bake until tops are golden brown, approx. an additional 5 to 10 minutes.

Place halves on a cutting board and with a sharp serrated knife cut into slices of desired thickness. Serves 6

Sour Cream Bran Muffins

INGREDIENTS

1 stick unsalted butter (8 tbsp.), softened to room temperature in a large bowl

¼ cup firmly packed light brown sugar

1 large egg

1 generous cup sour cream

¾ cup raisins

⅓ cup dark unsulfured molasses

1 cup unbleached all-purpose flour

1 tsp. baking soda

¼ tsp. salt

¾ cup toasted bran

¼ cup toasted wheat germ

PREPARATION

Add the brown sugar to the softened butter in the bowl and beat with a wooden spoon until the mixture is light and fluffy. Add the egg and beat until it is well combined. Add the sour cream, raisins, and molasses and combine the mixture well.

Into a bowl sift together the flour, baking soda, and salt. Add this mixture plus the bran and the wheat germ to the butter mixture and stir the batter gently until it is just combined (the batter should be lumpy).

Preheat the oven to 400 degrees. Spoon the batter into a buttered twelve-cup muffin tin, filling each cup about two-thirds full. Bake the muffins for 15–20 minutes, or until well browned, and a wooden toothpick inserted in the center of one tester muffin comes out clean. Makes 12 muffins

---

Raspberry-Lemon Corn Muffins
Adapted from Gourmet magazine, Condé Nast Publications

INGREDIENTS

1 cup unbleached all-purpose flour

1 cup yellow cornmeal

¾ cup granulated sugar, preferably organic

1 tbsp. baking powder

½ tsp. salt

2 tbsp. finely grated fresh lemon zest

1½ sticks unsalted butter, melted and cooled

¾ cup milk (2% low-fat OK)

2 large egg yolks

1 large egg

2 cups fresh raspberries

1½ tbsp. granulated sugar for sprinkling on top

PREPARATION

Preheat oven to 400 degrees. Whisk together flour, cornmeal, sugar, baking powder, salt and lemon zest in a large bowl. In a separate bowl whisk together the melted/cooled butter, milk, yolks and whole egg, then stir into the flour mixture briefly, until just combined. Very gently stir in the raspberries.

Generously butter a 12-cup muffin pan and divide the batter evenly among the cups. Bake in the middle of the preheated oven for 10 minutes. Remove from oven and sprinkle tops of muffins with the remaining 1½ tbsp. of granulated sugar. Return muffins to the oven and continue to bake for an additional 10–12 minutes, or until the tops are golden and a tester comes out clean. Allow muffins to cool in the pan for approx. 10 minutes, and then remove from the pan and continue to cool on a rack. Makes 12 muffins

Banana Bran Muffins

INGREDIENTS

1 cup unprocessed wheat bran

1 cup buttermilk (low-fat OK)

½ stick (4 tbsp.) unsalted butter, softened to room temperature in a large bowl

¼ cup dark brown sugar, packed

2 extra-large eggs, at room temperature

½ cup unsulfured molasses

1 tbsp. grated orange zest

1 tsp. vanilla

1½ cups unbleached all-purpose flour

¾ tsp. baking powder

¼ tsp. baking soda

½ tsp. kosher or sea salt

1 cup raisins

1 large ripe banana or 2 medium ripe bananas, cut in large diced pieces (should be enough banana to equal 1 to 1½ cups

½ cup chopped walnuts

Butter for greasing muffin tins

PREPARATION

Combine the bran and buttermilk in a small bowl and set aside.

Add the sugar to the bowl with the butter and cream with a hand-held electric mixer on high speed for approximately 3 minutes, or until the mixture is light and fluffy. With the mixer on low, add the eggs, one at a time. Scrape the bowl and then add the molasses, orange zest and vanilla. Add the bran-buttermilk mixture and combine, still using low speed on the mixer. The mixture will look curdled.

In a separate bowl sift together the flour, baking powder, baking soda and salt. With the mixer on low speed, slowly add the flour mixture to the batter and mix just until combined. Using a rubber spatula, fold in the raisins, bananas and walnuts.

Preheat oven to 350 degrees. Generously butter the muffin cups of a 12-cup muffin tin. Fill the cups full and bake in the preheated oven for 25–30 minutes, or until a cake tester (I use a wooden toothpick) comes out clean. Cool in the pan for several minutes, and then remove to a rack to continue cooling. Muffins should be served warm or room temperature. Makes 12 muffins

Sue's Tips:

Guests who come for dinner typically bring a bottle of wine - Always appreciated.

However, if you know your host/hostess is fond of margaritas, consider bringing a premium bottle of tequila (e.g. Patróne® or Romance® by Milagro. "Smooth" move.

Sour Cream Coffee Cake

(Recipe from the kitchen of Sheila Lockhart – a family favorite since 1960)

INGREDIENTS

1 cup (16 tbsp.) butter, softened to room temperature in a large bowl

1¼ cups sugar (preferably organic)

2 eggs

1 cup sour cream

1 tsp. vanilla

2 cups unbleached all-purpose flour

1½ tsp. baking powder

½ tsp. baking soda

½ tsp. salt

Topping:

(Stir topping ingredients together in a small bowl and set aside)

¾ cup finely chopped nuts (Sheila prefers pecans)

3 tbsp. sugar (preferably organic)

1 tbsp. cinnamon

PREPARATION

Add the sugar and eggs to the softened butter and beat with a wooden spoon until light and fluffy. Add the sour cream and vanilla and stir to combine.

Sift together the flour, baking powder, baking soda and salt. Add to the butter/sour cream mixture and stir just until well combined.

Preheat the oven to 350 degrees. Grease and lightly flour a tube pan and pour half of the batter into the pan. Sprinkle with half of the topping. Pour rest of the batter into the pan, and sprinkle the remaining topping over top. Bake in the preheated oven for approx. 50 minutes, or until a wooden toothpick comes out clean when inserted into the middle of the cake. Serve warm or at room temperature.

Birthday Celebration, The Wharf
Alexandria, VA, 2002

Blueberry Sour Cream Muffins

INGREDIENTS

¼ lb. (8 tbsp.) unsalted butter, softened to room temperature

¾ cup plus 1 tbsp. granulated sugar, preferably organic

2 large eggs

2 tsp. vanilla

1 cup sour cream

2 cups unbleached all-purpose flour

¼ tsp. baking soda

½ tsp. salt

2 generous cups fresh blueberries, rinsed and picked over

PREPARATION

In a bowl cream together the butter and ¾ cup sugar. Beat in the eggs, one at a time, and then beat in the vanilla and sour cream.

Sift together the flour, baking soda and salt and stir this mixture into the batter gently, until the flour is just incorporated, and then gently stir in the blueberries.

Preheat the oven to 375 degrees. Butter a 12 cup muffin pan generously, and divide the batter into the cups. Sprinkle the tops with the remaining 1 tbsp. sugar. Bake the muffins in the middle of the oven for 25 to 30 minutes, or until a tester comes out clean, and the tops of the muffins are golden brown.

Allow muffins to cool in the pan for 5–10 minutes and then remove to a rack to continue cooling. Makes 12 muffins

Pumpkin Sour-Cream Coffeecake

Adapted from Gourmet magazine, Condé Nast Publications

INGREDIENTS

⅓ cup sugar (preferably organic)

4 tbsp. butter (½ stick), softened

⅓ cup (generous) tinned pumpkin puree

¼ cup sour cream

1 egg

2 tbsp. (generous) grated orange rind

1¼ cups sifted flour

1 tbsp. double-acting baking powder

½ tsp. baking soda

¼ tsp. nutmeg

¼ tsp. salt

⅓ cup milk

Streusel Topping:

¼ cup firmly packed light brown sugar

3 tbsp. cold butter, cut into bits

2 tbsp. sugar (preferably organic)

2 tbsp. flour

½ tsp. cinnamon

⅓ cup chopped walnuts

PREPARATION

In a bowl, cream together the sugar and softened butter. Add the pumpkin, sour cream, egg and orange rind, and beat the mixture until well combined. Into a bowl sift together the flour, baking powder, baking soda, nutmeg and salt. Add the flour mixture to the pumpkin mixture alternately with the milk and blend until just combined.

Pour the batter into a buttered 8-inch square baking pan. In a mini-food processor, place all streusel ingredients except for the walnuts. Pulse the mixture quickly until it resembles coarse meal. Spread the streusel evenly over the batter and top it with the chopped walnuts.

Bake the coffeecake in a preheated 375 degree oven for 45 minutes, or until a wooden toothpick inserted in the center comes out clean. Let the cake cool in the pan for 10 minutes before cutting into squares. Serve warm or at room temperature. Serves 4–8

Flour - Bleached vs Unbleached

I normally use King Arthur Flour® - Never Bleached. Never Bromated®. I specify unbleached flour in my recipes because flour that is bleached is normally bromated. What this means is that bromine (a heavy, volatile, corrosive liquid element) is combined with a substance chemically. Among other things, this process is used in producing dyes. My attitude is that we all ingest enough chemicals in our lives, so using unbleached flour assures that this is one less chemical your body has to process.

Desserts

If you're consternating over what to serve for dessert for a special occasion, almost everyone appreciates home-made cookies served with a premium quality ice cream. You will note a recurring theme with most cookie recipes included in this book: They are very rich, mainly because of the quantity of butter (naturalmente). The butter makes the cookies not only delicious, but very crispy. I do not make cookies often, because I have no control – meaning that half of them are gone before they ever make their way into a storage container.

A dessert Toni made when peaches were in season was "Peach Melba" – so elegant, and so easy to throw together. Here's what to do: Peel and slice some ripe peaches (in season, preferably locally grown). Place desired amount in attractive individual serving bowls (something crystal is a good choice), top with premium vanilla ice cream, and then spoon gourmet quality Raspberry Sauce (also referred to as "Melba Sauce," available in better quality food stores) over the ice cream and peaches. Totalmente stupendo!!

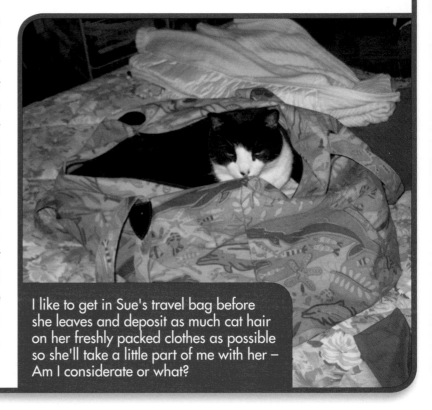

I like to get in Sue's travel bag before she leaves and deposit as much cat hair on her freshly packed clothes as possible so she'll take a little part of me with her – Am I considerate or what?

Testimonial

Very few things are truly unique, but "Cooking With Clyde" is one of them. Sue doesn't just offer sumptuous recipes; she tells delicious stories – about her beautiful Italian mother teaching her to cook, fun meals shared with family and friends, and the humorous hypothetical musings of her beloved cat Clyde.

Sue, Pat, and Clyde live down the hall from me in our condominium building, so I often encounter wonderful aromas when I pass their door. Happily, Sue is as generous as she is talented and often calls offering to bring me a portion – the gourmet version of Meals on Wheels

As a friend fortunate enough to enjoy Sue's cooking, I can attest to her culinary skill. As a cat-lover, I can corroborate her claim that, indeed, Clyde has no equal. Anyone who appreciates well-told stories, well-prepared food, or well-loved companions (and who doesn't?) will appreciate "Cooking With Clyde."

Melanie Scarborough
Neighbor and Cat Sitter for Clyde
Alexandria, VA

Ginger Crisps

INGREDIENTS

2 sticks unsalted butter at room temperature (very soft)

1 cup firmly packed light brown sugar

1 large egg yolk

1 tsp. vanilla

½ cup well chopped crystallized ginger

¼ tsp. ground ginger

1½ cup unbleached all-purpose flour

¾ tsp. double-acting baking powder

½ tsp. salt

PREPARATION

In a bowl cream together the butter and the brown sugar. When very well combined, beat in the egg yolk, vanilla, crystallized ginger, and the ground ginger. Place the flour, baking powder and salt into a sifter, and sift directly over the bowl. Combine the batter well.

Drop 12 teaspoons of the batter about 3 inches apart onto an un-greased baking sheet and bake the cookies in batches in the middle of a preheated 350 degree oven for 12 minutes, or until they are just golden brown. Let the cookies cool on the sheets for 5 minutes, then transfer them carefully with a spatula to a rack and cool completely before serving, or placing in an airtight storage container. Makes approx. 50 cookies

Three dozen for me,
1 dozen for Sue & Pat

Bermuda, 1969
Jackie Kennedy had nothing over Toni!

Pecan Cookies

Note: This is my mother's recipe. These cookies are decadently rich, worth every calorie

INGREDIENTS

2 sticks butter (½ lb.), softened in a large bowl to room temperature

2 cups hard packed dark brown sugar

2 large eggs

2 tsp. vanilla

2 cups unbleached all-purpose flour

1 tsp. baking powder

1 6-oz. bag pecan chips (or approx. 1½ cups)

Whole pecans for decorating cookies

PREPARATION

Add sugar to bowl with softened butter and cream together, 1 cup of sugar at a time. Add eggs and blend well. Stir in vanilla. Sift the flour and baking powder together twice, and then stir into the butter mixture. Last, add pecan chips and stir to combine well and evenly.

Preheat oven to 350 degrees. Lightly grease a non-stick cookie sheet and drop cookie dough from a tsp. onto the sheet (each cookie should be about the size of a tbsp.). Press a pecan lightly onto the top of each cookie. There should only be 12 cookies per baking sheet because they spread out a lot as they're baking. Bake for 13-15 minutes. The cookies should be a very deep brown color, and slightly browner around the edges.

Remove cookies from sheets with a sturdy spatula immediately upon removing from the oven, place on a rack to cool. As the cookies cool they become very crispy.

Lemon Curd Cheesecake with Blueberries

Lemon Curd:

1½ tsp. finely grated lemon zest

½ cup fresh lemon juice

½ cup sugar (preferably organic)

3 large eggs

½ stick unsalted butter, cut into tbsp., then each tbsp. cut in half

Crust:

5 tbsp. unsalted butter, melted

1½ cups gingersnap crumbs (crumbs should be very fine – use mini food processor)

2 tbsp. sugar, preferably organic

⅛ tsp. salt

Filling:

3 (8-oz.) packages cream cheese, softened to room temperature

1 cup sugar, preferably organic

3 large eggs

¾ cup sour cream

1 tsp. vanilla

½ cup red currant jelly

8 oz. container of fresh blueberries

PREPARATION

For lemon curd: Whisk together the zest, juice, sugar and eggs in a heavy saucepan. Add butter in pieces (1 or 2 at a time) and over moderate heat, whisk the mixture until the butter is melted and the curd is thickened and some bubbles appear on the surface (this should take 5–10 minutes). Remove from heat and set aside.

For crust: Preheat oven to 350 degrees. Stir together all crust ingredients in a bowl, then press onto the bottom and 1 inch up the sides of a 9 inch springform pan. Place the pan on top of a shallow baking pan and bake in the middle of the oven for 10 minutes. Remove pan from the oven and cool completely on a rack.

For filling: With an electric mixer set at medium speed, beat together the cream cheese and sugar in a bowl until very smooth. Reduce the speed to low and add the eggs, one at a time, until each egg is thoroughly incorporated. Add the sour cream and vanilla and continue to beat at low speed until these ingredients are also thoroughly blended.

Pour approx. two thirds of the cream cheese filling into the crust, then spoon half of the lemon curd over the filling. Note: the lemon curd should be well stirred with a whisk before using. With a knife, gently swirl the curd into the filling. The goal is to create a marbleized effect. Avoid touching the crumb crust with the knife so that crumbs do not get mixed in with the filling. Repeat procedure with remaining cream cheese filling and curd.

Reduce oven temperature to 300 degrees. Bake cheesecake until set, but the center should still tremble when the pan is gently shaken, approx. 50 minutes. Do not be concerned that the center appears loose, because it will continue to set as it cools. Transfer the springform pan to a rack and run a knife around the top edge of the cake to loosen. Cool on the rack completely, which will take about 2 hours. Place in refrigerator and chill, covered, for at least 4 hours.

Before serving, melt currant jelly in a small heavy saucepan over low heat, and remove from the heat. Add the fresh blueberries to the melted jelly and stir gently to coat berries evenly. Set aside to bring to room temperature, or slightly warm. Spoon a generous portion of the berries on each cheesecake slice. Serves 10

I couldn't eat another bite – for at least 10 more minutes!

Glazed Lemon Poppy-Seed Cake

Adapted from Gourmet magazine, Condé Nast Publications

INGREDIENTS

1½ cups unbleached all-purpose flour

1 tsp. baking powder

1 tbsp. grated fresh lemon zest

¼ tsp. salt

2 sticks unsalted butter, softened

¾ cup sugar, preferably organic

2 large eggs

1 tbsp. poppy seeds

¾ cup confectioners sugar

2 tbsp. fresh lemon juice

PREPARATION

Preheat oven to 375 degrees. Butter a 9-inch round cake pan.

Place the flour, baking powder, lemon zest and salt in a bowl and whisk together.

In a separate bowl beat the butter and sugar together with an electric mixer at medium speed until pale and fluffy, which should take 2–3 minutes. Beat in the eggs, one at a time, until combined with the butter mixture. Reduce speed to low and add the flour mixture and poppy seeds and mix until just combined.

Transfer the batter to the prepared cake pan, smoothing the top, and bake for ½ hour in the middle of the oven, or until a wooden pick inserted in the center of the cake comes out clean and the top is golden brown. Cool cake in the pan on a rack for 5 minutes, then invert onto a decorative serving dish or plate.

Whisk together the confectioners sugar and lemon juice in a small bowl until smooth. Spoon the glaze over the warm cake, spreading it with a spatula to drizzle over the edge. Let stand for about 15 minutes, or until the glaze is set.

Serve the cake warm or at room temperature. Serves 8–10

Chocolate Turtle Cheesecake

INGREDIENTS

2 cups vanilla cookie crumbs (best using mini food processor)

6 tbsp. melted butter

1 (14-oz.) bag of caramels (Kraft® Classic preferably)

1 (5 oz.) can evaporated milk

1½ cups chopped pecans (lightly toasted)

2 (8-oz.) packages cream cheese, softened to room temperature in a mixing bowl

½ cup sugar

1 tbsp. vanilla

2 eggs

½ cup semi-sweet chocolate chips, melted

PREPARATION

Preheat oven to 350 degrees. To make crust, mix crumbs with melted butter. Press as evenly as possible on bottom and sides of an 8 ½ to 9-inch springform pan. Bake for 10 minutes and set aside.

In saucepan over low heat, combine the caramels and evaporated milk. Cook, stirring often, until the candy melts and the mixture is very smooth. Cool for 5 minutes and spoon evenly over the crust. Do not let the caramel mixture come quite to the edge of the crust. Top with the toasted chopped pecans. Note: To toast pecans, spread evenly in a shallow baking dish (a pie plate is good), and bake at 350 degrees for approx. 10–15 minutes, or until the pecans are lightly browned.

To softened cream cheese in bowl, add sugar, vanilla and eggs. With a hand electric mixer, combine ingredients well. Next add melted chocolate, continue to mix until chocolate is thoroughly incorporated, and pour this mixture evenly over the pecans. Note: Chocolate can be melted in a double boiler, or place in a very small baking dish, and bake at 350 degrees for approx. 5–10 minutes.

Bake cheesecake for 30 minutes. Remove from oven and cool on a rack completely. Refrigerate overnight before serving.

Serves 8–10

Oatmeal Chocolate Chunk Coconut Cookies

INGREDIENTS

1¼ cups sweetened flaked coconut

¾ cup (or 4 oz.) almonds with skins, coarsely chopped

1½ cups unbleached all-purpose flour

1 tsp. cinnamon

1 tsp. baking soda

1 tsp. salt

¼ tsp. nutmeg

2½ sticks unsalted butter, softened to room temperature in a large bowl

¾ cup firmly packed light brown sugar

½ cup granulated sugar, preferably organic

1 large egg

1½ tsp. vanilla

1¾ cups old-fashioned rolled oats (not quick cooking oats)

12 oz. semisweet chocolate chunks (or chocolate chips if chunks are not available)

PREPARATION

Preheat oven to 350 degrees. Place coconut in a shallow baking dish (pie pan is good) and place chopped almonds in another baking dish, and bake in oven, stirring several times, until the coconut is a nutty brown color and the almond skins have turned a slightly deeper shade of brown and are aromatic (should take 10–15 minutes). The coconut will still have white flakes mixed in with the nutty toasted flakes. Do not expect it to all be an even nutty brown color. Remove the almonds and coconut from oven and set aside to cool. Increase oven temperature to 375 degrees.

Sift together the flour, cinnamon, baking soda, salt and nutmeg and set aside. Add the sugars to the butter in the large bowl and with an electric hand mixer, beat together until light and fluffy. Next beat in the egg and vanilla. Add the flour mixture and beat briefly just until incorporated. Remove as much cookie batter as possible from the beater blades. With a wooden spoon, stir the rolled oats, the toasted coconut, the toasted almonds, and the chocolate chunks into the cookie dough.

Arrange rounded tbsp. of dough about 3 inches apart on ungreased baking sheets and with moistened (if necessary) fingers, gently flatten the mounds into 3 inch rounds. Bake cookies in batches in the middle of oven until golden brown, 13–15 minutes. Cool cookies on the baking sheets for 1 minute and transfer with a spatula to a rack to cool completely. Makes approx. 5 dozen cookies

I feel like I've been rode hard & put away wet.

47

Orange Cheesecake Brownies

Adapted from Gourmet magazine, Condé Nast Publications

Cheesecake Batter:

1 8-oz. package cream cheese, softened to room temperature

⅓ cup granulated sugar, preferably organic

1 tbsp. finely grated fresh orange zest

1 large egg

1 tbsp. unbleached all-purpose flour

Chocolate Batter:

6 tbsp. unsalted butter

2 oz. unsweetened chocolate, in pieces

2 oz. good quality bittersweet chocolate (not unsweetened)

1 cup sugar, preferably organic

1 tsp. vanilla

2 large eggs

⅔ cup unbleached all-purpose flour

½ tsp. salt

PREPARATION

Preheat oven to 350 degrees. Butter and flour an 8-inch square baking pan, knocking out all excess flour.

For cheesecake batter: In a bowl stir together the cream cheese, sugar and orange zest with a wooden spoon until smooth. Beat in the egg until blended well and stir in flour.

For the chocolate batter: In a heavy saucepan melt the butter and both kinds of chocolate over low heat, stirring, until smooth and remove from the heat. Cool the mixture for 10 minutes and then stir in the sugar and vanilla. Add eggs, 1 at a time, beating well with a wooden spoon until the mixture is glossy and smooth. Stir in the flour and salt until just combined.

Spread chocolate batter evenly in prepared pan. Drop cheesecake batter by large spoonfuls onto the chocolate batter and run a knife through the batters to make decorative swirls. It will take a couple minutes to do this. The goal is to have the batters blended well together while maintaining a marbleized appearance.

Bake brownies in the middle of the oven for 50 minutes, or until the cheesecake mixture is pale gold and a wooden toothpick tester comes out clean. Cool brownies completely in pan on a rack before cutting into 16 squares. Leftover brownies (good luck if there are any) should be kept refrigerated, and brownies may be eaten chilled or at room temperature. Makes 16 brownies

Sugar

Recipes that include sugar usually (if not always) say "preferably organic." Here is why: organic sugar contains just one ingredient – pure, natural, organic evaporated cane juice. The evaporation process produces perfect sugar crystals, rich in flavor and molasses. You will note that organic sugar is not pure white, but has a slight caramel color. I won't debate whether organic sugar is more wholesome and better for you than other basic white processed cane sugars, but I do contend that it definitely tastes better and enhances your recipes.

Lemon Coconut Cookies

INGREDIENTS

1 cup sweetened flaked coconut, toasted and cooled

2 sticks unsalted butter, softened to room temperature in a large bowl

½ cup granulated sugar, preferably organic

2 tbsp. freshly grated lemon zest

1 tsp. vanilla

¼ tsp. lemon extract

¼ tsp. coconut extract

2 cups unbleached all-purpose flour

¼ tsp. salt

Confectioners sugar for sprinkling on the cookies

PREPARATION

Preheat oven to 350 degrees. Place coconut in a shallow baking dish (pie pan is good) and bake in oven, stirring several times, until the coconut is a nutty brown color (should take 10–15 minutes). The coconut will still have white flakes mixed in with the nutty toasted flakes. Do not expect it to all be an even nutty brown color. Remove from oven and set aside to cool.

Add the sugar to the softened butter and with an electric mixer cream the mixture until it is light and fluffy. Next beat in the zest, vanilla, and both extracts. Add the flour and salt and beat the mixture until it forms dough. Remove as much cookie batter as possible from the beater blades. With a wooden spoon, stir the toasted coconut into the cookie dough and chill for one hour.

Halve the dough and on 2 sheets of wax paper form each half into a log that is approx. 10 inches long, using the wax paper as a guide. Chill the logs, wrapped in the wax paper, for at least 4 hours, or overnight.

Preheat the oven to 300 degrees. Cut the logs into slices slightly larger than ¼ inch thick with a very sharp knife and arrange the slices 2 inches apart on lightly buttered baking sheets. Bake the cookies in the middle of the oven for 25 to 30 minutes, or until they are pale golden, and transfer the cookies to a rack, and immediately sprinkle them very generously with the confectioners sugar. Makes approx. 5 dozen cookies

Chocolate Mint Cheesecake Squares

Crumb Crust:

1 9-oz. package thin chocolate wafers, crushed to crumbs in a food processor (my preference is Nabisco® Famous Chocolate Wafers)

⅓ cup melted butter

¼ tsp. nutmeg

¼ cup sugar, preferably organic

Cheese Filling:

4 packages (8 oz. each) cream cheese, softened to room temperature in a large bowl

1 cup sugar, preferably organic

1 tsp. vanilla

1 tsp. pure peppermint extract

1 cup sour cream

4 eggs

12 oz. semi-sweet chocolate, melted and cooled

PREPARATION

Combine all crust ingredients in a bowl and stir to combine well. Press evenly on the bottom of a 13 x 9 inch baking pan and refrigerate until needed.

Add sugar, vanilla and peppermint extract to the cream cheese in the bowl and beat with an electric mixer on medium speed until very smooth and well blended. Add the sour cream and continue to beat on medium speed until also blended. Add the eggs, one at a time, beating on low speed after the addition of each egg, just until blended. Stir melted chocolate into the batter until well combined and pour over reserved chocolate crumb crust.

Preheat oven to 325 degrees. Bake cheesecake for approx. 45 minutes, or until the center is almost set. This means that when you shake the baking pan the middle will jiggle slightly. Cool completely on a rack. Cover and refrigerate at least 4 hours or overnight. Cut into squares to serve. Store any leftover cheesecake in the refrigerator. Serves 12–16

Buttermilk Glazed Pineapple Carrot Cake

INGREDIENTS

2 cups unbleached all-purpose flour

1½ tsp. baking soda

½ tsp. salt

1½ cups sugar, preferably organic

2 tsp. cinnamon

3 eggs

¾ cup buttermilk (low-fat is OK)

½ cup canola oil

2 tsp. vanilla

¾ cup well drained crushed pineapple

2 cups finely grated carrots (there should not be any liquid)

½ cup coarsely chopped pecans

1 generous cup flaked coconut

Buttermilk Glaze:

⅔ cup sugar (preferably organic)

¼ tsp. baking soda

⅓ cup buttermilk (low-fat OK)

5 tbsp. butter

2 tbsp. light corn syrup

½ tsp. vanilla

PREPARATION

Preheat the oven to 350 degrees. Sift the flour, baking soda, salt, sugar and cinnamon together into a bowl. In a separate bowl beat the eggs with the buttermilk, oil and vanilla and add to the dry ingredients. Mix until smooth.

Fold in the pineapple, carrots, nuts and coconut and pour into a greased 9 x 13 inch baking pan. Bake 45 to 50 minutes, or until the center of the cake springs back when lightly touched.

While cake is baking prepare glaze. Combine all the glaze ingredients except the vanilla in a small saucepan, bring to a boil, and cook over medium heat, stirring frequently, at a gentle boil for five minutes. Remove from the heat and stir in the vanilla.

When the cake is done, remove from the oven and immediately prick the cake all over with a fork. Slowly pour the buttermilk glaze evenly over the cake. Cool in the pan before cutting.

Toasting Nuts, Sesame Seeds, Coconut & More

I find the easiest way to toast nuts, sesame seeds, coconut, or almost any other ingredient is to do the following: Preheat the oven to 325 degrees. Place ingredient in a shallow oven-proof baking dish and place in middle of the oven. The time it takes to toast an ingredient varies depending on the quantity and type, and whether you want it to be lightly browned or a deep brown color. It is important to check every several minutes and stir the ingredient, to assure even browning and also to assure that you are not overcooking it.

If you prefer a stove-top method, then place the ingredient in a heavy non-stick skillet over moderately low heat. Cook stirring frequently, until you have achieved the desired shade of brown. I seem to have better luck using the oven method, but if I'm toasting a very small amount, I tend to use the stove-top method. Either way, you will have better results if you are not toasted when you are toasting.

Lemon Cheesecake Pie with Strawberry Glaze

(This recipe of Toni's was reserved for very special occasions, e.g. a birthday celebration, holidays, etc. This dessert would make any event a celebration.)

Crust:

9 honey graham crackers, each measuring 9 x 2½ inches, crushed finely (should equal approx. 1 ¼ cups of graham cracker crumbs – I use a mini-food processor)

5 tbsp. butter, melted

¼ cup sugar, preferably organic

Filling:

1 8-oz. package cream cheese, softened to room temperature in a bowl

2 tbsp. butter, softened to room temperature in same bowl as cream cheese

½ cup sugar, preferably organic

1 large egg

2 tbsp. unbleached all-purpose flour

⅔ cup milk

¼ cup fresh lemon juice

2 tbsp. grated lemon peel

Strawberry Glaze:

¼ cup water

¼ cup sugar, preferably organic

1 tbsp. cornstarch

1 16-oz. package frozen strawberries, thawed in a colander (just berries, no sugar or syrup added)

PREPARATION

Make crust: Blend crust ingredients in a bowl until well combined and press onto bottom and sides of an 8-inch pie plate that has deep sides. Chill in refrigerator while making the filling (for at least 15 minutes, or until set).

For the filling, cream together the cream cheese and butter, then stir in the sugar until well combined. Add the egg and stir until it is incorporated into the mixture. Add the flour and stir in. Add the milk and stir until combined. Finally, stir in the lemon juice and lemon peel. Pour into the unbaked pie shell. Preheat oven to 350 degrees and bake the pie for 35–40 minutes, or until the middle of the pie does not appear to be loose when gently shaken.

While the pie is baking make the strawberry glaze: Combine the water, sugar and cornstarch in a small saucepan and cook over moderate heat, stirring, until the mixture reaches the boiling point. Add the thawed strawberries, reduce heat and simmer until the mixture is glossy and thickened. Set aside and cool to room temperature.

When the pie has been removed from the oven, allow it to cool for approx. 15–20 minutes, and then spread the strawberry glaze over top. Chill well before serving. This pie is just as good if chilled overnight and served the next day. Serves 8–10

Note: My mother typically did not use a fruit glaze on her pie, but instead spread lots of lightly sweetened whipped cream on top (freshly whipped of course). Also, she would reserve several tbsp. of the graham cracker crumbs and would sprinkle these crumbs on top of the whipped cream. If this sounds better to you than the fruit glaze, go for it, and know that it will be the "Toni Original."

Mamma Mia Toni With Her Million Dollar Smile

Dearborn's Famous Brownies

(My friend Tricia obtained permission from Dearborn (an engineer who also resides in Maui) to publish his locally famous brownie recipe, which she vows is the most amazing recipe for people who prefer the "fudgey" (as opposed to the "cakey") type of brownies.)

INGREDIENTS

3 squares (3 oz.) unsweetened chocolate (good choice is Baker's®)

¼ lb. (8 tbsp.) butter

1 cup plus 2 tbsp. sugar (preferably organic)

2 eggs

½ cup unbleached all-purpose flour

½ tsp. salt

½ tsp. baking powder

½ tsp. vanilla

1 cup coarsely chopped walnuts

1 cup semi-sweet chocolate chips (preferably Ghiradelli®)

PREPARATION

Melt the chocolate and butter in a small saucepan over low heat until liquid. Set aside and cool for awhile. Place the sugar and eggs in a bowl and mix together. In a separate bowl combine the flour, salt and baking powder.

Add the chocolate mixture to the sugar mixture and combine. Next add the flour mixture and stir to combine. Stir in the vanilla. Add the walnuts and chocolate chips and stir to combine.

Preheat the oven to 275 degrees. Pour the batter into a 9 x 9 inch greased and floured Pyrex baking pan and bake for 50 minutes EXACTLY. Do not use the "toothpick" test to determine whether the brownies are cooked completely. The brownies will be crispy on the outside but soft on the inside. Allow to cool in the pan for approx. 10 minutes before cutting into squares.

Alexandria, VA, 1997
Pat with Clyde, Sue, Tricia

Clyde's Cookies

INGREDIENTS

8 tbsp. (1 stick) butter, softened in a bowl to room temperature

1 cup firmly packed light brown sugar

1 egg

1 tbsp. vanilla

1 cup all-purpose unbleached flour

½ cup unsweetened cocoa powder (preferably organic)

½ tsp. baking soda

¼ tsp. salt

1 cup white chocolate baking pieces (I use Ghirardelli® Classic White Premium Baking Chips)

1 cup bittersweet chocolate baking chips (I use Ghirardelli® 60% Cacao Premium Baking Chips)

½ cup coarsely chopped pecans, lightly toasted

PREPARATION

Add the brown sugar to the softened butter and beat together until creamy. Beat in the egg and the vanilla until the mixture is fluffy. Stir in the flour, cocoa powder, baking soda and salt until well blended. Stir in the white chocolate chips, dark chocolate chips, and chopped pecans.

Preheat the oven to 350 degrees. Drop the batter by tbsp. onto ungreased baking sheets. There should be 15 cookies per sheet, evenly spaced. Bake the cookies in the preheated oven for 14–15 minutes, or until the cookies are almost set in the center. Cool the cookies on the baking sheets for 2 minutes, then transfer cookies to wire racks to cool completely. The cookies should be crispy after they are completely cooled. Makes 45 cookies

Lime Almond Cheesecake

Adapted from Gourmet magazine, Condé Nast Publications

Crust:

½ stick (4 tbsp.) unsalted butter

1¼ cups slivered blanched almonds, lightly toasted

¼ cup sugar, preferably organic

Filling:

2 lbs. cream cheese, softened to room temperature

1½ cups sugar, preferably organic

1½ tbsp. fresh lime juice

A pinch of salt

1 tsp. almond extract

4 large eggs

Topping:

1 16-oz. container sour cream

¼ cup sugar, preferably organic

1 tbsp. fresh lime juice

1 tsp. grated lime zest

PREPARATION

Preheat oven to 350 degrees and butter the bottom and sides of a 10-inch springform pan.

Make crust: Melt butter and cool slightly. In a food processor pulse toasted almonds until finely ground and transfer to a bowl. Sprinkle buttered sides of the springform pan with 3 tbsp. of the almonds, and knock any excess back into the bowl. Stir butter and sugar into the almonds until combined well and press evenly onto the bottom of the pan.

Make filling: In a large bowl beat the cream cheese and sugar together with an electric mixer on low speed for several minutes. Add the lime juice, a pinch of salt and the almond extract and beat until smooth. Add the eggs, one at a time, beating well after each addition. Pour filling into the pan and bake cheesecake for 45 minutes. Remove from the oven (keep oven set at 350 degrees) and let stand for 10 minutes.

Make topping while the cheesecake is baking: Place sour cream in a bowl and let it stand at room temperature for 30 minutes. Add to the sour cream the sugar, lime juice and lime zest and whisk together until very smooth and well blended.

After the cheesecake has been removed from the oven and allowed to stand for 10 minutes, drop spoonfuls of the topping around the edges of the cheesecake and spread gently over the entire cake, smoothing evenly. Bake cheesecake for an additional 10 minutes and transfer immediately to the refrigerator. Chill uncovered for 8 hours, then cover until ready to cut and serve. The cheesecake will keep well for up to 2 days. Serves 10–12

I love a warm cheerful fire – I hate it when my feet go to sleep.

Chocolate Chip Cookies

(I have been asked by many people who have sampled these cookies whether they contain any sort of illegal drug because they are so addictive).

INGREDIENTS

2 sticks (16 tbsp.) unsalted butter, softened to room temperature in a large bowl

1 cup firmly packed light brown sugar

1 cup firmly packed dark brown sugar

1 tbsp. vanilla

2 large eggs

2½ cups unbleached all-purpose flour

2 tsp. salt

1 tsp. baking soda

2 tbsp. ground coriander

3½ cups coarsely chopped walnut pieces

4½ cups semisweet chocolate chips

PREPARATION

Add the light brown sugar to the softened butter in the large bowl. Beat until it is creamy and well combined. Repeat process with the dark brown sugar. Stir in the vanilla. Beat in the eggs, one at a time, until very creamy and well combined.

In another bowl, place the flour, salt, baking soda and coriander. Stir to combine well, and add to the butter mixture. Stir until the flour is completely incorporated into the butter. Stir in the walnuts and chocolate chips. Chill the cookie dough, covered, for one hour.

Butter two cookie sheets. Form the dough with your hands into balls that are approx. 1½ inches in diameter, or the size of a very large walnut, and place a couple inches apart on the cookie sheets. There should be 12 cookies per sheet. Preheat the oven to 375 degrees, place one cookie sheet in the middle of the preheated oven and bake for 15 minutes, or until they are a very deep golden brown. Remove the cookies from the oven and put in the second baking sheet. Allow the cookies you have removed from the oven to cool for about 8–10 minutes on the sheet before removing to a rack to cool completely. Put more unbaked cookies on this sheet so that when you remove the next batch from the oven, you're ready to go with the next batch. Makes about 6–7 dozen cookies

---

Baked Bananas with Coconut & Almonds

(Neruppu Vazhai) Note: If you are serving Indian food, this is a nice dessert accompaniment, since the origin of the dish is from India)

INGREDIENTS

3 ripened firm bananas

¼ cup fresh orange juice

¼ cup dark brown sugar

½ cup grated unsweetened coconut

¼ cup slivered blanched almonds

½ tsp. ground cardamom

2 tbsp. melted butter

Ice cream to accompany (vanilla or rum raisin are good choices)

PREPARATION

Preheat the oven to 400 degrees.

Peel the bananas and slice them lengthwise, then crosswise into 3 pieces. Arrange the bananas in a single layer in a shallow buttered baking dish. Pour the orange juice over the bananas and sprinkle evenly with the sugar, coconut, almonds and cardamom. Pour the butter over top, and bake in the preheated oven for 25 minutes. The bananas should be very soft, and the almonds browned.

Place scoops of ice cream in individual serving bowls and spoon the bananas with the sauce on the sides of the ice cream. Serve immediately. Serves 6

Butter

I consider the phrase "butter substitute" an oxymoron. You must realize that I came from the household of Toni, where butter was one of the major food groups. It would have been nothing short of heresy to consider substituting anything for butter in my mother's kitchen.

My mother was really on target regarding so many things when it came to cooking and ingredients. I remember clearly when margarine was first introduced as an alternative to butter. My mother did go so far as to purchase some just to see what all the hype was about, and the look on her face after she tasted it was indescribable. Suffice to say the margarine was thrown in the garbage, and she said to me "Not only does that stuff taste terrible, it's full of harmful chemicals, and I can't imagine how anyone's digestive system could even handle that." Now, many years later, it has come to light that hydrogenated oils are extremely bad for your health, and, in fact, the body has a difficult time processing them.

My husband, Pat, has many nicknames for me, one of which is "butter queen." He also says things such as, "Have a little bread with your butter." I am a bit over the top with my addiction to and adoration of butter, but Toni may have even been worse. She put butter on just about everything. I'll give you an example: My mother would place shredded wheat biscuits on a broiler-proof dish, then slather then with butter and broil them until the butter was melted and the tops were browned. Yum!

Also, my mother frequently made corn on the cob; as I mentioned, York County Silver Queen corn is the best I've ever eaten. Toni had these little soufflé dishes in which she would pour a generous amount of melted butter and place a little brush (very cute, with little corn cobs on the end) next to each dish. So you never had to utter the words, "Pass the butter" in our home when eating corn because everyone had their own, which was lavishly spread on each ear consumed. Was my mother considerate or what!

Cuban Flan

INGREDIENTS

⅔ cups sugar (preferably organic)

1 tsp. water

4 eggs

1 can Eagle Brand® sweetened condensed milk (14 oz.)

1 can whole milk (use the Eagle Brand®) scrape out any residual milk

Pinch of salt

1 tsp. vanilla

1 can Pet® evaporated milk (12 oz.)

PREPARATION

Preheat the oven to 100 degrees. The flan will be baked in a round glass ovenproof dish, or a round non-stick pan, that is approx. 8 to 9 inches in diameter. Put the baking dish in the oven so that it will be slightly warmed when you add the caramelized sugar.

Put the sugar in a non-stick skillet and sprinkle with the water. Cook over medium heat, watching carefully, and stirring occasionally, until the sugar starts to caramelize. Once the sugar starts to caramelize, stir continually to assure it does not burn. It may be necessary to turn down the heat a bit. When done, the sugar should be caramelized into a chestnut, light brown color.

Remove the warmed baking dish from the oven and quickly pour the caramel into the dish, holding, turning and tilting the dish so that the caramel coats the entire bottom and a little of the sides. It is important to complete this procedure quickly because the caramel will start to harden immediately. Set the prepared dish aside.

Increase the oven temperature to 350 degrees. Beat the eggs in a bowl with a whisk. In a separate bowl, place the evaporated milk, condensed milk and whole milk, in the order listed. Beat gently with a whisk to combine. Add a pinch of salt and the vanilla; stir gently to combine. Add the eggs to the milk mixture and whisk gently until combined. Pour this mixture into the prepared caramelized baking dish.

Place the baking dish inside a larger baking dish and fill it with water to reach halfway up the side of the flan dish (Shelley calls this a *baño de Maria*). Place carefully in the center of the preheated oven and bake for 1 hour and 10 to 15 minutes. Check the flan after an hour and test with a knife (it should come out clean) and if not done, check every five minutes until it is done.

Remove carefully from the oven and lift the dish containing the flan from the larger baking dish containing the water and set on a rack to cool for approx. 10 minutes. Run a knife around the edge of the flan to loosen it. Put a dish (with a raised edge) that is larger than the flan pan on top of the flan dish. Use the cooling rack, and flip the flan dish over quickly so that the baking dish will be sitting on the larger serving dish. When the flan dish is lifted, the flan should slide off intact with the caramel surrounding it. Refrigerate to cool, and remove 20 minutes before serving.

Shelley

Before Shelley relocated to London many years ago, we formed a close friendship while working together (and playing harder than we worked).

When she comes across the pond for visits, our reunions are always infused with two of the universal bonds that draw all humans closer – laughter and sharing fabulous food.

Shelley has shared with me, and now you, this marvelous recipe.

Women in Black
Washington, DC, 1985

Birthday Celebrations
Alexandria, VA, 1984

Peach & Blueberry Crisp

INGREDIENTS

½ cup granulated sugar, preferably organic

2 tbsp. all-purpose unbleached flour (or almond flour)*

2 tsp. fresh lemon juice

1½ tsp. grated lemon rind

1 tsp. cinnamon

3 cups sliced peeled ripe fresh peaches

2 cups fresh blueberries

Topping:

½ cup old-fashioned rolled oats

⅓ cup all-purpose unbleached flour (or almond flour)*

3 tbsp. firmly packed dark brown sugar

½ tsp. cinnamon

¼ tsp. nutmeg

3 tbsp. butter, softened to room temperature

PREPARATION

In a large bowl, combine sugar, flour, lemon juice, lemon rind and cinnamon. Stir in the peaches and blueberries until well mixed. Spread in a 9-inch square baking pan.

Preheat oven to 350 degrees. In a small bowl, combine all topping ingredients except for the butter. Then stir in the softened butter until combined and crumbly. Sprinkle evenly over the fruit. Bake the dish for 30 to 35 minutes, or until the topping is browned and the fruit is tender. Serve warm. Serves 6–8

Note: Once I invited a couple to dinner and when I asked about preferences, allergies, etc., I was advised that everyone in the family had allergic reactions to wheat. I had planned on making this recipe, so improvised and instead of regular wheat flour I used "almond flour." Here is a good example of improvising by necessity with the end result being improved. I liked this dessert even better using the almond flour. However, it is very expensive, and the recipe is totally delicious using the regular flour as specified.

Gingerbread Jamaican Style

INGREDIENTS

2 sticks (16 tbsp.) unsalted butter

1 cup unsulfured molasses

2⅓ cups unbleached all-purpose flour

1 tbsp. baking powder

1 tsp. allspice

½ tsp. baking soda

½ tsp. salt

¼ tsp. cinnamon

⅛ tsp. nutmeg

⅛ tsp. cloves

½ cup firmly packed dark brown sugar

2 large eggs

⅔ cup sour cream (low-fat is OK)

½ cup finely chopped crystallized ginger

3 tbsp. finely chopped fresh gingerroot (easiest in a mini-food processor)

PREPARATION

Melt the butter in a medium saucepan with the molasses over low heat until the butter is melted. Remove from heat and stir butter and molasses together until well combined. Set aside to cool.

Sift together into a large bowl the flour, baking powder, allspice, baking soda, salt, cinnamon, nutmeg and cloves and set aside.

When the butter/molasses mixture has cooled, stir in the brown sugar, eggs and sour cream until well combined. Add this mixture to the flour mixture and combine. Gently stir in the chopped crystallized ginger and fresh gingerroot.

Preheat oven to 350 degrees. Pour the batter into a greased 10 by 5 by 3 inch baking dish and bake for 45–50 minutes, or until a cake tester inserted in the center comes out clean. Serves 10–12

Grapefruit Cake

INGREDIENTS

1½ cups sifted cake flour

Note: If you do not have cake flour on hand, you can substitute all-purpose flour by measuring 1½ cups of flour and then removing 3 tbsp. before sifting

¾ cup sugar, preferably organic

1½ tsp. baking powder

1 tsp. salt

¼ cup water

¼ cup canola oil

3 eggs, separated

3 tbsp. fresh grapefruit juice (ruby red or pink, sweet)

1 tsp. grated grapefruit rind

¼ tsp. cream of tartar

Cream Cheese Frosting:

1 8-oz. package cream cheese, softened to room temperature in a small bowl

1 tbsp. grapefruit juice

2 tsp. grated grapefruit rind

¾ cup sifted confectioners' sugar

4 drops yellow food coloring

1 medium ruby red (sweet) or pink (sweet) grapefruit, well peeled, seeds removed, and sectioned

PREPARATION

Sift together flour, sugar, baking powder and salt into a bowl. Make a well in the center and add water, oil, egg yolks, grapefruit juice and rind. Beat until very smooth. In a separate bowl beat egg whites with cream of tartar until stiff but not dry. Gradually pour the cake mixture over the egg whites and fold in very gently until just blended. Do not stir.

Preheat the oven to 350 degrees. Pour the batter into an ungreased 9-inch springform pan and bake for 30 minutes, or until the top is lightly browned and springs back when touched lightly with a finger. Invert cake onto a rack and cool thoroughly. Loosen edges of cake carefully and remove from pan.

For frosting, beat cream cheese until fluffy. Add grapefruit juice and rind. Gradually blend in sugar and beat until well blended. Stir in food coloring. Take one of the grapefruit sections, crush it, and add to frosting.

When cake is completely cooled and removed from the pan, cut it crosswise with a serrated knife to make two layers. Spread half of the frosting over one layer and top with half of the grapefruit sections. Top with second layer, spread remaining frosting over and garnish with remaining grapefruit sections.

Don't put a freshly washed warm mattress cover on the bed and think you'll be able to actually make the bed in the near future.

Heavenly French Chocolate Silk Pie

INGREDIENTS

¾ cup butter (12 tbsp.), softened to room temperature in a medium-sized bowl

1 scant cup of sugar (preferably organic) Note: Set aside 2 tbsp. of sugar for beating into egg whites

3 large or extra-large eggs, whites & yolks separated, brought to room temperature

2 tsp. vanilla

3 1-oz. squares of unsweetened chocolate (good quality)

Topping:

1 cup heavy whipping cream

¼ cup powdered (confectioners) sugar

½ tsp. vanilla

Pie Crust

Garnish: 1 1-oz. square of unsweetened chocolate, mint leaves (optional)

PREPARATION

Add sugar (except for the 2 tbsp.) to the butter in the bowl, a little at a time, and combine with an electric hand mixer. Beat until all sugar is incorporated, and the mixture is light and fluffy which should take several minutes.

Melt chocolate in a double boiler. Slowly add the melted chocolate to the butter mixture and beat at low speed with the electric mixer until the mixture is smooth and creamy.

Add yolks to the pie filling mixture, one at a time on medium speed, beating until smooth and each yolk is incorporated before adding the next yolk.

With electric mixer (clean blades first) beat egg whites until stiff, gradually adding the sugar while beating, one tbsp. at a time. Fold in the egg whites gently with a large spatula along with the vanilla.

Put the mixture in a deep dish prepared (baked) pie shell. Either use your favorite crust recipe or buy a good quality frozen shell, or use a packaged mix. A graham cracker crust is a very good choice for this pie. Place filling in the pie plate evenly distributed on top of the baked pie crust and refrigerate.

Make topping: Beat whipping cream just until it starts to form stiff peaks. It is important to not overdo it or the cream will be a buttery texture, which is not what you want! Add the powdered sugar and vanilla to the cream, and continue beating until fluffy and stiff. Remove the pie from the refrigerator and spread the whipped cream topping on top.

Use a vegetable peeler to make shavings and/or curls with the chocolate square for garnish, and also garnish with some fresh mint leaves if desired. Return the pie to the refrigerator and allow it to chill completely (at least for one hour). The pie is great either served cold, or serve it closer to room temperature, especially if you like a creamier consistency. Serves 10–12

Maggie (aka Margaret)

I first met Maggie when she was living in West Virginia, and she subsequently relocated out west to Boulder, Colo. Even though we have never resided in the same area, our friendship has not suffered as a result of distance.

When I spent a weekend with Maggie and her husband at their cabin overlooking the Continental Divide, the only thing that rivaled the spectacular view was Maggie's Heavenly French Chocolate Silk Pie.

Boulder, CO, 2003
Happy Together Again

Debbie

Debbie is originally from North Carolina. She has never lost her Southern accent or her Southern charm.

Debbie's food contributions to our girlfriend get-togethers include such delicacies as "salad in a bag" (all ingredients included, ready to toss), and Dump Cake (don't ask). However, on one birthday celebration we were flabbergasted when she made a cake from scratch that was wonderful. The recipe has been in her husband's family forever, and she is happy to share it.

I Want to Kiss the Bride
Richmond, VA, 1987

Holiday Party At Sue's
Alexandria, VA, 1986

Hotmilk Cake with Caramel Icing

INGREDIENTS

4 eggs

2 cups sugar, preferably organic

2 cups all-purpose unbleached flour

2 tsp. baking powder

1 cup whole milk

¼ lb. (8 tbsp.) butter

1 tsp. vanilla

Caramel Icing:

4 cups dark brown sugar (firmly packed)

½ lb. (16 tbsp.) butter

1 cup table or heavy cream (additional cream may be necessary for proper consistency)

1 tsp. vanilla

PREPARATION

Place eggs in a bowl and beat. Stir in the sugar. Sift together the flour and baking powder and stir into the egg mixture.

Heat the milk with the butter in a small saucepan over moderately low heat until hot (do not boil!). Add the hot milk and butter combination a little at a time to the cake batter, stirring to combine after each addition, and then stir in the vanilla.

Preheat oven to 375 degrees. Pour the batter into 2 greased 9-inch round cake pans. Bake for 20–30 minutes, or until a cake tester comes out clean. Remove from the oven and set on a rack to cool.

Make icing: Place all ingredients except the vanilla in a large sauce pan and cook over moderate heat until the sugar has dissolved. Bring to a boil (if you have a candy thermometer it should register 238 degrees). While the icing is reaching the boiling point, stir occasionally. Remove from the heat and stir in the vanilla.

The icing must be cooled before frosting. The easiest option is to place the icing in the refrigerator. It may be necessary to stir a little extra cream into the icing to get the desired consistency once it has been cooled. Spread some icing on one of the layers, top with the second layer, and ice cake on the top and sides.

Pumpkin Ginger Cheesecake Pie

Adapted from Gourmet magazine, Condé Nast Publications

Crumb Crust:

5 tbsp. unsalted butter, melted

1½ cups gingersnap crumbs (if available, try Trader Joe's® Triple Ginger Snaps-YUM!)

2 tbsp. sugar, preferably organic

⅛ tsp. salt

Filling:

¾ cup sugar, preferably organic

¼ cup coarsely chopped crystallized ginger

8-oz. package cream cheese, softened to room temperature in a large bowl

2 large eggs

¼ cup milk (low-fat OK)

1 tbsp. unbleached all-purpose flour

½ tsp. nutmeg

¼ tsp. allspice

¼ tsp. cloves

¼ tsp. salt

1 cup canned solid-pack pumpkin

PREPARATION

For crust: Preheat oven to 350 degrees. Stir together all crumb ingredients in a bowl and press evenly on the bottom and up the sides of a 9–9 ½ inch pie plate (4-cup capacity). Bake in preheated oven for 15 minutes, remove from oven and cool on a rack for 45 minutes.

For filling: Place sugar and ginger in a mini-food processor and pulse until the ginger is very finely chopped and the sugar and ginger are mixed together. Add the sugar mixture to the cream cheese and mix with a hand immersion blender until very smooth. Add the eggs, milk, flour, nutmeg, allspice, cloves and salt and continue to beat with the blender until just combined. Pour ⅔ cup of the filling mixture into a measuring cup and set aside.

Add the pumpkin to the filling remaining in the bowl and beat just until combined with the immersion blender.

Preheat the oven to 350 degrees. Pour the pumpkin filling mixture into the cooled gingersnap crust. Pour the reserved filling mixture from the measuring cup onto the top of the pumpkin filling and with a spoon, gently swirl into the pumpkin mixture to create a marbleized effect. Make sure that you do not dip the spoon too deeply into the pie crust dish or you may dislodge some of the pie crust crumbs on the bottom.

Place the pie plate on top of a baking sheet and bake in the preheated oven just until the center is set, which should take 45 minutes to 1 hour. Transfer the pie dish to a rack and cool to room temperature, about 2 hours. Cover the pie loosely with foil, place in refrigerator and chill for at least 4 hours before serving. Serves 8

Sue's Tips:

Scientific testing has verified when a person is in love a molecular substance called PEA (phenylethylamine) courses thru the veins. Chocolate contains PEA. Enough said.

Snickerdoodles

(From the kitchen of Toni – of all the cookies my mother made in my childhood, these are the ones that bring back the fondest memories of producing a fabulous aroma in the kitchen. If you purchase a Snickerdoodle in a bakery or food store, more often than not it will be a soft cookie. These are very crispy.)

INGREDIENTS

2½ cups all-purpose unbleached flour

2 tsp. cream of tartar

1 tsp. baking soda

½ tsp. salt

2 sticks butter (16 tbsp.), softened in a large bowl to room temperature

1½ cups sugar, preferably organic

½ tsp. almond extract

2 eggs

2 tbsp. sugar, preferably organic

2 tbsp. ground cinnamon

PREPARATION

Preheat the oven to 400 degrees. Sift together the flour, cream of tartar, baking soda and salt. Cream the butter with 1½ cups sugar until light and fluffy and then beat in the almond extract. Beat in the eggs, one at a time. Combine the butter mixture with the flour mixture and stir with a wooden spoon until well combined.

In a small dish whisk together (or use a fork) the remaining 2 tbsp. sugar and the cinnamon. With your hands, roll the dough into small balls (about one inch in diameter) and roll them in the cinnamon/sugar mixture. Place the balls about 2 inches apart on an ungreased baking sheet and bake for 10–12 minutes. Remove from oven and use a spatula to put the cookies on a rack to cool.

Toni loved to play cards - Especially when she won! | York, PA, 1977

Lemon Meringue Pudding

INGREDIENTS

1 cup sugar, preferably organic

3 tbsp. flour

2 tbsp. butter, softened to room temperature

4 eggs, separated

1⅓ cups milk

Juice from 1½ medium sized lemons

1½ tbsp. grated lemon rind

Fresh fruit for garnish, if desired (for example, blueberries, strawberries, raspberries).

PREPARATION

Place the sugar and flour in a large bowl and stir together. Add the butter and stir until the butter is incorporated.

Separate the eggs, placing the yolks in the bowl with the butter and sugar mixture, and put the whites in a separate bowl and set aside. Blend the egg yolks thoroughly into the sugar mixture until light and fluffy. Add the milk, lemon juice, and lemon rind to the mixture and stir the batter until well combined.

Beat the egg whites with a hand electric mixer until they are stiff but not dry and fold the egg whites gently into the batter.

Preheat the oven to 325 degrees. Butter a 9-inch square glass or ceramic baking pan and pour the mixture into the pan. Bake the pudding for 35 to 45 minutes, or until it is puffed and lightly browned on top. Let the pudding cool to room temperature and then place in the refrigerator to chill. The pudding will separate into two layers, with custard on the bottom and a cake-like mixture on the top.

Spoon the chilled pudding into small serving bowls, and if desired, place fruit decoratively in the bowls around the edges of the pudding. Serves 6–8

Fruit Pizza

Sugar Cookie Crust:

¾ cup powdered sugar

½ cup (8 tbsp.) butter, softened to room temperature

1 egg

½ tsp. vanilla

¼ tsp. almond extract

1⅓ cups unbleached all-purpose flour

½ tsp. baking soda

½ tsp. cream of tartar

Filling:

1 8-oz. package cream cheese, softened to room temperature

½ cup sugar, preferably organic

1 tsp. vanilla

2 tsp. freshly grated lemon zest

Glaze:

½ cup sugar, preferably organic

1½ tbsp. cornstarch

½ cup fresh orange juice

¼ cup fresh lemon juice

½ cup water

Mixed fresh fruit (good choices are strawberries, blueberries, raspberries)

PREPARATION

Make crust: Cream together the sugar and softened butter in a medium bowl. Add the egg, vanilla and almond extract and combine thoroughly. Stir in the flour, baking soda and cream of tartar.

Prepare a pizza pan (approx. 12" in diameter) for baking: Place a round of parchment paper cut to the same size as the baking pan on the bottom. With your hands, mash the cookie dough onto the bottom and sides of the baking pan evenly. The amount of dough prepared will be more than is needed for the crust, especially since it is recommended that the crust be thin.

Preheat the oven to 350 degrees and bake the cookie crust for 20 minutes, or until a deep golden brown. Remove from the oven and cool completely.

While the crust is baking, mix all filling ingredients together in a small bowl and set aside.

Make the glaze by mixing together all glaze ingredients in a saucepan and cook over medium heat until the glaze comes to a boil. Continue to cook, stirring, until the glaze thickens. Remove from the heat and cool to room temperature.

When the crust has cooled completely, spread the filling evenly over top. Arrange the fresh fruit in a decorative pattern on the filling. Note: Have fun with this! The sky's the limit as to how creative you can be.

After the fruit is decoratively arranged on top of the filling, spoon some of the glaze evenly over top. The amount of glaze the recipe makes is more than you should need since the glaze should be spread on top generously but not excessively.

Refrigerate dessert for at least an hour before serving.

Serves 8

No more pictures today, please...

Journal Entry: Woke up Sue by catapulting (no pun intended) myself off the end table onto her stomach, got back in Sue's favor by allowing her to return to bed for another hour after serving me breakfast; first nap of the morning about to take place; more later...

Gingerbread Cupcakes with Lemon Cream-Cheese Frosting

Adapted from Gourmet magazine, Condé Nast Publications

INGREDIENTS

1¼ cups unbleached all-purpose flour

1½ tsp. ground ginger

1 tsp. cinnamon

¼ tsp. ground cloves

½ tsp. allspice

¼ tsp. salt

2 tbsp. of unsalted butter, softened

½ cup sugar, preferably organic

½ cup unsulfured molasses

1 large egg

1 tsp. baking soda

8 oz. cream cheese, softened to room temperature in a large bowl

4 tbsp. unsalted butter, softened to room temperature

½ tsp. vanilla

1¼ cups confectioners sugar

1 tbsp. freshly grated lemon zest

2 tsp. fresh lemon juice

PREPARATION

Sift together the flour, ginger, cinnamon, cloves, allspice and salt into a bowl and set aside. Add the sugar to the softened butter and beat until fluffy. Beat in the molasses and the egg until smooth.

In a measuring cup combine the baking soda with ½ cup boiling water and stir to dissolve the baking soda. Stir the baking soda mixture into the butter mixture, then add the flour mixture and stir to combine the ingredients well.

Preheat the oven to 350 degrees. Line twelve ½-cup muffin tins with paper liners and spoon the batter equally into the liners. Bake the cupcakes in the preheated oven for 20–25 minutes, or until a tester comes out clean. (Note: the cupcakes will be flat or slightly indented on top). Remove the cupcakes from the baking pan, transfer to a rack and let them cool.

While the cupcakes are baking, cream together the cream cheese and butter. Add the vanilla and the confectioners sugar, and beat until fluffy and smooth. Beat in the zest and lemon juice and chill the frosting for at least 30 minutes. Spread the frosting on the cupcakes after they have cooled. (Note: The frosting will very generously frost all the cupcakes, with some left over). Makes 12 cupcakes

Chocolate Mint Dream Cookies

I took singing lessons from a wonderful teacher (and friend) named Gwen Sharp. The first time I made these cookies for her she literally got tears in her eyes and claimed they were the best cookies she had ever eaten in her life. Making these cookies for her was always the best way to show my appreciation for all her support and encouragement.

INGREDIENTS

1 cup semi-sweet chocolate morsels

10⅔ tbsp. butter, softened to room temperature in a large bowl

½ cup sugar, preferably organic

1 egg

¼ cup light corn syrup

1 tsp. pure peppermint extract

1 ¾ cup sifted unbleached flour

1 tsp. cinnamon

2 tsp. baking soda

¼ tsp. salt

Additional sugar for rolling cookies

PREPARATION

Melt chocolate morsels in a double boiler over hot water and remove from heat. Add sugar to the softened butter and beat well with a wooden spoon until very creamy. Add the egg and beat until combined. Stir in the melted chocolate, corn syrup, and peppermint extract. Note: Use a spatula to assure you get as much chocolate as possible.

Sift together the sifted flour, cinnamon, baking soda and salt. Stir the flour mixture gradually into the butter mixture. Refrigerate the cookie dough for at least an hour, which will make it easier to form the cookies.

Preheat oven to 350 degrees. Shape the dough into small balls (about the size of a walnut) and roll the balls in sugar. Place cookies about 3 inches apart on un-greased cookie sheets. Bake for 12–15 minutes and remove from oven. Cool completely on a rack before placing in an airtight storage container.

Gwen's Annual Singing Recital
June 2007

Sue's Tips:

It is not possible to be in a bad mood and sing at the same time.

Meat

Toni's favorite meat was lamb, so it's not surprising there are quite a few lamb recipes included in the meat section. I wonder if a passion for lamb can be a genetically transmitted trait, because about 95 percent of my relatives adore lamb. My mother's typical preparation of lamb is, to this day, one of my favorites and unlike some of the lamb recipes included in this book that are more complex and require a lot of ingredients, this procedure couldn't be easier. Here's what you do: Buy loin lamb chops, highest quality available (this is the filet mignon of lamb) and sprinkle each side with garlic pepper and salt (or Herbamare®). Broil until cooked so they are medium rare (light pink on the inside) and serve with mint jelly on the side. Buono, Buono!!!

Parody from Clyde – Sung to the turn of "My Favorite Things"
Five o'clock wake ups & scratching of sofas, Saturday brunches with eggs & mimosas, Here in the kitchen with Sue as she sings, These are a few of my favorite things

Testimonial

When you sit down at Sue's table to experience her divine creations, you are partaking in one of the most sensual rewards of life. There is essence in good food, power and love in delicious nourishment. Amid the joy in Sue's process of cooking, she brings love to the table. Each dish is an expression of her spark, an offering to eat, drink and be merry – together. It is not an exaggeration to say that Sue's cooking transforms her guests from the inside out.

If you are reading this, it means you have discovered Sue and can now begin to experience her gleeful approach to cooking, and celebrate life more fully through your taste buds. Congratulations on your discovery of this fine woman and exemplary chef. Let the feast begin!

Erin Glenn-Hash
Life Coach
Lincoln, NE

Luscious Lamb Chops

INGREDIENTS

4–6 loin lamb chops, approx. 1½ inches thick

Garlic pepper (for sprinkling on lamb chops)

1 tbsp. butter

1 tbsp. Worcestershire sauce

1 tbsp. fresh lemon juice

1 tbsp. gin

½ tsp. Herbamare® or salt

Mint jelly (Optional)

PREPARATION

Place lamb chops in a foil lined shallow broiler-proof baking dish. Melt butter over low heat in small saucepan; remove from heat and add Worcestershire sauce, lemon juice, gin and Herbamare®.

Sprinkle chops liberally with garlic pepper, then spoon marinade over top of chops. Let sit for approx. ½ hour; turn chops, sprinkle again with more garlic pepper, and again spoon marinade over top. Continue to marinate for another ½ hour.

Preheat broiler and broil about 6–8 inches from the heat for approx. 5 minutes on each side, which should result in rare chops, pink on the inside. Cook a little longer if you want them less pink, but be sure the chops are not too well done, because then they won't be "luscious" any longer. Serve with mint jelly on the side if desired. Serves 2–3

Beef Stroganov with Shiitake & Cremini Mushrooms

INGREDIENTS

3 tbsp. unbleached all-purpose flour

1 tsp. salt

¼ tsp. black pepper

1½ lbs. filet mignon, cut crosswise into ¼ inch thick pieces

2 tbsp. extra virgin olive oil

4 tbsp. butter

⅔ cup chopped shallots

1 cup chopped sweet yellow onions

1 large garlic clove

½ cup medium dry sherry

½ lb. shiitake mushrooms, rinsed, stems discarded and caps thinly sliced

½ lb. cremini mushrooms, rinsed, stems trimmed and sliced thinly

¾ cup beef broth

1 tsp. dried chervil

½ tsp. Hungarian paprika

2 tbsp. freshly grated lemon rind

2 tsp. Worcestershire sauce

¼ cup finely chopped fresh parsley leaves (flat-leaf)

1 cup sour cream

Additional ¾ tsp. salt and ¼ tsp. pepper for seasoning

Thin egg noodles to accompany (cook according to package directions)

PREPARATION

Mix flour, salt and pepper together in a bowl and add filet mignon pieces. Toss well with hands to completely coat all pieces of meat. There should not be any loose flour left in the bowl. In a large heavy skillet heat the olive oil and 2 tbsp. of the butter over moderately high heat. Add the meat in batches and cook very briefly, just until lightly browned on both sides. The meat should still be pink in the center. Transfer the meat as cooked with a slotted spoon to a bowl and set aside.

Add remaining 2 tbsp. of butter to the skillet and cook the shallots and onion over moderate heat, stirring, until softened. Add garlic and cook for another minute. Add the sherry and simmer until the cooking liquid is almost evaporated.

Add shiitake and cremini mushrooms and cook, stirring, until tender and the liquid they give off is almost evaporated. Add the beef broth and simmer for 1 minute. Stir in the chervil, paprika, lemon rind, Worcestershire sauce, parsley and sour cream, and simmer for a couple of minutes (do not boil). Return the beef to the skillet with the additional salt and pepper and gently simmer just until heated, which should take no more than a couple of minutes. Serve Stroganov over buttered thin egg noodles. Serves 3–4

Chinese Roast Pork

Adapted from Gourmet magazine, Condé Nast Publications

INGREDIENTS

A 2-lb. boneless fresh pork loin, cut lengthwise into 2 thick strips

Marinade:

⅓ cup soy sauce

2 tbsp. dry Sherry

1 tbsp. red curry paste

2 tbsp. ketchup

1 tbsp. sugar (preferably Turbinado/raw)

1 tbsp. fresh lemon juice

1 tbsp. honey

4 large garlic cloves, finely chopped

2 tbsp. peeled and minced fresh gingerroot

Sauce:

6 tbsp. soy sauce

3 large cloves garlic, minced

2 tbsp. honey

2 tbsp. red-wine vinegar

2 tbsp. toasted sesame oil

¾ tbsp. chili oil (hot oil)

PREPARATION

Combine all the marinade ingredients in a bowl and mix well. Add the pork loin and submerge. Let the pork marinate, covered and chilled, for at least 4 hours, or overnight.

Preheat the oven to 350 degrees. Arrange the pork on a rack in a roasting pan, and add enough hot water to the pan to measure about ½ inch. Roast the pork in the preheated oven, basting it with the marinade occasionally, for 1 hour and 30 minutes.

While the pork is roasting, make the sauce, by combining all sauce ingredients well in a serving bowl.

When pork is done, transfer to a carving board and let it stand, covered with foil, for 15 minutes. Cut the pork crosswise into thin slices, and arrange either on a platter, or put slices directly onto serving plates. Spoon some of the sauce over the pork, and serve the rest on the side. Serves 4

What to Serve Guests

When I am preparing food for good friends, I normally am well aware of things they particularly like or dislike, and adjust my menu accordingly. However, if you are entertaining guests for the first time, or a long amount of time has passed since you have cooked for them, you will do yourself a favor if you leave nothing to chance regarding food preferences, as well as finding out about any allergies or dietary concerns. A question I usually ask people is, "What don't you like to eat?" Nothing is worse than spending a lot of time and effort making a fabulous meal, only to find out that a guest is either allergic to, or simply not fond of what has been prepared.

For example, have you ever spent hours preparing a really special decadent dessert for a guest, and then had the person say, "Oh, none for me thanks. I'm on a diet." As annoying as that may be, the upside of that scenario means there will be more left over!

Lamb Burgers with Fresh Mint Sauce

INGREDIENTS

2 tbsp. fresh lemon juice

4 tbsp. cider vinegar

4 tbsp. water

1 tbsp. soy sauce

2 medium cloves garlic, minced

2 tbsp. sugar, preferably organic

¼ tsp. anchovy paste

1 tsp. dried hot red pepper flakes

½ cup minced fresh mint leaves

1 large egg

1 lb. ground lamb, lean

¼ generous tsp. cinnamon

⅛ tsp. nutmeg

⅔ cup finely chopped onion

⅓ cup fresh bread crumbs

½ tsp. salt

¼ tsp. pepper

PREPARATION

In a small serving bowl, stir together the lemon juice, vinegar, water, soy sauce, garlic, sugar, anchovy paste, red pepper flakes, and mint until well combined and the sugar is dissolved.

In a bowl combine well the egg, lamb, cinnamon, nutmeg, onion, bread crumbs, salt and pepper. Form the mixture into 4 patties – they will be approx. 1 to 1½ inches thick. Broil the burgers on a foil-lined broiler pan (or broiler safe baking dish) under a preheated broiler approx. 6 to 8 inches from the heat for 6 minutes. Turn the patties and broil them for an additional 6 minutes. Transfer the burgers to serving plates and spoon the sauce over them; serve remaining sauce on the side. Serves 4

There are friends, family, & then me...a friend who is family

Oriental-Style Marinated Flank Steak

INGREDIENTS

2 tbsp. finely chopped fresh gingerroot

1 tbsp. sunflower oil

1 tbsp. toasted sesame oil

2 tbsp. firmly packed dark brown sugar

3½ tbsp. soy sauce

3½ tbsp. Sherry vinegar

3 scallions, using only white part

3 medium garlic cloves

1½ tbsp. fresh lemon juice

¼ tsp. dried hot red pepper flakes

1-lb flank steak

PREPARATION

Peel gingerroot and blend in mini-food processor enough to make 2 tbsp. To the gingerroot in the processor, add all remaining ingredients until the mixture is smooth and well combined. Place the flank steak in a shallow dish and pour the marinade over it, turning to coat well. Let the steak marinate, covered and chilled, overnight.

Preheat the broiler and place the steak on a broiler pan, or broiler-safe shallow baking dish, and broil the steak approx. 3–4 inches from the heat for 4–5 minutes on each side for medium rare meat. Alternately, you could grill the steak on an oiled rack set about 4 inches over glowing coals for 5–6 minutes on each side for medium rare meat.

Let the steak stand for about 5 minutes and then slice it thinly across the grain. Serves 2–3

Middle Eastern Style Meatballs with Orzo

INGREDIENTS

1 lb. lean ground lamb

3 large cloves garlic, finely chopped

1 egg

1 tsp. salt

¼ tsp. pepper

¼ tsp. ground allspice

⅓ cup crumbled feta cheese

⅓ cup chopped shallots

1 tbsp. red wine vinegar

1 tsp. dried oregano

½ cup pine nuts

2 tbsp. chopped Italian (flat-leaf) parsley

1 tbsp. olive oil

2 tbsp. olive oil for frying meatballs

PREPARATION

Serve with Orzo with Feta and Cherry Tomatoes (See p.129).

In a large bowl, mix by hand the ground lamb with all of the ingredients listed, except for the extra 2 tbsp. of olive oil.

In a large heavy non-stick skillet, heat the remaining 2 tbsp. of olive oil over moderately high heat until hot but not smoking. Form the lamb mixture into balls, to a size of your choice.

Cook the meatballs in the hot olive oil until browned on all sides and cooked but still slightly pink in the middle. The time it will take to do this depends on the size of the meatballs prepared. Serve the meatballs over Orzo with Feta and Cherry Tomatoes. Serves 3–4 as an entrée

Note: If you wish to make the meatballs as an appetizer instead of a main course, form the lamb mixture into very small meatballs. If you do this, you could serve the appetizer meatballs with a dipping sauce, but they are so delicious they really stand on their own.

Lamb London Broil with Scallion Ginger Sauce

Adapted from Gourmet magazine, Condé Nast Publications

INGREDIENTS

2 lbs. boneless leg of lamb, butterflied (should be about 1½ inches thick)

¼ cup soy sauce

1 tbsp. fresh lemon juice

2 tbsp. grapeseed oil

⅓ cup (generous) minced shallots

2½ tbsp. chopped peeled fresh gingerroot

6 tbsp. unsalted butter, softened to room temperature

3 tbsp. minced scallions (white part)

PREPARATION

In a shallow baking dish slightly larger than the lamb whisk together the soy sauce, lemon juice, grapeseed oil, shallots and 1½ tbsp. gingerroot. Add the lamb, turn to coat well on both sides, and marinate, covered and chilled, for 8–10 hours. Remove the lamb from the refrigerator approx. 45 minutes before cooking.

In a small bowl, cream together the butter, remaining 1 tbsp. gingerroot, and scallions. Set aside.

When ready to cook lamb, remove it from the marinade, and put the marinade in a small saucepan. Preheat the broiler, and place the lamb on a broiler pan. Broil approx. 4–6 inches from the heat, turning it once, for approx. 8–10 minutes on each side for medium-rare meat (light pink in the center, which is ideal). When done, transfer the lamb to a platter and let it stand for 10 minutes. Pour any juices that have accumulated on the platter into the saucepan with the marinade and bring to a boil. Immediately reduce the heat to low and whisk in the butter mixture. The sauce should not be brought to a boil. When the butter is incorporated, the sauce will be slightly thickened but not thick.

Slice the lamb thinly across the grain. Spoon the scallion ginger sauce over each portion of lamb before serving.

Serves 4

Bobotie *(Curried Lamb Loaf with Custard) Adapted from Gourmet magazine, Condé Nast Publications*

INGREDIENTS

1 slice whole-wheat bread, torn by hand into ½ inch pieces

1 cup plus 3 tbsp. milk

1 large onion, chopped

3 tbsp. unsalted butter

4 large garlic cloves, finely chopped

1½ tbsp. curry powder

2 tbsp. fresh lemon juice

1 tbsp. sugar

3 tbsp. raisins

4 tbsp. finely ground almonds

1 tsp. salt

½ tsp. pepper

2 lbs. lean ground lamb

2 tbsp. orange marmalade

2 large eggs

1 tsp. tumeric

PREPARATION

In a small bowl, soak the bread crumbs in 3 tbsp. of milk. In a large skillet, cook the chopped onion in the butter over moderate heat, stirring occasionally, until the onion is softened. Reduce heat to low and add the garlic and the curry powder. Stir to combine with the onions and cook for about a minute. Add the lemon juice, sugar, raisins, ground almonds, salt and pepper and cook the mixture, stirring, for approx. 5 minutes.

Remove the skillet from the heat and stir in the lamb, bread crumbs, marmalade, and 1 of the eggs. When the mixture is well combined, transfer it to a 13 x 9 inch baking dish and pat it into a level loaf. Bake in a preheated 375 degree oven for 30 minutes. Remove from the oven and carefully pour off the fat in the pan. Reduce oven temperature to 325 degrees. In a small bowl whisk together the remaining 1 cup of milk, the remaining egg, and the tumeric. Pour the custard over the lamb mixture, and continue to bake for another 10 minutes or until the custard is just set. Bobotie is good served with brown rice. Serves 6

Spicy Veal Meatballs with Tomato Sauce

INGREDIENTS

Fresh Tomato Sauce with Thyme (see p. 165)

Other accompaniments: thin spaghetti noodles or rice (optional)

For Meatballs:

1 lb. ground veal

½ cup finely chopped onion

3 large cloves garlic, minced

¼ cup finely chopped sweet red bell pepper

1 egg

2 tbsp. grated Parmesan cheese

⅓ cup fresh bread crumbs (I prefer whole grain or whole wheat bread)

2 tbsp. chili sauce

1 tbsp. chopped fresh tarragon leaves

¼ tsp. nutmeg

1 tsp. chili powder

½ tsp. Herbamare® or salt

¼ tsp. black pepper

2 tbsp. extra-virgin olive oil

2 tbsp. butter

PREPARATION

In a large bowl mix together with your hands all ingredients listed above (except for the olive oil and butter) until well combined.

Heat the olive oil and butter over moderate heat in a large heavy non-stick skillet until hot. Form the meat mixture into balls approx. 2 inches in diameter and add to skillet. Brown the meatballs on all sides until firm and cooked through, which should take approx. 10–12 minutes per batch. Remove with a slotted spoon as meatballs are cooked and set aside.

Right before serving, add cooked meatballs to the tomato sauce and stir to coat well and reheat the meatballs. Serve alone, or over spaghetti or rice. Note: My preference is to eat them alone – that is not to say by myself, but without the spaghetti/rice. Serves 3–6, depending on whether you add the spaghetti or rice.

Steak with Shallot Butter Sauce

INGREDIENTS

2 filet mignon steaks (about 8 oz. each)

Herbamare® or salt and black pepper

2 tbsp. butter

1 tbsp. garlic flavored extra-virgin olive oil (Olave® is a good choice)

½ cup chopped shallots

3 tbsp. red wine vinegar

1 tbsp. finely chopped fresh parsley

PREPARATION

Sprinkle one side of the steak with Herbamare® and pepper. Heat 1 tbsp. of the butter and the olive oil in a heavy skillet. When it is hot and just starting to brown, add the steaks, seasoned side down. When in the pan, sprinkle the other sides with Herbamare and pepper. Cook the steaks on one side until well browned, then turn and brown on the other side. Depending on how rare you like the steaks, cook from 3–5 minutes per side.

Remove the steaks to a dish and cover loosely with aluminum foil to keep warm. Reduce the heat to medium low, and add the shallots and the vinegar to the skillet. Cook until the shallots are softened and the vinegar has reduced slightly. Remove the skillet from the heat. Add the remaining tbsp. butter and swirl until melted. Stir in the parsley and spoon the sauce over the steaks before serving.

Note: The sauce should be prepared as rapidly as possible after the meat has been transferred to a platter. Serves 2

I want it so rare a good vet could bring it back.

Moroccan Lamb

INGREDIENTS

½ cup white raisins

Dry sherry wine

¼ cup safflower oil

1½ lbs. lean lamb meat, cut into small (about 1½ inch) cubes

1 large white onion, finely chopped

4 large garlic cloves, finely chopped

½ tsp. salt

¼ tsp. black pepper

¼ tsp. red pepper flakes

½ tsp. tumeric

1 14-oz. can diced tomatoes, drained

½ cup chicken broth

Brown rice

Fried onion pieces (optional) – prepared with no hydrogenated oils or fats (e.g. Trader Joe's® brand)

PREPARATION

Put raisins in a small bowl and pour enough sherry over them so that they are covered. Set aside and soak for at least fifteen minutes.

Heat oil in a skillet and brown the lamb cubes over moderately high heat until browned. Remove lamb with a slotted spoon and set aside. Pour off approx. half of the liquid that remains in the pan and return to the heat. Reduce heat to moderate and add the onions and garlic to the skillet and cook, stirring occasionally, until the onions are softened. Stir in the salt, pepper, red pepper flakes and tumeric. Return the lamb cubes (and any juice that accumulated on the dish) to the skillet and add the raisins, including the sherry, tomatoes, and enough chicken broth to cover the mixture, which should be approx. ½ cup.

Bring to a boil, cover and simmer for one and one-half hours. While dish is cooking, prepare brown rice according to package directions. Put some brown rice on each serving dish and spoon serving of lamb over top. If desired, sprinkle fried onion rings on top of each serving, and serve extra on the side. Serves 3–4

Braised Pork Ribs with Orange & Soy Sauce

INGREDIENTS

3 racks (about 2 lbs. each) lean baby back pork spareribs

4 tbsp. (generous) finely chopped fresh gingerroot

8 cloves garlic

4 cups freshly squeezed orange juice

¾ cup soy sauce

¼ cup firmly packed dark brown sugar

1 tsp. black pepper

PREPARATION

Cut each rack in 2–3 pieces. Arrange in a single layer in a large flameproof roasting pan. You will probably need to use 2 pans unless you have something that's super large. Sprinkle ribs with salt. Preheat oven to 450 degrees. Place ribs in oven and roast for approx. 45 minutes and pour off any fat that has been rendered.

While the ribs are roasting make sauce: In a mini-food processor, pulse to chop enough fresh gingerroot to equal 4 generous tbsp. Add garlic cloves to processor and pulse with gingerroot to combine and to chop the garlic. In a large saucepan combine the orange juice, soy sauce, brown sugar, gingerroot, garlic and pepper and bring to a boil over moderately high heat. Reduce heat and simmer for 10 minutes and then set aside.

After fat has been poured off the ribs, pour sauce over ribs, turning ribs to coat. Cover the baking pans tightly with aluminum foil. Reduce oven temperature to 325 degrees and return ribs to oven. Roast, basting occasionally, with the sauce for 2 ½ to 3 hours, or until the meat is extremely tender, and is falling off the bones. Transfer the ribs to an ovenproof serving dish. Reduce oven heat to 200 degrees and keep the ribs warm in the oven.

Pour the orange soy sauce from the roasting pans into a saucepan. Skim fat if necessary, but it normally won't be because of the fat rendering procedure, coupled with the fact that the ribs used should be lean. Bring the sauce to a boil, uncovered, stirring occasionally, until it is reduced to about 2 cups and is syrupy. Spoon the sauce over the ribs, and if any is left over, serve on the side if desired. Serves 6

Veal Scallopini with Mushrooms & Herb Sauce

INGREDIENTS

2 tbsp. extra-virgin olive oil

1 lb. veal scallops, sliced approx. ¼ inch thick (See Note)

Herbamare® or salt and pepper for sprinkling on veal

1 cup chicken broth

4 tbsp. minced shallots

4 oz. chopped Baby Bella (Cremini) mushrooms, rinsed, tips of stems removed

2 tbsp. minced fresh chives

2 tbsp. minced fresh tarragon leaves

1 tbsp. minced fresh parsley leaves

1 tbsp. fresh lemon juice

2 tbsp. salted butter

PREPARATION

In a large skillet heat the oil over moderately high heat until it is very hot but not smoking. Pat the veal dry with paper towels thoroughly. Sprinkle each veal scallop with Herbamare® and pepper. Sauté the veal for approx. 45 seconds on each side in batches if necessary (it should be lightly browned). It is extremely important to not overcook the veal! Remove the veal to a plate and set aside. Pour off any fat and/or liquid that remain in the pan and add the broth, scraping up any brown bits.

Reduce the heat to moderately low and add the shallots, mushrooms, chives, tarragon and parsley and gently boil the sauce until it is reduced by about half. Add the lemon juice and the butter and continue to cook, stirring until the butter is just melted. Return the veal to the skillet with any juices that have accumulated on the plate and turn to coat with the sauce, and briefly reheat for about 30 seconds. Put the veal on 2 serving plates, and spoon the sauce over each portion. Serves 2

Note: In most high quality food stores, veal scallops can be purchased already in the "scaloppini" state – meaning, they have already been cut thinly and are recipe ready. If veal is not available thinly sliced, then veal slices must be placed between pieces of wax paper and pounded with a mallet until they are ¼ inch thick. The success of this recipe depends on buying veal that is high quality and very tender.

Toni's Famous Spare Ribs

(In York, PA, where my parents lived and I was raised, these ribs truly were famous. Whenever my mother announced that she was making her ribs, we would swoon with joy and anticipation. She also frequently made them for dinner parties, and figured on about ¾ to 1 lb. of ribs per person (assuming the ribs are very lean with a minimal amount of fat). The sauce for these ribs is very sweet. The sauce ingredient amounts given should be doubled (or tripled) depending on the quantity of ribs. The same goes for the onion and lemon slices.

INGREDIENTS

2¼ lbs. baby back lean pork spare ribs

1 large onion, thinly sliced

1 large lemon, thinly sliced (remove seeds)

Sauce:

1 cup catsup

⅓ cup Worcestershire sauce

1 tsp. chili powder

⅔ cup brown sugar, firmly packed

1 tsp. salt

Several dashes of Tabasco sauce

2 cups pineapple juice

PREPARATION

Mix all of the sauce ingredients together in a saucepan and heat over moderate heat until the sauce is at a low boil. Reduce heat to low and simmer for approx. 10–15 minutes, and set aside.

Preheat oven to 450 degrees. Place ribs in a roasting pan and bake for approx. ½ hour. Remove from oven and pour off any excess fat. Note: If the ribs are lean, there should be very little excess fat to pour off.

Sprinkle onion slices and lemon slices evenly over the ribs. Reduce the oven temperature to 350 degrees. Pour sauce over the ribs. Cover the baking dish with a lid or aluminum foil and bake the ribs for one hour, basting about every 15 minutes. Remove the lid or foil after one hour and continue to bake, basting every 15 minutes or so, for an additional 1½ hours. The sauce should be thickened, and the ribs fork tender with the meat falling off the bones. Serves 3–4

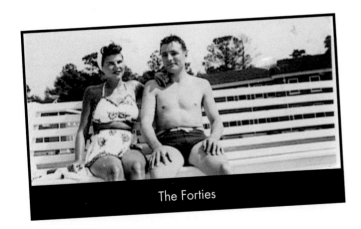

The Forties

The Forties

Marinated Flank Steak

(Another recipe from Toni – of all my marinade recipes, this is my favorite one – and not just for sentimental reasons..)

INGREDIENTS

¼ cup soy sauce

3 tbsp. honey

2 tbsp. red wine vinegar

2 large garlic cloves, minced

1½ tbsp. finely chopped fresh gingerroot

¾ cup light oil (sunflower, safflower, or grapeseed)

1 large shallot, chopped (to equal approx. ¼ cup)

1 flank steak (1–2 lbs.)

PREPARATION

Combine all marinade ingredients in a baking dish large enough to hold the flank steak in a single layer. Whisk ingredients together until the oil is incorporated. Add the flank steak and marinate for a MINIMUM of 12 hours, turning the steak occasionally. I typically put the flank steak in the marinade the day before I am serving it and allow it to marinate overnight (at least 24 hours).

Remove the steak from the marinade and place it on a broiler pan. Preheat the broiler and broil the flank steak to your desired degree of doneness, preferably so that it is pink on the inside, which should take 3–5 minutes on each side. Or if preferred, cook on an outside grill. Serves 2–6 (figure that a lb. of meat will serve 2–3 people)

Spring, 1985, York, PA

Lemon Lamb Shanks with Potatoes

INGREDIENTS

2 lbs. good quality lean lamb shanks, all excess fat removed

¼ cup olive oil

1 lb. small red-skinned potatoes, cut in half lengthwise

1 lb. small white onions, peeled and trimmed

2 cups chopped fresh tomatoes (seeds removed)

1 6-oz. can tomato paste

4 large garlic cloves, finely chopped

¾ cup dry red wine

2 tbsp. red wine vinegar

1 tsp. salt

3 small bay leaves

1 large strip (approx. 3 inches) of lemon peel

¼ lb. feta cheese, crumbled

PREPARATION

Heat the olive oil in a heavy Dutch oven or large non-stick pot over moderate heat and brown the lamb shanks on all sides. Remove the meat and set aside. Brown the potatoes and onions in the fat remaining in the pot. Return the lamb shanks to the pot.

Place the tomatoes, tomato paste, garlic, wine, vinegar and salt in a bowl and combine with an electric immersion blender (or use a food processor) until the mixture is smooth. Pour the tomato mixture over the lamb shanks. Add the bay leaves and lemon peel. Bring to a boil, reduce heat to low, cover and simmer for at least 2 hours, or until the meat is tender to the point where it is falling off the bones.

Remove the pot from the heat, and remove the lamb shanks from the pot and also remove and discard the bay leaves. Keep the pot covered. When the lamb shanks are cool enough to handle, remove all the meat from the bones, assuring that all fat is discarded. Cut or tear the lamb into pieces.

Return the lamb pieces to the pot and add the feta cheese. Remove the lid, and cook over moderately low heat until mixture is thoroughly heated and the cheese has melted. Serves 4

Lamb Burgers with Tapenade

INGREDIENTS

4 cloves garlic, minced

1 tsp. salt

1½ tsp. ground cumin

1 tsp. ground coriander

1 tsp. sweet Hungarian paprika

½ tsp. ground cinnamon

½ tsp. cayenne

1¼ lbs. ground lamb

¼ cup finely chopped fresh cilantro

Tapenade:

1½ cups brine-cured large green olives, pitted

½ cup loosely packed finely chopped fresh parsley (flat-leaf)

¼ cup slivered almonds, toasted

2 tbsp. fresh lemon juice

⅓ cup extra-virgin olive oil

3 tbsp. mayonnaise

Accompaniment: Tandoori Naan Flatbread

PREPARATION

In a bowl, mash minced garlic with the salt to make a paste. Then blend in the cumin, coriander, paprika, cinnamon and cayenne. Add ground lamb to the bowl and sprinkle the chopped cilantro over top. With hands, mix together the lamb with the other ingredients until everything is evenly distributed. Form lamb into 4–6 patties.

In a mini-food processor, place the olives, parsley, toasted almonds and lemon juice. Pulse scraping down the sides occasionally until the mixture is finely chopped. With the motor running, add the olive oil in a steady stream, blending to form a paste. Add the mayonnaise and pulse just until combined. With a small spatula, remove tapenade from the processor and put in a small serving dish or bowl.

Brush a large non-stick skillet (grill style, with ridges) with olive oil and heat over moderate heat until hot. Add the burgers and cook, turning once, for approx. 7–10 minutes per side. Burgers should be a light pink color on the inside. Serve with tapenade on the side. *Tapenade is also included in the "Appetizer" Section.*

Note: My favorite way to eat this dish is to cut a piece of the burger, wrap it in a small piece of Naan, and put a dollop of tapenade on top. Serves 4

Lamb Chops with Sun-Dried Tomato Butter

INGREDIENTS

4 tbsp. unsalted butter

1 large garlic clove

¼ cup chopped sun-dried tomatoes, packed in oil, drained

½ cup toasted walnuts

¼ tsp. ground coriander

¼ tsp. cayenne pepper

1 tbsp. chopped flat-leaf (Italian) parsley

2 tsp. fresh lemon juice

¼ tsp. salt

⅛ tsp. black pepper

2 lbs. loin lamb chops (8 chops, approx. 1 inch thick)

Herbamare® and garlic pepper for sprinkling on chops

PREPARATION

Place unsalted butter in a mini-food processor. When the butter has softened a bit, add the remaining ingredients, except for the lamb chops. Pulse until the ingredients are finely chopped. The mixture will be lumpy.

Preheat the broiler. Pat the lamb chops dry with paper towels and sprinkle chops on both sides with Herbamare® and garlic pepper. Broil on the rack of a broiler pan (or other broiler-proof shallow baking dish) for approx. 5–6 minutes on each side (10–12 minutes total), turning once, for medium-rare meat. Put chops on serving plates and spoon tomato butter generously over top. Serves 4

Tricia

Tricia resides in the Kihei area of Maui. She and I met at college and discovered quickly that we were soul mates in addition to being sisters (sorority sisters that is).

Tricia is one of the most persuasive individuals I've ever known. Like the time she got us into one of the best restaurants in New Orleans (during Mardi Gras!) without a reservation by convincing the maitre d' it was his error that we weren't on the list.

Happily, her persuasive powers resulted in her procuring this authentic recipe for a dish that is, according to Tricia, famous, a local favorite, and the "real deal."

Beach Bunnies, Maui, 1989

White Water Rafting, Colorado River, 2006

Mardi Gras
New Orleans, 1974

Azekas Ribs

INGREDIENTS

2¼ cups shoyu (or soy sauce)

1 cup dark toasted sesame oil

¾ cup sugar, preferably organic

½ cup honey

12 large scallions, sliced (white part)

3 tbsp. minced fresh garlic

3 tbsp. thinly sliced fresh gingerroot

5 lbs. flat beef ribs (preferably organic)

PREPARATION

Mix together all of the ingredients listed except for the ribs. Place the ribs in the marinade and soak for at least 24 hours (longer is better). These ribs can be either broiled or barbecued.

Note from Tricia: She prefers broiled because the ribs can be broiled in the marinade, and any extra marinade left in the pan can be used as additional sauce.

To broil: Preheat broiler and broil ribs approx. 8 inches from the heat until very brown and cooked through (10–20 minutes).

Beef Filet with Caramelized Onions & Blue Cheese

INGREDIENTS

3 tbsp. salted butter

4 cups thinly sliced sweet yellow onion

1 large garlic clove, minced

½ tsp. salt

¼ tsp. black pepper

2 center-cut beef filets (approx. ½ lb. (8 oz.) each

Olive oil

Salt and pepper for sprinkling on filets

2 tbsp. (generous) blue cheese

PREPARATION

Melt the butter in a large nonstick skillet over moderately high heat. Add the onions and sauté for approx. 10 minutes, or until the onions start to caramelize. Deglaze the pan with ¼ cup water to moisten the onions and lift any sugars that are on the bottom of the pan. Cook the onions for another several minutes, or until most of the liquid has evaporated. Add the garlic, salt and pepper, stir to combine and set aside.

Preheat the oven broiler. Rub both sides of the filets with olive oil and sprinkle both sides with salt and pepper. Place the filets on a broiler pan and broil approx. 6 inches from the heat for 6–8 minutes on each side, until the meat is medium rare, turning only once. When the filets are almost done (about a minute to go), remove from oven and spread one tbsp. of blue cheese on top of each filet. Return to oven and broil for an additional 30–60 seconds, or until the filets are perfectly cooked and the blue cheese is melted on top.

Put on serving dishes and arrange the caramelized onions in a circle around each filet. Serve as soon as possible after removing from the oven. Serves 2

Marinated Lamb Cutlets

INGREDIENTS

½ cup grapeseed oil

⅓ cup soy sauce

¼ cup red wine vinegar

Juice of ½ lemon (approx. 2 tbsp.)

1 tbsp. Worcestershire sauce

1 tsp. dry mustard

¼ tsp. black pepper

1 lb. boneless lamb cutlets, 1 to ½ inches thick, all fat trimmed/removed

Mint jelly

PREPARATION

In a broiler safe shallow baking dish, whisk together all ingredients except for the lamb. Add the lamb, turning to coat all sides, and marinate refrigerated and covered loosely, for at least 4–6 hours, preferably overnight. Occasionally rotate the lamb to the other side.

Preheat the broiler. Pour the marinade out of the baking dish and discard, but leave a small amount in the dish with the lamb. Broil approx. 6 inches from the heat for 4–5 minutes on one side, turn and continue to broil an additional 4–5 minutes. The meat should be pink inside for the best flavor.

Remove meat and on a cutting surface, cut the lamb diagonally into thin slices. Spoon some of the juices from the broiling/baking dish over each serving. Serve mint jelly on the side. Serves 2

Veal Parmesan

(Note: I added eggplant to this recipe because I love eggplant, and feel that it makes this dish extra special. If you are not fond of eggplant, just follow the recipe and leave out the preparation and inclusion of the eggplant in the final assembly of the dish)

INGREDIENTS

1½ lbs. eggplant (Note: If available, use Italian baby eggplants)

2 tbsp. butter

2 tbsp. extra-virgin olive oil

2 eggs

½ tsp. salt

¼ tsp. black pepper

½ cup fresh bread crumbs, finely processed (easiest in a mini-food processor)

1 cup grated Parmesan cheese

1½ lbs. veal scaloppini

1 tbsp. butter

1 tbsp. extra-virgin olive oil

8 oz. sliced mozzarella cheese

Tomato Sauce:
4 tbsp. olive oil

2 medium red onions, sliced thin

4 large garlic cloves, finely chopped

1 tsp. dried basil

1 tsp. dried oregano

2 tsp. firmly packed light brown sugar

1 28-oz. can chopped Italian tomatoes with puree

1 tsp. Herbamare®

½ tsp. black pepper

PREPARATION

Peel eggplant and slice into rounds about ½ inch thick. Place on paper towels and sprinkle with salt. Allow the eggplant to stand for at least ½ hour – beads of water will form on the top. When ready to cook, press tops of eggplant slices with paper towels to remove all excess moisture.

Heat 1 tbsp. of the butter and 1 tbsp. of the olive oil over moderate heat in a large heavy non-stick skillet. Add eggplant slices in a single layer in the skillet and cook until nicely browned and beginning to soften. Turn the eggplant to the other side and continue to cook until the other side is also browned and the eggplant slices are very soft. Remove to a plate lined with paper towels and continue with second batch in same manner, adding another tbsp. of both butter and olive oil. Set eggplant aside.

Make tomato sauce: Heat olive oil in a large saucepan over moderate heat and add the sliced onions. Cook stirring occasionally, until the onions are very soft and just beginning to brown. Add the garlic, basil, oregano, brown sugar and tomatoes. Simmer sauce for ½ hour to 45 minutes, then add the Herbamare® and pepper. Set aside.

In a small shallow dish (pie plate is good for this) mix the eggs with the salt and pepper. On a separate dish mix together the Parmesan cheese and the bread crumbs. Pat the veal scaloppini very dry with paper towels.

Wipe the skillet clean with paper towels. Add another tbsp. of butter and a tbsp. of olive oil, and heat over moderately high heat until very hot but not smoking. Dip the veal pieces first in the beaten egg, and then immerse both sides in the bread crumb mixture. Put immediately in the hot skillet and sauté for approx. 3–4 minutes on each side. The bread crumbs should adhere to the meat and be a deep golden brown color.

Place the veal in a large rectangular baking dish in a single layer. Place the eggplant slices on top of the veal. Spoon the tomato sauce over the eggplant slices. Finally, top with the sliced mozzarella cheese.

Preheat oven to 325 degrees and bake the veal for approx. 10 to 15 minutes, or until heated through and the cheese is melted. Serves 4

Note: In a good food store, veal scallops can be purchased already in the "scaloppine" state – meaning, they have already been cut thinly and are recipe ready. If not available, then veal slices must be placed between pieces of wax paper and pounded with a mallet until they are approx. ¼ inch thick. The success of this recipe depends on buying veal that is high quality and very tender.

French Rack of Lamb with Roasted Red Pepper Coulis

INGREDIENTS

1 8-bone rack of lamb, cut in half

1 tbsp. extra-virgin olive oil for searing

2 tsp. whole-grain mustard (for rubbing on lamb rack)

1 cup fresh whole wheat bread crumbs (1 large slice of bread)

1 tbsp. chopped fresh garlic (2–3 cloves, depending on size)

1½ tbsp. chopped fresh parsley

1 tsp. dried rosemary (or 2 tsp. chopped fresh rosemary)

¼ tsp. Herbamare® or salt

⅛ tsp. black pepper

2 tbsp. extra-virgin olive oil

Sauce:

1 very large red bell pepper, roasted in oven, then peeled, membranes & seeds removed (See p. 213)

2 tbsp. balsamic vinegar

3 tbsp. honey

½ tsp. dry mustard

¼ cup Dijon mustard

1 tsp. crumbled dried rosemary

PREPARATION

Heat olive oil in large heavy skillet over moderately high heat until very hot, but not smoking. Add lamb rack (cut in half), and brown for 2 minutes on each side, turning once. Transfer to a 13 x 9-inch baking dish, fatty sides up. Spread each lamb rack half with 1 tsp. of mustard.

In a mini-food processor pulse the bread to equal 1 cup. Add the garlic, parsley, rosemary, Herbamare® and pepper and pulse until combined. Add the olive oil and pulse just until combined. Pat the bread crumb mixture evenly over the lamb racks, pressing gently so the crumbs adhere.

To make the sauce, combine all sauce ingredients in a mini-food processor and pulse until combined and very smooth. Set aside and keep at room temperature until needed.

Preheat oven to 350 degrees. Roast lamb racks for 35–45 minutes, or until the desired doneness (lamb should be light pink to very pink on the inside). Remove from the oven and let sit for several minutes before carving racks into individual chops. Spoon a generous amount of sauce on each serving plate and serve remainder on the side. Serves 2

Clyde's Clips:

Cats are masters at communicating non-verbally. One of the best ways to let a human know you want something is by staring with unrelenting perseverance, for example, at an empty food bowl. For added drama I usually raise my hackles a bit. Here's what I do to Sue sometimes: I stare until she relents and gives me some food, and then I sniff it disdainfully and walk away. Self-denial is worth witnessing her reaction.

Sheila ("Peach")
In Loving Memory 2.28.56–10.16.10

Sheila (Peach) and I first met at work, and I was her supervisor – well, not really. The Dalai Lama says you should know what all the rules are so that you can learn how to break them properly. She was a master at accomplishing this.

The rewards and blessings I have received from having a best friend like Peach are too numerous and immeasurable to be detailed here. Thirty years of her friendship made the sun shine more brightly, the birds sing more sweetly, and my laughter more uncontrolled and constant. You will never be forgotten, and could not have been loved more.

The recipes that appear in this cookbook contributed by Peach are:

Sour Cream Coffee Cake and…

Bethany Beach, DE, 1991

Sherry-Glazed Corned Beef
(from the kitchen of Sheila Lockhart)

INGREDIENTS

3 lbs. corned beef, any excess fat removed

2 medium onions, peeled and halved

2 whole large garlic cloves, peeled

2 bay leaves

6–8 whole cloves

Glaze:

½ cup dry sherry

½ cup granulated brown sugar

2 tbsp. molasses

Cabbage to accompany (2 large heads)

Butter, salt and pepper

PREPARATION

Place corned beef, fat side down, in a large cooking pot (Dutch oven) along with the onions, garlic, bay leaves and cloves. Cover with cold water and bring to a boil. Reduce heat and simmer beef, partially covered, as slowly as possible for 3 ½ to 4 hours, or until the meat is very tender when tested with a fork. Remove from the pot, drain, and place on an ovenproof baking dish, fat side up. If there is any remaining fat on top of the beef, remove it with a sharp knife.

Preheat oven to 350 degrees. Combine all glaze ingredients in a small saucepan and simmer over medium heat until the sugar is dissolved and the glaze is slightly syrupy.

Spoon the glaze over the beef, coating thoroughly, and bake for 30 minutes, basting several times. Slice the beef diagonally and place on a serving dish. Cover meat with some of the glaze from the baking dish. Serve hot or at room temperature.

While beef is in the oven, cut the cabbage into large chunks and place on a vegetable steamer and steam just until tender! It should not be mushy! Place the cabbage in a large serving bowl and toss gently with a generous amount of softened butter, and salt and pepper to taste. Serves 6

Quality of Ingredients

Ever hear the expression "garbage in, garbage out?" If you cook with inferior quality ingredients, it is too pejorative to say that the end result will be garbage. However, the end result with inferior ingredients will be just that – inferior.

This does not mean you have to follow Toni's philosophy, which was, "If it costs more then it must be better." Of course, in many cases, if something costs more it is in fact better. However, good quality ingredients are readily available that are not the most expensive, and in some instances may even be the least expensive.

Some good examples are olive oil and different kinds of vinegar (e.g. balsamic, red or white wine, etc). If you are in a quality food store purchasing either of these two items, you may be overwhelmed with the choices. If you have my mother's attitude, which is actually the least confusing, but the most detrimental to your bank account, just buy the most expensive brand available. I tend to buy something in the mid-range price, and I am almost always pleased with the result.

A lot of recipes call for chicken broth. I prefer to use "Organic Free Range Chicken Broth," which is available in most food stores. When using soy sauce, my normal choice is Kikkoman® Naturally Brewed Tamari Soy Sauce. If a recipe calls for garlic flavored olive oil, a good choice is Olave® Extra Virgin Olive Oil (Garlic).

When purchasing fresh ingredients (meat, fish, vegetables, and other produce), the most important thing is to assure what you are buying is as fresh as possible. Do not be tempted to buy things that are about to be past their prime (as noted in the "Sell By" date) and may have a reduced price. There are better ways to save money (e.g., a "two for one" Happy Hour.)

Ground Lamb in Cashew Nut Sauce with Chickpeas *(Keema Matar)*

INGREDIENTS

2 lbs. lean ground lamb

4 tbsp. grapeseed oil

2 cups (generous) finely chopped sweet yellow onions

4–6 large garlic cloves, or enough to equal one very generous tbsp. of finely chopped garlic

1½ tbsp. finely chopped fresh gingerroot

1 tsp. ground cumin

2 tsp. ground coriander

1 tsp. tumeric

½ tsp. cayenne pepper

2 bay leaves

1½ tsp. Kosher salt

3 cups fresh seeded & chopped fresh tomatoes

3 tbsp. cashew nut butter

1 15½ to 16-oz. can chickpeas, drained and rinsed in cold water

½ cup hot water

1 cup chicken broth

2 tsp. *garam masala*

1 tsp. Kosher salt

Brown rice to accompany

PREPARATION

Place lamb in large heavy non-stick skillet and cook over moderate heat until any fat has been released and the meat is no longer pink. As it is cooking, stir and break into small pieces. Pour off excess grease and drain lamb well on paper towels. Set aside.

Heat the oil in a large heavy non-stick pot and add onions. Over medium heat, cook the onions until they turn a caramel brown and are very soft. This should take 20–25 minutes. Stir frequently to assure the onions brown evenly and do not burn. Add garlic and ginger to the onions and cook for an additional minute. Add cumin, coriander, tumeric, red pepper and bay leaves. Stir to combine and add the cooked lamb. Add salt, chopped tomatoes, cashew nut butter and chickpeas.

Add ½ cup of hot water and the chicken broth. Bring the contents to a boil, then reduce heat to low and simmer, covered, for about 45 minutes, or until the sauce is thickened. Check and stir occasionally to assure the sauce is not sticking and burning. When done, turn off heat and stir in *garam masala*. Add an additional 1 tsp. Kosher salt. Serve over rice that has been cooked according to package directions. Serves 6–8

Braised Lamb Shanks with Orzo & Feta Cheese

INGREDIENTS

2 lbs. lean lamb shanks

¼ cup extra-virgin olive oil

1½ cup chopped white onions

1 28-oz. can crushed tomatoes, not drained

1 tsp. dried oregano

½ tsp. salt

¼ tsp. black pepper

1 cup orzo (rice-shaped pasta)

¼ cup minced fresh parsley leaves

8 oz. crumbled Feta cheese

½ cup dry vermouth

PREPARATION

Trim as much of the fat as possible off the lamb shanks. Heat olive oil in a large pot (Dutch oven) over moderately high heat and brown the lamb shanks on all sides. Transfer to a plate and set aside. To the fat remaining in the pot, add the onions. Reduce heat to moderately low and cook, stirring, until the onions are softened. Return the lamb shanks to the skillet, add the crushed tomatoes, oregano, salt and pepper and bring the mixture to a boil. Simmer the mixture, covered, for approx. 3 hours, or until the lamb is very tender.

When the lamb is almost ready, prepare the orzo in salted boiling water according to package directions; drain and set aside.

Remove the lamb shanks from the pot and turn off the heat. When the shanks are cool enough to handle, remove all meat from the bones and cut into small pieces. Note: This is much easier to do (plus you'll get the maximum amount of meat and it's easier to assure that a minimum amount of fat is included) if you do it with your hands. Return the meat to the pot and add the cooked orzo, parsley, Feta and the vermouth. Stir gently to combine. Cook the lamb mixture over moderately low heat for 5–10 minutes, or until thoroughly heated. Serves 4

German-Style Beef Pot Roast with Horseradish

INGREDIENTS

3 tbsp. extra-virgin olive oil

1½ lbs. boneless chuck roast (cut into small cubes, all fat removed)

1 medium onion, chopped

2 large garlic cloves, minced

½ tsp. salt

¼ tsp. pepper

2 cups coarsely chopped fresh carrots

4 small potatoes (Yukon gold), diced (not peeled)

1½ cup beef broth

3 oz. jar whipped Horseradish

¼ tsp. celery salt

3 bay leaves

Spaetzle or thin egg noodles to accompany (cooked according to package directions)

PREPARATION

Heat the olive oil over moderate heat in a heavy frying pan until hot. Add the beef and cook, stirring occasionally, until browned on all sides. Add the onion and garlic and cook, stirring occasionally, for approx. 5 minutes. Stir in salt and pepper and remove from heat.

Place the carrots, potatoes, beef broth and Horseradish in a crock pot. Stir in the celery salt and bay leaves. Add the beef/onion mixture. Cook on the slow setting for 6 hours. Serve over spaetzle or egg noodles.

Note from Ute: Don't be afraid of the large amount of Horseradish – it will mellow out and taste great (Es Schmeckt wunderbar!!)

Guten Appetit!!

Ute

A native of Germany, Ute is my beloved sister-in-law who resides in Frederick, Md.

I do not have many authentic German recipes in my repertoire, so I was excited when Ute offered to provide one. As with most of my friends, some of our most joyful memories include hanging in the kitchen, drinking wine while we work together to get a memorable meal on the table. Happiness is having family who are also treasured friends.

Luray, VA, 2006
Premium Wine Tasting Weekend

Cleveland Browns Stadium,
Nov. 2001

Beef Filet Tips with Cucumber Dill Sauce

Adapted from Gourmet magazine, Condé Nast Publications

INGREDIENTS

1½ lbs. filet mignon

1½ cups peeled, seeded, thinly sliced cucumbers

1 tbsp. butter

1 onion, thinly sliced (approx. 1½ cups)

1½ cups thinly sliced mushrooms

½ tsp. salt

¼ tsp. pepper

½ cup sour cream

3 tbsp. dried dill weed

1 tbsp. mild mustard

½ tsp. dried basil

2 cups chopped fresh tomatoes (seeded)

1 tbsp. grapeseed oil

Herbamare® or salt

PREPARATION

Cut the filet mignon into small (about ¾ inch) cubes and pat them dry with paper towels.

Spread cucumber slices on paper towels and let sit for at least ½ hour; pat the tops dry with more paper towels.

In a heavy skillet, heat the butter and sauté the onion over moderately high heat until softened. Add the cucumber, mushrooms, salt and pepper; sauté for 5–10 minutes, or until the cucumber is only slightly softened. Stir in the sour cream, dill, mustard and basil and cook the mixture, stirring, until it is hot. Stir in the tomatoes and reduce the heat to the lowest setting possible; cover and keep warm.

In a separate heavy skillet, heat the oil over high heat until hot but not smoking. Add the beef cubes and cook quickly, for approx. 3 minutes, until browned on all sides, but still pink inside. Sprinkle the meat liberally with Herbamare®.

Divide the meat among serving plates and spoon the cucumber sauce over the beef. Optional: Garnish the plates with sliced tomatoes sprinkled lightly with fresh parsley. Serves 4

Song Parody – "My Furry Valentine"

My furry valentine, Sweet comic pal 'o mine
You make me smile with my heart

Your looks are laughable, so photographable
You are my favorite work of art

Is your figure less than sleek –
Are you at times a little meek?
You have always won my heart –
from the start

Don't change your fur for me –
Come here and purr for me
Stay little pal 'o mine stay
Each day is Valentine's Day

Lamb in Fragrant Spinach Sauce *(Saag Gosht)*

INGREDIENTS

6 tbsp. grapeseed oil

2½ lbs. boneless lean lamb, all excess fat removed, cut into 1½ inch cubes

3 medium onions, thinly sliced

8 large cloves garlic, finely chopped

3 tbsp. finely chopped fresh gingerroot

1 tbsp. ground cumin

2 tbsp. ground coriander

¼ tsp. cayenne pepper

1 tsp. tumeric

1 cup seeded chopped fresh tomatoes

1 green chili pepper, finely chopped (to equal 2–3 tbsp.)

½ cup plain yogurt (not low-fat) "Greek style"

2 cups water

1 tbsp. Kosher or sea salt

1 cinnamon stick (approx. 3 inches long)

9 whole cloves

3 small bay leaves

6 cardamom pods

2 large bags of fresh spinach (10 oz. each), rinsed well, stems removed

4 tsp. *garam masala*

Cooked brown rice to accompany

PREPARATION

In a heavy large non-stick frying pan heat 2 tbsp. of the oil over moderately high heat until hot but not smoking, and in it brown the lamb, patted dry first, in batches. As each batch is browned transfer the lamb to a heavy non-stick oven-proof casserole dish that has a lid. Add the remaining 4 tbsp. of oil to the skillet and add the sliced onions. Cook the onions over moderate heat, stirring frequently, until they are a deep caramelized golden brown color, and very soft. This should take 20–25 minutes.

When onions are done, add the garlic and gingerroot and cook for an additional minute. Add the cumin, coriander, cayenne pepper and tumeric and stir rapidly for about 15 seconds. Add the chopped tomatoes and chopped green chili and cook for 3–5 minutes, stirring occasionally, until the tomato is cooked and the entire mixture is turned into a thick pulpy concoction. Add the yogurt, stir to combine, and simmer for 1 minute.

Add the water and salt to the skillet and over moderate heat bring to a boil. Pour this mixture over the browned lamb cubes in the casserole dish.

Cut a double layer of cheesecloth about 6 inches square. Put cinnamon stick, whole cloves, bay leaves and cardamom pods in the center, bring up the four corners of the cheesecloth to wrap the spices, and tie them to form a bag. Add the spice bag to the casserole dish and submerge it.

Preheat the oven to 350 degrees. Cover the casserole dish with a piece of foil, and then place the casserole lid over the foil. Braise the lamb, covered, in the preheated oven for 2 hours, at which time the lamb should be fork tender. Remove from the oven and take off the lid. Remove the spice bag and squeeze hard to extract as much juice as possible into the casserole dish (it is more efficient and easier to do this using a rubber glove). Discard the spice bag.

Place the spinach in a very large heavy pot and cook it, uncovered, over moderate heat, adding no additional water other than the water that clings to the spinach after rinsing it. You probably cannot add all of it at once. As the spinach steams and starts to soften, add additional spinach until it all fits in the pot. Stir continually just until all the spinach is softened. It is very important not to overcook the spinach. When it is just softened the spinach should still retain a bright green color. Place cooked spinach in a colander and set aside. Note: You can wait to cook the spinach until the lamb is close to being fully cooked.

Place the cooked spinach in a bowl and finely puree it with an immersion blender or in a food processor. Stir in the garam masala. Add the seasoned spinach to the lamb, stirring very gently to combine well. Return the cover to the casserole dish, and return the casserole to the oven and cook for an additional 5 minutes. Serve the *Saag Gosht* over cooked brown rice. Serves 6

Note: As is the case with most braised dishes, this one will taste better with keeping, meaning to make it several hours in advance, allow to rest at room temperature before reheating and serving. Also, it keeps extremely well if refrigerated up to 2 days. If refrigerated, bring to room temperature before reheating.

Veal Scaloppini with Brown Butter & Capers

INGREDIENTS

¼ cup unbleached all-purpose flour

¾ tsp. salt

½ tsp. black pepper

2 tbsp. extra-virgin olive oil

1 lb. thinly sliced (no more than ¼ inch thick) veal scaloppini

4 tbsp. unsalted butter

2 tbsp. red-wine vinegar

2 tbsp. small capers

1 tbsp. chopped fresh flat-leaf parsley

PREPARATION

Stir together flour, ½ tsp. salt and ¼ tsp. pepper with a fork on a plate and set aside.

Place olive oil in a 12-inch heavy skillet. Heat oil over high heat until it is very hot and shimmers. Pat veal dry with paper towels and lightly dredge on both sides in the flour mixture, shaking off excess. Cook veal in olive oil for about 2 minutes on each side, turning once, until browned and just cooked through. Transfer veal to a plate and cover with foil to keep warm.

Discard oil from skillet and wipe with a paper towel. Add butter to the skillet and cook over medium heat until a nutty brown color and fragrant. Reduce the heat to low and stir in the vinegar, capers, and the remaining ¼ tsp. salt and ¼ tsp. pepper and cook briefly to combine. Return veal to skillet, sprinkle with the parsley, stir gently to coat veal with butter and evenly distribute the parsley. Cook just to heat through, about a minute. Serves 2–3

Note: In most high quality food stores, veal scallops can be purchased already in the "scaloppini" state – meaning, they have already been cut thinly and are recipe ready. If veal is not available thinly sliced,, then veal slices must be placed between pieces of wax paper and pounded with a mallet until they are ¼ inch thick. The success of this recipe depends on buying veal that is high quality and very tender.

Veal Scaloppini with Mushrooms

INGREDIENTS

2½ tbsp. butter

2 tbsp. extra-virgin olive oil

1 lb. veal scallops, sliced approx. ¼ inch thick (See Note)

2 tbsp. chopped shallots

¼ cup dry vermouth

¼ cup chicken broth

2 tbsp. sour cream

½ tsp. salt

¼ tsp. pepper

½ lb. mushrooms, rinsed, trimmed and sliced

PREPARATION

In a large skillet, heat 1½ tbsp. of the butter and 1 tbsp. of the olive oil until hot but not smoking. Sauté the veal scallops in batches on both sides until lightly browned. Do not overcook the scallops – cook approx. 2 minutes per side. Transfer to a plate as cooked and cover plate with aluminum foil to keep warmed.

Add the shallots to the same skillet and sauté until tender but not browned. Add the vermouth and chicken broth and cook, stirring, until brought to a boil. Simmer until liquid is reduced by about half. Keep an eye on it as it is simmering to assure you do not reduce it by more than half. Add sour cream and stir with a whisk until well combined, then season with salt and pepper.

In a separate skillet while the sauce is being reduced, sauté the mushrooms in the remaining 1 tbsp. butter and 1 tbsp. olive oil. Add mushrooms and veal to the sauce. Stir to coat veal with sauce and reheat briefly – do not overcook. Serve immediately. Serves 3–4

Note: In many high quality food stores, veal scallops can be purchased already in the "scaloppini" state – meaning, they have already been cut thinly and are recipe ready. If not available, then veal slices must be placed between pieces of wax paper and pounded with a mallet until they are ¼ inch thick. The success of any veal recipe depends on buying veal that is high quality and very tender.

Lamb in Fragrant Garlic Cream Sauce *(or as they would say in India "Rogan Josh")*

INGREDIENTS

3 lbs. lean boneless lamb (preferably from the leg), cut into 1½ inch cubes (remove all excess fat – if you buy lean, good quality lamb, there shouldn't be a lot)

⅓ cup melted *usli ghee* (If not available, use 8 tbsp. of sweet (unsalted) butter)

2 tbsp. *usli ghee* (if not available, use 1 tbsp. unsalted butter plus 1 tbsp. grapeseed oil)

1 tbsp. minced garlic cloves

2 tsp. ground cumin

2 tsp. ground cardamom

1 tsp. *garam masala*

¼ cup half and half

Brown rice as an accompaniment (cooked according to package directions)

Marinade:

4 medium onions (white or yellow), peeled and quartered

3 tbsp. finely chopped fresh gingerroot

2 tbsp. ground coriander

¾ tsp. cayenne pepper

2½ cups Greek All Natural Strained Yogurt

½ cup sour cream

1 tbsp. Kosher salt

PREPARATION

Place all of the marinade ingredients in a food processor (or an electric blender) and process until the ingredients are finely pureed. Place the lamb cubes in a large bowl and pour the marinade and the melted *ghee* over it. Mix thoroughly to coat the meat pieces with the marinade and let the meat marinate for approx. ½ to 1 hour at room temperature.

Transfer the meat along with the marinade to a heavy non-stick pot (Dutch oven). Bring the mixture to a gentle boil over medium-low heat. Reduce the heat to low and simmer, covered, until the lamb is very tender. If you have used high quality lamb, this should take no more than 2 hours. Stir occasionally to assure that the sauce is not sticking to the bottom of the pan.

Heat the 2 tbsp. of *ghee* in a small skillet over moderately high heat. When it is very hot, add the garlic and, stirring rapidly, cook for about 15 seconds. Immediately add the cumin, cardamom, and *garam masala* and cook for only about 5 more seconds. Turn off the heat and pour the perfumed butter and spices over the meat. Add the half and half and stir to distribute the ingredients. Let the meat stand at room temperature for 2 hours.

When ready to serve, reheat the meat until hot and serve over brown rice. Serves 6–8

Testimonial

As long-time and dear friends, Sue and I have shared many experiences, many laughs, and many meals since high school. I can attest that her recipes are filled not only with scrumptious and carefully chosen ingredients, but also with love, delight and good humor. Discover Sue's wonderful spirit as you prepare her dishes, and absorb her joyous approach to the art of cooking and sharing memorable food with great friends.

Dr. Jeff Neff
Professor, Western Carolina University
Cullowhee, NC

Sue's Tips:

I am amazed that so many people who entertain in their homes, and especially servers in restaurants, remove cutlery and dishes from the table before all diners have finished eating.

One of the earliest doctrines my mother espoused was to never, ever start clearing anything away from the table until each and every person was completely done with their meal. To do so is not only disruptive but rude. When things are being cleared prematurely, the diner or diners who are still eating may feel they need to hurry up and finish.

I am a very slow eater, so when I'm with my husband in a restaurant he always finishes first. About 95% of the time a server will come to the table to snatch his plate before I'm done. He normally says, "Please leave my plate alone – my wife is still eating." Often he gets a look of incomprehension, like "So what? Your plate is empty." But sometimes the servers actually give an indication that they get it, and realize that it was disruptive to our dining experience to be rushing things along. Enlightenment is a wonderful thing!

Lamb & Feta Patties with Bell Pepper Relish
Adapted from The Gourmet Cookbook (2004), Condé Nast Publications

For Relish:

¾ cup cider vinegar

¼ cup sugar, preferably organic

⅔ cup water

1 orange bell pepper

1 red bell pepper (both peppers cored, seeded and cut into ½ inch pieces)

⅓ cup (generous) golden raisins

1 apple, peeled, cored, and cut into ½ inch pieces

1 tsp. mustard seeds

⅛ tsp. cayenne pepper

½ tsp. salt

For Patties:

⅓ cup coarsely chopped fresh mint leaves

1 slice whole wheat bread, torn into several pieces

2 generous tbsp. coarsely chopped

shallots

2 cloves garlic

1 lb. lean ground lamb

1 large egg

¼ lb. crumbled feta cheese

½ tsp. salt

¼ tsp. black pepper

PREPARATION

For the relish: Combine the vinegar and sugar in a large heavy saucepan and bring to a boil, stirring until the sugar is dissolved and boil uncovered for 1 minute. Add the remaining relish ingredients, reduce heat to moderately low, and simmer briskly uncovered, stirring occasionally, until the peppers and apple are tender, and most of the liquid is evaporated. This should take approx. 30 to 45 minutes.

For the patties: Pulse mint leaves in a mini-food processor to equal ⅓ cup. Add the bread, shallots and whole garlic cloves and pulse until the mixture is well combined and all ingredients are finely chopped. Transfer this mixture to a medium bowl and add the lamb, egg, feta, salt and pepper. Blend with your hands just until combined. Do not overwork the mixture. Form into 4 large patties.

Preheat broiler and broil patties about 6 inches from the heat, turning once, until they are browned but still just slightly pink in the center, approx. 8 to 10 minutes total. Serve with the relish. Serves 2–4

Sweet & Sour Pork *(Bears no resemblance to what you might get at "Takee Outee")*

INGREDIENTS

1 lb. boneless pork tenderloin

3 tbsp. dry sherry

1¼ tsp. salt

¼ tsp. black pepper

1 tbsp. cornstarch

½ cup water

1 tbsp. tomato ketchup

¼ cup sugar, preferably organic

1 tbsp. soy sauce

1 tbsp. red wine vinegar

4 tbsp. sunflower oil

1 large green bell pepper, cored, seeded, and thinly sliced

1 large red bell pepper, cored, seeded, and thinly sliced

1 medium onion, sliced into thin ring slices

Brown rice to accompany (cooked according to package directions)

Batter:

2 egg yolks

2 tbsp. unbleached all-purpose flour

3 tbsp. water

PREPARATION

Cut the pork loin into small strips (about ½"wide), place in a bowl and sprinkle with 2 tbsp. of the sherry, ¼ tsp. salt and the pepper. Stir to coat evenly and set aside.

Mix the cornstarch with a little bit of the water until dissolved in a small bowl, then add the rest of the water, ketchup, sugar, soy sauce, remaining 1 tbsp. of sherry, the vinegar, and the remaining 1 tsp. salt. Stir until the sugar is dissolved and set aside.

Beat together the egg yolks, flour and 3 tbsp. water to make a smooth batter. Pour over the pork strips and stir to coat evenly. Heat 3 tbsp. of the oil in a large heavy skillet over moderately high heat until very hot but not smoking. Add the pork strips to the skillet in a single layer (do in 2–3 batches) and cook for approx. 2–3 minutes on each side. The pork should be well browned on both sides. Remove pork strips with a slotted spoon after each batch is cooked and put on a large plate lined with a paper towel.

When all pork strips are cooked, add remaining tbsp. of oil to the skillet and then add the sliced peppers and onion rings. Stir fry vegetables for approx. 10 minutes, stirring frequently, or until the vegetables are softened but still firm, and not mushy. Add the soy sauce mixture to the skillet and cook, stirring, until thickened. Add the cooked pork strips and continue to cook, stirring, just until the pork strips are heated through, which should only take a couple of minutes. Serve over cooked brown rice. Serves 2–3

Clyde's Clips:

Pat can take it or leave it if I sit on his lap. So naturally I do it on a regular basis. Sue on the other hand goes ballistic with pleasure when I'm on her lap, so I typically only do this when there's something in it for me, like licking her ice cream bowl.

Filet Mignon with Gorgonzola Tomato Topping

Marinade:

2 tbsp. balsamic vinegar

2 tbsp. chopped shallots

1 tbsp. extra-virgin olive oil

3 cloves garlic, crushed (use garlic press)

¼ tsp. dried thyme

¼ tsp. black pepper

2 filet mignon steaks, (6 to 8 oz.) each

Herbamare® or salt for sprinkling

Topping:

1 cup chopped fresh tomatoes (seeds removed)

½ cup crumbled Gorgonzola cheese

¼ cup shredded fresh basil leaves

2 tbsp. chopped fresh chives

½ tsp. Herbamare® or salt

¼ tsp. black pepper

PREPARATION

In a small bowl, whisk together all of the marinade ingredients. Place the filets in a shallow broiler-proof baking dish and spoon the marinade over the steak. Set aside.

Preheat broiler. In a serving bowl, combine the topping ingredients and stir gently until blended.

Sprinkle the filets with Herbamare®. Broil the steaks approx. 4–6 inches from the heat for approx. 5–7 minutes on each side for medium rare meat. When the steaks are turned, sprinkle the other side also with Herbamare®. Note: It is difficult to state exactly how long the steaks should be cooked, because it depends on the thickness of the meat, oven temperatures may vary, etc. The most important thing is to be sure that the filets are not overcooked. At the very most, they should be light pink inside, and preferably (for best flavor and moistness) they should be medium rare, which is a darker shade of pink, but not red.

Any marinade left in the baking dish can be spooned over the steaks before serving, Spoon some topping onto each serving plate and serve the rest on the side. Serves 2

Never compromise – that assumes you're going to agree to give up something.

Asian Pork Tenderloin with Shiitake Mushrooms

Adapted from Gourmet magazine, Condé Nast Publications

INGREDIENTS

1 lb. boneless pork tenderloin, all excess fat trimmed

All-purpose flour for dredging pork

2 tbsp. unsalted butter

1 tbsp. grapeseed oil

¾ cup chopped shallots

6 oz. *shiitake* mushrooms, stems discarded and caps sliced thinly

¼ cup Calvados cognac (preferably, or use ¼ cup brandy)

¼ cup water

⅓ cup apricot preserves

¼ cup heavy cream

Marinade:

¼ cup fresh orange juice

2 tbsp. oyster sauce

2 tbsp. soy sauce

1½ tbsp. toasted sesame oil

1½ tsp. five-spice powder

½ tsp. dried thyme

3 large garlic cloves, minced

PREPARATION

In a large bowl stir together marinade ingredients. Add pork to marinade, tossing to coat completely. Marinate pork, covered and chilled, for at least 2 hours, turning pork at least once.

Preheat oven to 200 degrees. Remove pork from marinade and cut into 1 inch thick slices. Put flour on a plate, and dredge pork slices thoroughly in the flour, shaking off any excess. In a large heavy skillet heat 1 tbsp. of the butter and the oil over moderately high heat until hot but not smoking and sauté the pork for approx. 5 minutes on each side. The pork should be nicely browned. Transfer the pork to an ovenproof dish and keep warm in the preheated oven.

Add the remaining 1 tbsp. of butter to the skillet and sauté the shallots, stirring, for several minutes or until softened. Add the mushrooms and sauté, stirring, for approx. 5 minutes, or until the mushrooms release their liquid, and it is mostly evaporated. Add Calvados (or brandy) and cook until also mostly evaporated. Add water and preserves and cook, stirring, until well combined. Stir in the cream. Add pork and simmer for approx. 5 minutes. Serves 2–3

All of the entrées or side dishes in this section could be consumed for breakfast, lunch/brunch or dinner, and as with all types of food, should be enjoyed whenever the spirit moves you. My mother used to make strawberry shortcake as an entrée she frequently served for lunch, and sometimes even dinner. Here's what she did: Make shortcake biscuits using Bisquick® (recipe on box). As an aside, this is one of the few things I can remember Toni making that was out of a box, and not from scratch. Then she would mash up a bunch of fresh strawberries in a bowl, with a little sugar added. The biscuits were put in serving bowls hot out of the oven with the mashed strawberries spooned generously over top, and milk poured over all. My sister made this version of strawberry shortcake for me recently, and the nostalgia produced when I took the first bite was overwhelming.

I had Sue at "meow"

Testimonial

One of my earliest, most vivid memories of my Aunt Susan's cooking prowess is the experience of arriving at her Alexandria, VA apartment with my family for a weekend visit and being sumptuously greeted by the aromas of the 3-meat, 4-cheese lasagna she had been preparing for us the entire day, including her own homemade tomato sauce to boot! It was (and probably still is) the best lasagna I've ever had.

Since then, I have always known that when she is cooking or baking something for me, whether it is simple or complex, I am in for a wonderful treat. By her example, Aunt Susan continues to regularly inspire me toward the sheer ease and true pleasure of cooking great food. Most of all, her food is such a natural manifestation of her love of giving and the immense love she has to give!

Liz Ference
Massage Therapist
Asheville, NC

Hot Shrimp Salad Sandwiches

INGREDIENTS

1 lb. fresh shrimp, shelled and deveined cooked and chopped

1½ cups grated Swiss cheese

⅔ cup scallions, sliced (white part only)

1 tsp. dried dill weed

½ cup mayonnaise

1 tbsp. tarragon vinegar (Note: If you do not have tarragon vinegar available or prefer, use 1 tbsp. white wine vinegar and ½ tsp. dried tarragon)

6 hamburger type rolls, whole grain or whole wheat

PREPARATION

Mix all ingredients in a bowl except for rolls. Divide shrimp mixture evenly among rolls and wrap individually in aluminum foil. Place on a baking sheet and bake at 350 degrees for ½ hour. Filling will be hot and cheese melted.

Note: These sandwiches are a great hit for road trips. When you remove them from the oven, put them in a thermal type carry bag, keeping them wrapped in their individual foil packets. If you're not the designated driver, have your cooler handy and break out some nice chilled white wine to go with these. La vida es Buena!

Sue & I believe in shared activities – She sharpens her knives, I sharpen my claws

Three-Cheese Tart with Fresh Tomatoes

Recipe provided by Susan (Flish) Mau of Tallahassee, FL

INGREDIENTS

1 pie shell (prepare your own or buy a frozen one, uncooked)

1 tbsp. extra-virgin olive oil

¾ lb. fresh tomatoes, seeded and sliced about ½ inch thick

2 large cloves garlic, minced

6 oz. soft goat cheese

¾ cup grated sharp cheddar cheese

¾ cup grated Gruyere cheese

½ cup finely shredded fresh basil leaves

3 large eggs

¾ cup whole milk

⅛ tsp. salt

½ tsp. black pepper

PREPARATION

Prepare pie crust per package instructions (or make your own) and bake in a preheated oven until browned and cool. Use either a deep dish pie pan or, if preferred, a quiche dish.

Heat olive oil in a skillet over moderately low heat and sauté the tomatoes and garlic, stirring gently, for approx. 1–2 minutes, or until the tomatoes are just slightly softened. Place in the bottom of the pie shell.

Sprinkle the 3 cheeses and the basil on top of the tomatoes. In a medium bowl, whisk together the eggs, milk, salt and pepper until well combined and pour evenly over the cheese in the pie pan/quiche dish. Cook in a preheated 375 degree oven for approx. 45 minutes. The center of the "tart" should appear to be firm when the dish is gently shaken. Serves 6

Lentils with Spinach & Goat Cheese

Adapted from Gourmet magazine, Condé Nast Publications

INGREDIENTS

2 tbsp. extra-virgin olive oil

1 large white onion, finely chopped

1 generous cup finely chopped fresh carrots

¾ cup chopped celery

2 bay leaves

½ tsp. salt

¼ tsp. black pepper

4 cups (32 fluid oz.) chicken broth

1¼ cups French green lentils

3 tbsp. mascarpone cheese

½ tsp. Herbamare® or salt

2 tbsp. unsalted butter

4 6-oz. packages baby leaf spinach

Crumbled goat cheese for sprinkling on top (approx. 3 oz.)

PREPARATION

In a large pot, heat olive oil over moderately low heat, then add the onions, carrots, celery, bay leaves, salt and pepper and sauté until the vegetables are slightly softened and golden, about 10–15 minutes. While the vegetables are cooking, in a separate saucepan, heat the chicken broth over moderate heat until it is simmering, not boiling.

Add the lentils to the vegetables and stir until the mixture is well combined. Add the heated stock and simmer, covered, until the lentils are tender and most of the stock is absorbed, about 45 minutes. Discard bay leaves and gently stir in the mascarpone cheese and the Herbamare®.

While the lentils are cooking, in a separate very large pot melt the 2 tbsp. of butter over moderate heat. Add the spinach gradually (as much as will fit in the pot at a time) and stir (I prefer to use a pasta pronged spoon). As the spinach begins to wilt, there will be more room in the pot to add more spinach leaves. Continue to add spinach, stirring, until all of the spinach is wilted and cooked through. Sprinkle the spinach lightly with Herbamare®. Turn off the heat and set aside. Note: If you have never cooked spinach this way before, when you start the process it's hard to imagine that this mass of raw leaves will turn into cooked spinach, but trust in the process. Actually, it's quite irritating, because you start off with this mountain of spinach, and by the time it's cooked, you have a disappointingly small amount left.

Finally, with the pasta spoon, lift the spinach from the pot and add to the lentils. There should be some watery-looking liquid in the bottom of the spinach pot – do not add this to the lentil mixture. Stir the spinach gently into the lentils.

Spoon a generous amount onto each serving plate, and sprinkle each serving generously with the goat cheese (approx. 2 tbsp. per serving). Serves 4–6

Sue's Tips:

A cat's meow can mean many different things. It can be loud and demanding (like when Clyde wants me to get up and feed him breakfast), or short and sweet, which means "I love you, and thank you for being my friend." Very tiny mews are an effective ploy cats use to get what they want, a carryover from being a kitten. Women sometimes follow this philosophy by using little girl voices to get what they want from men. Clyde is way more effective with this ploy than I ever was!

Sweet & Spicy Beans Baked with Beef

(This recipe is very similar to how my mother used to make her Baked Beans casserole, except that she did not add barbecue sauce, used dry mustard, and only used pork and beans. Also, if using meat in the dish, she added hot dogs instead of ground beef. Making it this way has proven to be more of a crowd pleaser.)

INGREDIENTS

1 lb. bacon

1 large onion, chopped

1 lb. lean ground beef

½ cup ketchup (generous)

½ cup (generous) bottled barbecue sauce (I use Sweet Baby Ray's® Award Winning Barbecue Sauce)

1 tsp. salt

¼ cup bottled spicy brown mustard

½ cup molasses

1 tsp. chili powder

1 tsp. ground black pepper

2 16-oz. cans small red kidney beans, rinsed and drained

1 16-oz. can butter beans, rinsed and drained

2 16-oz. cans pork and beans, undrained

PREPARATION

Cook the bacon until crisp, drain on paper towels and set aside. Put 1 tbsp. of the rendered bacon fat in a large pot/Dutch oven and add the chopped onions. Cook over moderate heat for approx. 5 minutes. Add the ground beef and cook, stirring occasionally, to break up any lumps, until the beef is no longer pink. Pour off excess fat (if the beef is lean, there should not be very much to pour off). Return the pot to the heat and add the ketchup, barbecue sauce, salt, mustard, molasses, chili powder, pepper and all of the beans. Stir the mixture until it is combined well. Transfer the mixture to a large oven safe casserole dish.

Preheat the oven to 350 degrees. Bake the casserole, covered, in the middle of the oven for 1 hour.

Serves 16–20 people as a side dish, or 8–10 as a main course

Open-Faced Turkey Sandwiches

INGREDIENTS

2 cups chopped cooked turkey (smoked if desired)

½ cup minced celery

⅓ cup mayonnaise

1½ tbsp. lemon juice

1 tbsp. finely chopped shallots

½ tsp. salt

¼ tsp. pepper

4 slices whole wheat bread, lightly toasted

3 egg whites

¾ cup grated Cheddar cheese

PREPARATION

In a bowl combine turkey, celery, mayonnaise, lemon juice, shallots, salt and pepper.

Place ¼ of the turkey mixture on each slice of bread. In another bowl, beat the egg whites with a pinch of salt with an electric mixer or hand beater until they hold stiff peaks. Gently fold in the Cheddar cheese and gently spread the cheese mixture equally over the turkey mixture.

Preheat the oven to 450 degrees. Arrange the bread slices on a baking sheet and bake for approx. 10 minutes, or until the tops are puffed and golden brown. Serves 4

I get grumpy when I'm sleep deprived – 19 hours just isn't quite enough.

Lentils with Vinaigrette & Chorizo

Adapted from Gourmet magazine, Condé Nast Publications

INGREDIENTS

2 cups French green lentils, picked over and rinsed

6 cups water

2 Turkish bay leaves

½ tsp. salt

½ cup plus 3 tbsp. extra-virgin olive oil

2 cups finely chopped onions

1 cup diced carrots

1 cup diced celery

2 tbsp. finely chopped garlic

½ tsp. dried thyme

1 tsp. Herbamare® or salt

¼ tsp. black pepper

¼ cup red wine vinegar

1 tbsp. Dijon mustard

¾ lb. (12 oz.) Chorizo smoked sausage, cut crosswise into ¼ inch slices

¼ cup finely chopped fresh flat-leaf parsley

PREPARATION

Bring lentils, water, and bay leaves to a boil in a large heavy saucepan. Reduce heat and simmer, covered, for 15 minutes. Stir in ½ tsp. salt and continue to simmer the lentils, covered, until tender, but not falling apart, about another 5 minutes.

While the lentils are cooking, heat 3 tbsp. olive oil over moderately low heat in a large heavy skillet and cook the onions, carrots, celery, garlic, thyme, ½ tsp. of the Herbamare®, and ⅛ tsp. of the pepper until the vegetables are just softened.

Make a vinaigrette by whisking together the vinegar, mustard, remaining ½ tsp. Herbamare® and remaining ⅛ tsp. pepper in a bowl. Add the remaining ½ cup olive oil in a slow stream, whisking until well blended.

Drain lentils in a colander, discard the bay leaves, and return lentils to saucepan, along with the cooked vegetables and the vinaigrette. Stir to combine and cover to keep warm.

In the same skillet used for the vegetables, without cleaning, add the sliced Chorizo and cook over moderate heat until the sausage is nicely browned on all sides, stirring frequently as it is cooking. Stir the Chorizo and the parsley into the lentils. Cook over low heat for a couple minutes, or until just heated through. Serves 4 as a main course

Blueberry Buttermilk Pancakes

INGREDIENTS

2 large eggs

1 cup buttermilk (low-fat OK)

½ cup low-fat milk

3 tbsp. butter, melted and slightly cooled

1½ cup unbleached flour

1½ tbsp. sugar, preferably organic

1½ tsp. baking powder

½ tsp. baking soda

½ tsp. salt

2 cups fresh blueberries, rinsed and picked over to remove any stems

Butter for pan

PREPARATION

In a large bowl thoroughly whisk the eggs. Add the buttermilk, milk and butter and whisk until well blended. Sprinkle the flour, sugar, baking powder, baking soda, and salt on top of the buttermilk mixture and whisk just until the dry ingredients are evenly moistened. Gently stir in the blueberries.

Place a small amount of butter on a griddle or in a large non-stick skillet and heat over medium heat until a fleck of water dropped on it sizzles. Make pancakes to your desired size by spooning batter in rounds on skillet or griddle. When they are ready to be flipped, you should notice some bubbles on the top, and the edges should be golden. Cook until golden brown on each side.

Serve with warm maple syrup. Serves 3

Prosciutto, Leek & Cheese Quiche

Adapted from Gourmet magazine, Condé Nast Publications | This is extremely rich and decadent. Worth the calories? You bet.

INGREDIENTS

Pie dough for a 9 to 10-inch quiche dish **OR** make your own from your own preferred recipe

1½ cups finely chopped leeks (white and pale green parts only)

1 tbsp. unsalted butter

6 oz. thinly sliced Prosciutto ham (trimmed of any excess fat)

1 cup coarsely grated Swiss or Gruyère cheese

1½ cups shaved Parmigiano Reggiano cheese

1 cup coarsely grated whole-milk mozzarella cheese

3 large eggs

⅛ tsp. nutmeg

¼ tsp. black pepper

1 8-oz. container crème fraîche

PREPARATION

Prepare pie crust in quiche dish and bake according to package directions, remove from oven, and set oven temperature at 350 degrees.

Rinse leeks well and cut off the very top and all of the greens on the bottom up to the portion that is pale green. Rinse well again. Cut leeks lengthwise and then crosswise to make small (about ½ inch) pieces. Melt butter over moderately low heat in a small skillet and sauté the leeks, stirring occasionally, for about 10 minutes, or until they are very tender. Set aside.

Slice Prosciutto into thin strips, and line the bottom of the warm pie shell evenly with the ham. Toss the cheeses together in a bowl and then spread evenly over the ham. Do not pack, sprinkle lightly. Next spread the cooked leeks on top of the cheese.

Whisk together the eggs, nutmeg and pepper until well combined, and then whisk in the crème fraiche until smooth. Carefully and slowly pour half of the egg mixture on top of the quiche filling, gently moving the cheese with a spoon to help the custard disperse more evenly. Slowly add the remaining custard in the same manner.

Cover the pie loosely with foil (foil should not touch the top of the cheese mixture) and place on a baking sheet. Bake for an hour and 15 minutes on the middle oven rack and then check the quiche. The center of filling should be puffed and set (the center should appear to be slightly loose but not liquid). If need be, bake for an additional 15 minutes. Remove from oven and cool on a rack for at least 20 minutes before serving, as the filling continues to set as it cools. Serve warm or at room temperature.

Serves 8 (main course), and more than that if served as a starter course

Does wine count as a serving of fruit?

Lamb & Lentil Gratin *Adapted from Gourmet magazine, Condé Nast Publications*

INGREDIENTS

1 medium white onion, chopped (to equal approx. 2 cups)

5 tbsp. extra-virgin olive oil

1¼ lbs. ground lamb (lean)

4 large garlic cloves, finely chopped

½ tsp. ground cinnamon (generous)

2 tbsp. finely chopped fresh mint leaves

2 cups chicken broth

1½ cups lentils, rinsed

3 tbsp. tomato paste

1 cup dry red wine

¼ cup finely chopped fresh flat-leaf (Italian) parsley leaves

1½ tsp. Herbamare® or salt

½ tsp. black pepper

2 slices whole wheat or whole grain bread, to equal approx. 1½ cups of coarse bread crumbs

6 oz. crumbled Feta cheese

PREPARATION

In a large skillet cook the onion in 2 ½ tbsp. of the oil over moderately low heat until it is softened. Add the lamb and cook, stirring and breaking up the lamb into small lumps, until the lamb is no longer pink. Carefully pour off any excess grease. If you have used high quality lean lamb, there should not be a large amount of grease.

Add the garlic, cinnamon, and the mint and continue to cook, stirring, for 2 minutes. Add the chicken broth plus 2 cups of water and bring the liquid to a boil. Add the lentils and simmer the mixture, covered, stirring occasionally, for 30 minutes. Add the tomato paste and the wine, continue to simmer uncovered for another 15 minutes, or until the lentils are tender but not mushy. Remove from heat and cool for 10–15 minutes. Stir in the parsley, Herbamare® and pepper and transfer the mixture to a 14-inch gratin dish.

Preheat the oven to 425 degrees. In a bowl toss together the bread crumbs, the remaining 2 ½ tbsp. of olive oil, and the Feta. Sprinkle the mixture evenly over the gratin, and bake in preheated oven for 10 to 15 minutes, or until it is heated through and the top is lightly browned. Serves 6

Reuben Quiche

INGREDIENTS

Pie dough for a 10-inch quiche dish (from a box mix or frozen **OR** make your own from scratch, your own preferred recipe (See Note Below)

1 tbsp. caraway seeds

8 oz. cooked corned beef, finely shredded (remove all traces of fat)

1 cup sauerkraut (not canned), squeezed and drained, but unwashed

2 cups Swiss cheese, grated

2 eggs, beaten

1 cup half and half

1 tbsp. Dijon mustard

½ tsp. dry mustard

¼ cup finely chopped shallots

PREPARATION

Press dough evenly on bottom and about half way up the sides of the baking dish. Sprinkle caraway seeds over pie crust. Preheat oven to 375 degrees. Prick crust with a fork and bake for 10 minutes.

Spread corned beef evenly over baked pie shell. Top with sauerkraut, then grated cheese. In a bowl, whisk together eggs, half and half, Dijon mustard, dry mustard, and shallots. Pour mixture evenly over cheese into the pie shell and bake 40 minutes. Let stand 5 minutes before cutting.

Note: If you really enjoy making your own pie crust, then knock yourself out and don't buy the prepared frozen or other prepared (in a box) pie crust. While I consider myself an excellent cook, I have always had trouble producing exceptionally good pie crust, and there are some good choices available that are acceptable alternatives to making your own.

Oyster & Spinach Casserole

INGREDIENTS

1 tbsp. butter

1 tbsp. safflower (or other light) oil

10 oz. fresh baby leaf spinach

1 large garlic clove, minced

12 oz. shucked oysters, drained on paper towels and patted dry

1 egg, beaten

½ cup panko (Japanese bread crumbs)

Herbamare® or salt and black pepper for sprinkling on oysters

¼ cup grated fresh Parmesan cheese

3 slices bacon, cooked until very crisp and crumbled

1½ tbsp. butter, melted

1½ tbsp. fresh lemon juice

PREPARATION

Heat the tbsp. of butter and the tbsp. of oil in a large pot (Dutch oven) over moderate heat until hot. Add the spinach and cook, stirring, until just wilted. Remove from the heat and stir in the minced garlic clove. Place the spinach on the bottom of a shallow casserole dish (a quiche style baking dish is good for this recipe).

Dip the oysters in the beaten egg, roll in the panko, and place on top of the spinach in a single layer (they will be close together). Sprinkle oysters with Herbamare® or salt and black pepper, and then sprinkle the oysters with the cheese and crumbled bacon. Combine the melted butter with the lemon juice and pour evenly over the oyster mixture.

Preheat the oven to 450 degrees. Bake the casserole for 10–12 minutes. Serves 2 as an entrée, 4 as a side dish

Judy

Judy has a wonderful home in Falls Church, Va. For me the best part is her kitchen, which I would kill for (well, maybe I wouldn't go quite that far).

Judy's career, travel, and constant get-togethers with her many friends result in her not spending a lot of time in her kitchen. But when she does, she comes up with some absolute winners. I know you will enjoy her recipe for Oyster & Spinach Casserole.

Birthday Celebrations

Falls Church, VA, Summer 2009

Sausage-Stuffed Zucchini

INGREDIENTS

2 medium zucchini squash (approx. ½ lb.)

2 tbsp. butter

½ lb. ground pork sausage (as lean as possible)

2 large garlic cloves, finely chopped

½ tsp. dried crushed rosemary

2 tbsp. sour cream

3 tbsp. finely minced fresh Italian (flat-leaf) parsley

½ cup fresh bread crumbs

¼ cup grated Parmesan cheese (plus extra for sprinkling)

½ tsp. Herbamare®

¼ tsp. black pepper

Fresh Tomato Sauce with Basil (see p. 167)

PREPARATION

Make tomato sauce (this can be done ahead and refrigerated until ready to use.) While the sauce is cooking, prepare sausage filling as follows: Trim off and discard the ends of the zucchini. Split the zucchini in half lengthwise. Using a melon ball cutter (be sure it is sharp), scoop out the pulp of each half and leave a thin shell for stuffing.

Heat the butter in a saucepan and cook the scooped-out pulp (chopped coarsely) until it is wilted. At the same time, cook the sausage, crumbling well with a spoon while cooking, until done. With a slotted spoon, add the sausage to the cooked (wilted) zucchini pulp. Add the garlic, rosemary, sour cream, parsley, bread crumbs, ¼ cup Parmesan cheese, Herbamare® and pepper. Set aside.

Preheat oven to 350 degrees. Pour the tomato sauce into a rectangular baking dish. Place each zucchini half on top of the tomato sauce. Fill the zucchini halves with the sausage mixture, and sprinkle each zucchini half with Parmesan cheese. Bake 20–30 minutes, or until the zucchini are tender and the filling is golden brown.

Serves 2 as an entrée, or 4 as a side dish

Zucchini Frittata

INGREDIENTS

1 large zucchini squash (about ½ lb.)

1 tbsp. butter

1 tbsp. extra-virgin olive oil

3 large eggs

2 egg whites

¼ cup whole milk

½ cup (generous) finely crumbled mild feta cheese

½ tsp. salt

⅛ tsp. black pepper

1 medium clove garlic, minced

¾ tsp. dried oregano

¼ cup finely grated Parmigiano-Reggiano cheese

PREPARATION

Trim ends from zucchini and slice lengthwise into quarters, and then cut cross-wise into ½ inch thick slices. Heat the butter and olive oil in a 12-inch ovenproof nonstick skillet over moderate heat. Add the zucchini and cook, stirring, just until tender, which should take about 10 minutes.

While the zucchini is cooking, place the eggs, egg whites, milk, feta, ¼ tsp. salt and the pepper in a bowl and whisk ingredients together until well combined. Set aside.

When the zucchini is tender, add the garlic, oregano and the remaining ¼ tsp. salt to the skillet and cook, stirring, for 1 minute.

Preheat the broiler. Pour the egg mixture over the zucchini in the skillet and cook, gently lifting up the cooked egg around the edges with a spatula occasionally to let the uncooked egg flow underneath. Cook on top of the stove for 3–5 minutes. The center of the frittata should still be moist.

Sprinkle the frittata with the Parmigiano-Reggiano and place the skillet 6 inches from the preheated broiler and cook until set, puffed and golden brown, which should take about 3 minutes.

Let cool for 5 minutes and then cut into wedges and serve warm or at room temperature. Serves 3–4

Tacos Para Beef

INGREDIENTS

2 tbsp. sunflower oil

1 large onion, chopped

½ cup chopped green bell pepper

3 large garlic cloves, finely chopped

1 lb. lean ground beef (good quality)

1 14–15 oz. can petite diced tomatoes (with juice)

⅔ cup chopped green olives with pimientos

½ cup sweet corn (canned or frozen)

⅓ cup raisins

2 tbsp. light brown sugar, firmly packed

1½ tbsp. red wine vinegar

1 tbsp. beef broth concentrate (I prefer Superior Touch™ Better Than Bouillon™ Beef Base)

3 tbsp. chili powder

1 tsp. ground cumin

3 drops Tabasco

12 corn taco shells (I use Old El Paso® Stand 'n Stuff® Yellow Corn Taco Shells)

Shredded lettuce

Grated cheese, Cheddar or Monterey Jack (I use a 4 Cheese Mexican mixture)

PREPARATION

Heat the oil in a large skillet over moderate heat. Add the onions and green pepper and cook until tender. Add the garlic and cook for an additional minute. Add the beef and cook, breaking up, until it is browned and cooked through. Add the tomatoes with juice, olives, corn, raisins, brown sugar, vinegar, beef broth concentrate, chili powder, cumin and Tabasco. Cook for 15 minutes, until flavors are well blended and the excess liquid has evaporated.

To serve, heat the taco shells. Place shredded lettuce on the bottom of the shell and top with a generous amount of the beef mixture. Place a generous amount of grated cheese on top of the beef mixture. Serves 6

Greek Pizza

INGREDIENTS

2 large pita pockets (7–8 inches in diameter)

4 medium fresh tomatoes, sliced

½ cup (generous) very thinly sliced red onion

2 tsp. dried oregano (or 4 tsp. fresh oregano leaves, crumbled)

½ tsp. black pepper

8 oz. feta cheese crumbled

Sautéed Bell Peppers:

1 tbsp. unsalted butter

1 tbsp. extra-virgin olive oil

3 medium garlic cloves, thinly sliced

1 red bell pepper, cored, seeded, & cut into ¼-inch thick strips

1 orange bell pepper, cored, seeded, & cut into ¼-inch thick strips

1 yellow bell pepper, cored, seeded, & cut into ¼-inch thick strips

2 tsp. drained capers, coarsely chopped

8 small Kalamata pitted olives, quartered

2 tbsp. pine nuts, lightly toasted

PREPARATION

Carefully cut the pita pockets with a sharp knife around the edges to make 4 rounds and place on 2 baking sheets (the pita pockets should not be touching).

For the bell peppers: Melt the butter and oil in a large (12-inch) heavy skillet over moderate heat. Add the garlic and cook, stirring, until softened, which should take about 1–2 minutes. Add the peppers, increase the heat to moderately high and cook, stirring, several minutes. Stir in the capers and olives, cover and cook, stirring occasionally, for approx. 10 minutes, or until the peppers are softened but not mushy. Remove from heat and stir in the pine nuts.

To assemble the pizzas: Top each pita round with sliced tomatoes. Place sliced red onion on top of the tomatoes. Spoon the bell peppers over the red onion. Sprinkle the oregano and pepper evenly over each pizza round. Divide the feta cheese evenly over top of each pizza round.

Preheat the oven to 450 degrees. Bake the pizza for 20 minutes, or until the crust is browned and crisp. Cut each round into 4 wedges. Serves 4–6

Zucchini Moussaka with Feta

INGREDIENTS

3 tbsp. extra-virgin olive oil (plus additional for brushing the zucchini)

1 lb. lean ground lamb

1 large white onion, chopped fine (approx. 2 cups)

3 large garlic cloves, finely chopped

½ cup dry red wine

1 14–15 oz. can diced tomatoes, drained

1 bay leaf

½ tsp. dried oregano

¼ cup minced fresh parsley leaves (preferably Italian flat-leaf)

⅛ tsp. ground nutmeg

¼ tsp. cinnamon

¼ tsp. allspice

1 tsp. Herbamare® or salt

2 lbs. zucchini squash

3 tbsp. unsalted butter

3 tbsp. all-purpose flour

1 cup milk

1 large egg

½ lb. Feta cheese, crumbled

PREPARATION

In a large heavy skillet, heat 1 tbsp. of the olive oil over moderate heat. Add the ground lamb and cook, breaking up the pieces well, until the lamb is thoroughly cooked and no longer pink. Remove the lamb with a slotted spoon and place in a bowl and set aside. Pour off all fat from the skillet and wipe with paper towels. Return skillet to the stove and heat the remaining 2 tbsp. of olive oil. Add the onions and cook, stirring occasionally, until softened. Add the garlic and cook for a minute. Return the lamb to the skillet along with the wine, drained tomatoes, bay leaf, and oregano. Cook over moderate heat, stirring, for approx. 20 minutes. Stir in the parsley, nutmeg, cinnamon, allspice, and Herbamare® and cook for another few minutes. Remove from heat, discard the bay leaf and set aside. NOTE: This sauce improves in flavor if you make it the day before and refrigerate in a covered container.

Cut the zucchini lengthwise into ½ inch slices. Arrange on a foil-lined broiler safe pan and brush the zucchini lightly with olive oil (unless you have a broiler pan that's way bigger than mine, you'll need to cook the zucchini in 2 batches). Preheat broiler and broil zucchini, about 6 inches from the heat, for approx. 4–5 minutes, or until they are softened and golden brown. Turn the zucchini, brush the other sides lightly with olive oil, and return to the broiler for an additional 4–5 minutes. Place half (or the first batch) of zucchini in a shallow baking dish (approx. 12 x 6 inches).

In a small saucepan, melt the butter over low heat, add the flour and cook the roux, stirring for 3 minutes. Add the milk in a stream, whisking, and bring the mixture to a boil. Reduce heat and simmer, stirring, for approx. 5 minutes. The mixture should be very thick. Remove from the heat and whisk in the egg.

Cover the zucchini with half of the lamb mixture, next sprinkle half of the Feta cheese on top of the lamb. Repeat the layers (2nd batch of zucchini, remaining lamb, remaining Feta), and as the final step, spoon the white sauce evenly over the casserole, smoothing the top with the spoon or a spatula.

Preheat the oven to 350 degrees and bake the moussaka in the middle of the oven for approx. 45 minutes or until it is golden on top. Let the moussaka stand for 10–15 minutes before serving. Serves 4–6

You can imitate me, you can copy me, but there is no substitute for perfection.

Moussaka with Eggplant à la Grecque

INGREDIENTS

1 large eggplant (1½ to 2 lbs..)

Spray olive oil (I prefer Spectrum Naturals® Organic Olive Spray Oil)

Butter for sautéing eggplant (approx. 2 tbsp.)

2 tbsp. butter

1½ large onions, finely chopped

1 to 1¼ lbs. lean ground lamb

1 large fresh tomato, seeded & chopped

3 tbsp. tomato paste

½ cup red wine

¼ cup chopped flat-leaf parsley

¼ tsp. cinnamon

1 tsp. Herbamare® or salt

½ tsp. black pepper

Topping:

4 tbsp. butter

3 tbsp. flour

2 cups milk

2 eggs, beaten until frothy

⅛ tsp. ground nutmeg

1 cup ricotta cheese

¾ cup grated Parmesan cheese

PREPARATION

Peel the eggplant and cut into slices (about ½ inch thick). Spray a large skillet generously with the olive oil, and add about ½ tbsp. butter to the skillet. When the butter and oil are very hot, cook the eggplant slices in batches over moderate heat until lightly browned on both sides and slightly softened. Remove eggplant from skillet as they are cooked and set aside.

When all of the eggplant is cooked and removed from the skillet, add 2 tbsp. of butter to the same skillet and cook the onions until they are transparent and just beginning to brown. Add the ground lamb to the onions and continue to cook, breaking up the lamb into small pieces, until the lamb is browned and no pink remains.

Add to the meat mixture the chopped tomato, tomato paste, wine, parsley, cinnamon, Herbamare®, and pepper and stir gently until combined. Simmer the mixture over low heat, stirring occasionally, until almost all of the liquid has been absorbed. Remove from heat and set aside.

Sue says it's as much fun to give as it is to receive – what a load of poppycock…

Make the topping: Melt the butter in a small saucepan over low heat and whisk in the flour. Meanwhile, in a separate small saucepan, bring the milk to a slow boil. Add the milk gradually to the butter-flour mixture, whisking constantly. When the mixture has thickened and is smooth, remove from the heat. Cool slightly and whisk in the beaten eggs, nutmeg and ricotta cheese. Set aside.

Preheat the oven to 375 degrees. Place half of the cooked eggplant slices on the bottom of a 9 x 12-inch baking dish. The eggplant will overlap slightly. Cover the eggplant evenly with half of the lamb mixture. Sprinkle the lamb mixture with half the Parmesan cheese. Cover the Parmesan with the remaining eggplant slices, followed by the remaining lamb mixture, and again sprinkle the lamb with the remaining Parmesan.

Pour the ricotta cheese topping slowly and evenly over the entire casserole. Bake one hour, or until the top is golden. Remove from the oven and cool 15–20 minutes before serving. Cut into squares and serve. Serves 5–6

Note that you can taste the flavors of this wonderful dish better if it is not served piping hot – it is delicious either warm or even at room temperature. Also, while it is fabulous the day it is made, the flavor improves if it is made the day before. Reheat before serving.

Eggplant Strata

(Adapted from "Vegetable Heaven" by Mollie Katzen)

INGREDIENTS

3 medium-sized red bell peppers, roasted (see p. 213)

2 cups ricotta cheese

1½ cups grated Parmesan cheese

1 tsp. salt

½ tsp. black pepper

⅛ tsp. (scant) cayenne pepper

1½ cups chopped scallions (white part only)

2 tsp. crumbled dried rosemary

Roasted Tomato-Garlic Sauce (see p. 164)

Olive oil for lightly greasing baking dish (or use spray olive oil, preferably organic)

1½ lbs. eggplant, cut horizontally into ½-inch slices

1 lb. zucchini, cut horizontally into ¼-inch slices

1 lb. smoked mozzarella cheese, thinly sliced

PREPARATION

Peel roasted peppers and remove seeds and membranes. Cut into strips, and set aside.

While the peppers are roasting, in a medium-sized bowl, combine the ricotta, Parmesan, salt, pepper, cayenne, scallions and rosemary. Mix well and set aside.

Make 1 recipe of Roasted Tomato-Garlic Sauce (see p. 164) and set aside.

Lightly grease with olive oil a 9 x 13-inch baking dish (2 ½ to 3 inches deep). Spread a double layer of eggplant slices on bottom of the baking dish, followed by a single layer of the sliced zucchini. Spoon on half of the ricotta mixture in small mounds, then place half the roasted pepper strips on top. Cover the peppers with half of the smoked mozzarella slices, then spoon half of the Roasted Tomato-Garlic Sauce evenly over top.

Spread a single layer of eggplant slices on top of the sauce, then repeat all layers, ending with the remaining sauce on top of the mozzarella.

Preheat oven to 350 degrees. Bake the strata for 1½ hours. If the top starts to become too brown, cover lightly with foil and continue baking.

Remove the dish from the oven, and let it sit for at least 10 minutes before serving. Cut into squares and serve hot, warm, or at room temperature. Serves 10–12

Note: This recipe is very easy to pull together if you roast the peppers in advance and refrigerate until ready to use. The Roasted Tomato-Garlic Sauce can also be made ahead (keeps in the refrigerator if tightly covered for up to two weeks). If you have the peppers and the sauce at the ready, you can pull this recipe together in about ½ hour!

Sue's Tips:

Cats may be independent, but they are also trusted friends. Clyde shares many characteristics of my girlfriends: He is always there for me, he makes me laugh, listens to me when I cry, and tells me the truth.

Italian-Style Quiche

INGREDIENTS

Pie crust dough for a 9 x 9½ inch quiche dish (boxed mix or frozen or make your own favorite recipe)

½ lb. sweet Italian sausage

2 tbsp. extra-virgin olive oil

1 onion, sliced thinly (should equal 1½ cups)

1 cup chopped red bell pepper

½ cup (generous) grated mozzarella cheese

¾ cup grated Fontina cheese

¼ lb. prosciutto, thinly sliced, cut into ½-inch strips

4 eggs

¼ cup Parmesan cheese

1 tbsp. flour

½ tsp. salt

⅛ tsp. nutmeg

⅛ tsp. black pepper

2 cups half and half

1½ tbsp. melted butter

PREPARATION

Make the pie dough and press into the quiche dish, bottom and sides. Assure that the crust is very thin. Set aside.

In a skillet heat the olive oil and sauté the sausage, crumbled, until it is nicely browned all over. Continue to break up the pieces of sausage as it is cooking into smaller pieces. When cooked completely, remove the sausage with a slotted spoon, put on a plate lined with paper towels and set aside. Add the onion and red pepper to the skillet and cook, stirring, until the vegetables are softened.

Place the sausage on the bottom of the pastry-lined quiche dish and top with the cooked onions and peppers. Sprinkle the mixture evenly with the Mozzarella and Fontina cheeses, and top the cheese with the prosciutto.

Place the eggs, Parmesan cheese, flour, salt, nutmeg and pepper in a bowl and whisk until combined. Add the half and half and melted butter and continue to whisk until well combined.

Pour the egg mixture over the ingredients already in the quiche dish, distributing the custard as evenly as possible.

Preheat the oven to 375 degrees and bake the quiche in the middle of the oven for 45 minutes, or until the custard is set and the top is lightly browned. Allow the quiche to cool enough so that it is not piping hot and serve warm. Serves 6–8

Journal entry:
Woke up Sue by meowing plaintively & loudly, ate breakfast, took morning nap, ate mid-morning snack, took pre-lunch nap, ate lunch, took post-lunch nap, spent quality time in the kitchen cooking with mamma mia Sue
xoxoxox

Eggplant Parmigiana

INGREDIENTS

1 large eggplant (1½ to 2 lbs.)

¼ cup extra-virgin olive oil

2 eggs

1½ cups fresh bread crumbs

¾ cup Parmesan cheese

1 8-oz. package sliced Mozzarella cheese

1½ cups grated Parmesan cheese

Sauce:

¼ cup extra-virgin olive oil

4 tbsp. unsalted butter

1½ cups chopped red onions

12 cloves garlic, finely chopped

1 12-oz. can tomato paste

1 can (28 oz.) chopped Italian-style Roma tomatoes, not drained

2 tbsp. firmly packed light brown sugar

4 tsp. dried oregano

2 tbsp. chopped fresh basil

2 tsp. salt

½ tsp. pepper

PREPARATION

Slice eggplant ¼ to ½ inch thick. Place in a single layer on paper towels and sprinkle with salt. Let eggplant sit for 1 hour, then with more paper towels, blot out the moisture (beads of water that will have gathered on the top of the eggplant slices). Note: This is an important step because this procedure removes the bitterness from the eggplant.

Heat ¼ cup of olive oil in a large skillet over moderate heat. Beat eggs with a fork in a shallow dish until whites and yolks are well combined. In a mini processor, blend bread crumbs and Parmesan cheese together until well combined and put on a plate or shallow dish. Dip eggplant slices first into egg, then crumbs (both sides), and add to the skillet (in batches) and sauté slices, turning once, until both sides are golden brown and crisp. Add more olive oil to the skillet as necessary. Set aside.

For sauce: Heat the butter and olive oil together in a large skillet. Add onion and sauté until softened. Next add all remaining sauce ingredients and bring slowly to a boil. Reduce heat to low and simmer for approx. ½ hour. The sauce should be very thick.

Note – you can either make the sauce while the eggplant is sitting on the paper towels for an hour (first step in the recipe), or you can make the sauce the day before and refrigerate until you're ready to assemble the eggplant casserole. This is my preference.

Arrange half of the eggplant slices on the bottom of a large baking casserole dish. Sprinkle with ¾ cup grated Parmesan cheese and half of the sliced Mozzarella cheese and cover with half of the tomato sauce. Arrange the remaining eggplant over the tomato sauce, cover with remaining ¾ cup Parmesan, then the rest of the sauce, and on the very top should be the remaining Mozzarella slices. Bake uncovered in a preheated 350 degree oven until heated through and the Mozzarella is lightly browned (about 25 minutes). Cut with a knife into six servings and remove carefully with a spatula. Serves 6

Always ask for a little more than you think you want.

Spinach Omelet with Goat Cheese

INGREDIENTS

1 6-oz. package of baby leaf spinach, larger stems removed

4 eggs

⅛ cup milk (regular or low-fat)

½ tsp. dried thyme

1 tsp. dried parsley leaves, or 2 tsp. fresh chopped parsley

¼ tsp. black pepper

¼ tsp. salt

1½ tbsp. butter

3 tbsp. chopped shallots

4 tbsp. crumbled goat cheese

PREPARATION

Place about a quarter cup of water in a large skillet and heat until it is boiling. Add spinach leaves and cook, stirring, until spinach is wilted and cooked. Remove spinach with a slotted spoon to a colander and with the spoon press out as much of the water as possible.

While the spinach is cooking, in a bowl, whisk together the eggs, milk, thyme, parsley, pepper and salt.

Melt butter in a heavy non-stick 10-inch skillet. Add shallots and cook, stirring, for a couple minutes until softened, but not browned. Add egg mixture to the skillet and cook over medium-low heat for about 5 minutes, or until the bottom is set but the eggs are not completely cooked. Sprinkle one side of the egg mixture with the spinach and the goat cheese. Using a large spatula, fold the omelet in half. Continue cooking for an additional 2–3 minutes or until the omelet is golden and the cheese is melted. Turn onto a plate and cut in half. Serves 2

Liz

Asheville, N.C., is a mecca for fabulous food. But some of the best food to be found in that area comes from the kitchen of my beloved niece, Liz, and her husband, Jason.

The best part of our visits to their home always center in the kitchen, where Liz and Jason work together like a finely tuned instrument, chopping, mixing, and combining ingredients to enchant and tantalize us. The incomparable bond our family shares is enhanced by the thoughtfulness and caring shown as they prepare remarkable food, infused with love and magic.

Liz and Jason were pleased to share their recipe for Vegetarian Pad Thai

York, PA, August 1997
Grandmother Toni Turns 80

Maui, Hawaii, 2003 | Family Vacation

Vegetarian Pad Thai

INGREDIENTS

1 lb. block of extra firm tofu, preferably organic

Juice from 2 limes to equal at least ¼ cup (if 2 limes do not yield this amount, use 3)

3 tbsp. Thai fish sauce

2 tbsp. firmly packed light brown sugar

2 tbsp. chili purée with garlic (or hot chili sauce if not available)

3 tbsp. canola or safflower oil

3 large garlic cloves, finely chopped

1 tbsp. finely chopped fresh gingerroot

1¼ cup julienne carrot strips (use baby-cut carrots – trim ends, cut lengthwise into very thin julienne strips)

Pad Thai rice noodles (about 3 ½ oz.) – a good brand is Annie Chun's™

1 tbsp. butter

2 eggs, beaten

2 cups fresh mung bean sprouts

1 generous cup loosely packed fresh cilantro leaves, chopped

¼ cup coarsely chopped roasted unsalted peanuts

¼ cup finely chopped roasted unsalted peanuts

PREPARATION

Line a plate with several layers of paper towels and place the tofu on them. Let stand to drain excess moisture for at least ½ hour. In a small bowl, combine the lime juice, fish sauce, brown sugar and chili purée and set aside.

In a large non-stick skillet heat 2 tbsp. of the oil over moderate heat. Add the garlic and gingerroot and cook for 30 seconds. Add the julienne carrot strips and sauté until softened but still firm. Remove from heat and set aside.

In a separate medium sized non-stick skillet heat the remaining tbsp. of oil over moderate heat. Pat the tofu all over with another paper towel to remove more moisture, and then cut two-thirds of the block of tofu into small (bite-size) pieces. Reserve the remaining one-third of the tofu block for another use. Add the tofu to the skillet and cook, stirring occasionally, until the tofu is lightly browned on both sides. Add the tofu to the carrot mixture, wipe the medium skillet with a paper towel and set aside.

While the tofu is cooking, boil water and cook the noodles according to the package directions. Drain noodles and add to the large skillet and stir to combine with the carrots and tofu. Stir in the lime juice mixture.

Add the butter to the medium skillet used to cook the tofu (that has been wiped clean) and melt over moderate heat. Add the beaten eggs and cook until they are just set. Break up with a spoon into very small pieces. Add the eggs to the large skillet along with the bean sprouts, cilantro and the ¼ cup of coarsely chopped peanuts and stir gently to combine all ingredients.

When you are ready to serve, reheat the Pad Thai over moderate heat for about 5 minutes until it is warmed. Sprinkle the ¼ cup of finely chopped peanuts evenly over each serving. Serves 2 (large portions) or 3–4 (smaller portions)

Cheesy Frittata

INGREDIENTS

1 tbsp. butter

1 medium red onion, thinly sliced (approx. 1½ cups)

1 medium red bell pepper, thinly sliced (approx. 1½ cups)

1 medium zucchini squash, thinly sliced (approx. 1½ cups) Note: to slice squash, trim ends, and cut squash in two pieces, lengthwise; then cut each half horizontally into thin slices.

1 cup diced fresh tomatoes, seeded

2 tbsp. chopped fresh basil

½ tsp. salt

¼ tsp. pepper

6 eggs

1 cup ricotta cheese

⅓ cup milk

1 large sausage (flavor of choice), approx. ¼ lb. - OPTIONAL

1 cup shredded Monterey Jack cheese (or mixture or Monterey Jack with cheddar and mozzarella cheeses)

PREPARATION

Melt the butter over medium-low heat in a 10-inch heavy non-stick skillet that is ovenproof. Add the onion, bell pepper and zucchini and sauté until the vegetables are softened, but not overcooked. Add the tomatoes, basil, salt and pepper and stir to combine. Cook for about a minute and remove from heat.

If you plan on adding sausage to the frittata, in a separate small skillet, while the vegetables are cooking, fry the sausage until nicely browned on all sides and set aside.

Place eggs, ricotta cheese and milk into a medium bowl. With an immersion blender, process until smooth. Pour the egg mixture over the cooked vegetables in the skillet. If using sausage, cut cooked sausage into ¼ inch slices and distribute evenly over the frittata. Push down so the sausage is covered with egg mixture.

Preheat the broiler. Cover the skillet and cook on the top of the stove over medium low heat until the bottom is set and the top is still slightly wet. Transfer the skillet to the oven and broil about 6 inches from the heat until the top is set, approx. 2–3 minutes. Sprinkle with the cheese and continue to broil for about another minute or until the cheese has melted. Cut into wedges and remove with a spatula to serve. Serves 4

Baked French Toast à L'orange

INGREDIENTS

12 bread slices, white or whole wheat

1 large orange (will use juice as well as rind)

6 extra large eggs

½ tsp. ground cinnamon

½ cup (8 tbsp.) butter

Maple syrup to accompany

PREPARATION

Place grater on a shallow pie plate or baking dish and grate enough orange rind to measure a generous 2 tbsp. Cut the orange in half and squeeze juice, which should measure at least ½ cup. If it is a bit more than ½ cup, that is fine.

Add juice, eggs and cinnamon to the orange peel and with a fork or whisk beat until well mixed.

Preheat oven to 450 degrees. Place 4 tbsp. of butter into each of 2 jelly-roll pans and place in preheated oven to melt butter, which will only take several minutes. Butter should be bubbling and just starting to brown. Remove baking pans from oven. Dip bread slices in egg mixture to coat well on both sides. Place bread in a single layer in baking pans, 6 slices per pan. Bake 6 minutes and with a spatula, turn bread slices and bake an additional 6 minutes, or until bread is golden brown on top. Serve with heated maple syrup. Serves 6

Mexican Lasagne

INGREDIENTS

2 tbsp. extra-virgin olive oil with garlic (Olave® is a good choice)

1 lb. extra lean ground beef

1 medium sweet yellow onion, chopped

3 large garlic cloves, minced

1 15-oz. container ricotta cheese

¾ cup sour cream

1 jar (4 oz.) chopped green chile peppers

½ cup chopped fresh cilantro leaves

2 tsp. ground cumin

½ tsp. salt

2½ cups chunky bottled salsa (medium)

4 whole wheat tortillas (8" in diameter), halved

3 cups shredded Mexican Blend cheeses (e.g. Sharp Cheddar, Monterey Jack, Asadero, Queso Blanco)

PREPARATION

Heat one tbsp. of the oil in a large nonstick skillet over moderate heat until hot. Add the ground beef and cook, breaking up the meat, for approx. 10 minutes, or until it is no longer pink. Remove the beef with a slotted spoon to a bowl and set aside.

Wipe the skillet with paper towels and add the second tbsp. of oil to the skillet. Add the onions and cook over moderate heat until softened and very lightly browned. Add the garlic and continue to cook, stirring, for 1 minute. Add onions and garlic to the beef mixture and stir until combined.

In a separate bowl combine the ricotta, sour cream, peppers, cilantro, cumin and salt.

Lightly grease a 13 x 9 inch baking dish with olive oil. Spread half of the salsa (1 ¼ cups) across the bottom of the baking dish. Arrange half of the tortillas evenly over the salsa (they should slightly overlap). Sprinkle the tortillas with half (1½ cups) of the grated cheese. Cover the cheese with half of the beef mixture. Spread half of the ricotta mixture evenly over the beef.

Continue layering by covering ricotta mixture with remaining tortillas. Spread 1 cup of salsa over the tortillas. Sprinkle 1 cup of the grated cheese over the salsa. Cover the cheese with the remaining beef, and cover beef evenly with the remaining ricotta mixture. Finally cover the ricotta mixture with the remaining ¼ cup of salsa, and sprinkle the remaining ½ cup of grated cheese over the salsa.

Preheat the oven to 350 degrees. Bake until the casserole is thoroughly heated and bubbling around the edges, which should take 30–40 minutes. After the casserole is removed from the oven, allow it to sit for 10 minutes before cutting into squares and serving. Serves 8

Sue's Tips:
Bright red can make anyone look good!

Banana Walnut Pancakes & Orange Butter

Adapted from Gourmet magazine, Condé Nast Publications

INGREDIENTS

Accompaniment: maple syrup

Orange Butter:

4 tbsp. unsalted butter, softened to room temperature

1 tbsp. finely grated fresh orange zest

1 tbsp. fresh orange juice

Pancakes:

1½ cups unbleached all-purpose flour

3 tbsp. sugar, preferably organic

1½ tsp. baking powder

½ tsp. baking soda

¼ tsp. salt

1½ cups well-shaken buttermilk (low-fat OK)

2 tbsp. unsalted butter, melted

2 large eggs

1 tsp. vanilla

2 ripe bananas, peeled and cut into small pieces

½ cup chopped walnuts, toasted

1 tbsp. unsalted butter for cooking pancakes

PREPARATION

Orange butter: Mix all ingredients together until orange juice is incorporated. This will take several minutes. Set aside.

For pancakes, whisk together the flour, sugar, baking powder, baking soda and salt in a bowl. In a separate bowl whisk together the buttermilk, 2 tbsp. of the melted butter, eggs, and vanilla until smooth. Add the flour mixture and whisk until just combined. Fold the banana pieces and the chopped walnuts into the batter gently.

Preheat the oven to 200 degrees. Melt part of the remaining tbsp. of butter in a large skillet over moderate heat until hot but not smoking. Using a measuring cup, pour ¼ cup batter per pancake into the hot skillet (3–4 pancakes will be able to be cooked at one time), and cook until bubbles appear on the surface and the undersides are golden brown. Flip pancakes with a spatula and cook until golden brown and cooked through. Transfer to an ovenproof dish, cover loosely with foil and place in preheated oven to keep warm. Add more butter to the skillet, and continue to make pancakes, placing in oven as they are done to keep warm.

Serve with orange butter and maple syrup. Makes 12–15 pancakes

"To invite a person into your house is to take charge of his happiness for as long as he is under your roof."

Brillat-Savarin

One of the best things about waking up in the morning is being able to look forward to your first nap of the day

Crustless Spinach Quiche

INGREDIENTS

1 10-oz. package frozen chopped spinach

¼ cup chopped scallions (white part)

1½ cups chopped fresh mushrooms (approx. ¼ lb.)

6 slices bacon, cooked until crisp and crumbled

Herbamare® or salt and black pepper

2 cups shredded Swiss or Gruyere cheese

3 eggs

¾ cup half and half

¼ tsp. ground nutmeg

PREPARATION

Thaw the spinach and squeeze out as much of the moisture as possible (most effective way is by hand). Layer the spinach, scallions, mushrooms and bacon in a well buttered quiche dish. Sprinkle mixture liberally with Herbamare® and black pepper. In a bowl, whisk together the eggs, half and half, cheese and nutmeg.

Preheat the oven to 375 degrees. Pour the egg mixture evenly over the spinach mixture and bake in preheated oven for approx. 30–45 minutes, or until set and nicely browned on top. Serves 6–8

Gingerbread Pancakes

Adapted from Gourmet magazine, Condé Nast Publications

INGREDIENTS

2 cups unbleached all-purpose flour

1 tsp. baking soda

½ tsp. baking powder

½ tsp. salt

1 tsp. ground cinnamon

1 tsp. ground ginger

½ tsp. ground nutmeg

¼ tsp. ground cloves

¼ tsp. ground allspice

3 large eggs

¼ cup packed dark brown sugar

½ cup well-shaken buttermilk (low-fat OK)

½ cup water

¼ cup brewed regular coffee

6 tbsp. unsalted butter, melted and cooled slightly

1 tbsp. molasses

Butter (or oil) for brushing skillet or griddle

Lemon curd to accompany or maple syrup

PREPARATION

Preheat oven to 200 degrees. Whisk together flour, baking soda, baking powder, salt and spices in a large bowl. Whisk together eggs and brown sugar in another bowl until smooth. Whisk in buttermilk, water and coffee until combined, then add the wet mixture to the flour mixture, continuing to whisk until combined. Whisk in the melted butter and the molasses.

Heat a griddle or large heavy skillet over moderate heat until hot enough to make drops of water scatter over its surface, and then brush with butter or oil. Working in batches, fill a ¼ cup measure with batter for each pancake, then pour onto the griddle or skillet and cook, turning over once, until deep golden on each side, approx. 1–2 minutes per side. Transfer each batch to a heatproof platter and keep warm in the oven until ready to serve. Serves 6

Note: Lemon Curd can be purchased in many food stores, but the preference would be to make your own (see p. 45).

Pasta

Considering my mother's Italian heritage, it is interesting that she did not make a lot of pasta dishes. However, she did have one signature pasta dish she called "Baked Italian Spaghetti." To prepare this concoction Toni mixed cooked ground beef with tomatoes, tons of garlic, tons of cheese, and cooked spaghetti noodles, and baked the casserole within an inch of its life until the top was very crusty, and the noodles were mushy. Believe it or not, it tasted fabulous. I tried to replicate this dish once, and decided that it is best left as a loving memory.

Pasta noodles should always be cooked "al dente," which means the pasta is tender but still firm to the bite. When you follow package directions for cooking pasta, be sure to test it for tenderness at least once before the prescribed cooking time has expired. Nothing ruins a great pasta dish quicker than mushy noodles.

By the way, did you know that an old Italian superstition dictates that it is bad luck to place salt in a kettle of water before it has reached the boiling point?

You can't touch this.

Testimonial

It is difficult not to become more personal with a casual acquaintance or daily work mate when they reveal themselves more intimately by cooking for you. It's like a portal to understanding the source and depth of their passions for life.

Such it was for me the first time my colleague of nearly 15 years, Sue Cassidy, cooked dinner for me and my wife. Prior to that time, I had always groveled for Sue to bring in her lemon curd cheesecake for my birthday each year. I still am not a great aficionado of cheesecake, but Sue's concoction was so perfectly blended and complex that it offered far more than the simple comfort of cool cheese and graham crackers like most cakes of its kind.

Sue has a wonderful appreciation for the magic that results from blending the ingredients of friends, wine and a thoughtfully prepared meal, that make such evenings greater than the sum of each part. Sue's love of her friends and the joy she extracts from eating and drinking with them can be tasted in everything she prepares. It would not be possible for me to forget the components of that fabulous meal: her "Lamb London Broil with Scallion Ginger Sauce" and "Marinated Lime Basil Shrimp" were among the memory-making dishes served.

Sue's marvelous cooking, combined with her whimsical smile and easy laughter can't be purchased in a jar or vacuum sealed. Sue and her food are made to be savored in the moment, and are the recipes for enjoying life.

Mark Irion
CEO, Dutko Worldwide
Washington, DC

Couscous with Tomato & Chives

INGREDIENTS

¾ cup chicken broth

1½ tbsp. unsalted butter

½ cup whole wheat couscous

½ cup chopped shallots

2 tbsp. minced fresh chives

½ cup seeded coarsely chopped fresh tomatoes

½ tsp. Herbamare® or salt

¼ tsp. black pepper

PREPARATION

In a small saucepan bring the broth and 1 tbsp. of the butter to a boil, stir in the couscous and remove from the heat. Cover, and let stand for 5 minutes.

Heat the remaining ½ tbsp. of butter in a small saucepan and sauté the shallots until they are tender. Add the shallots, chives, tomatoes, Herbamare® and pepper to the couscous and stir gently to combine all ingredients. Serves 2

Note: Couscous is really pasta, but is made from semolina, the gritty, coarse particles of wheat remaining after the finer flour has passed through the bolting machine.

When taking my picture, every side is my best side

Pasta Bolognese

INGREDIENTS

2 tbsp. extra-virgin olive oil

1 to 1¼ pound lean ground beef

6 large cloves garlic, finely chopped

1 tbsp. dried oregano

¼ tsp. crushed red pepper flakes

1¼ cups dry red wine

1 28-ounce can crushed tomatoes

2 tbsp. tomato paste

¾ tbsp. Kosher salt

1¼ tsp. black pepper

½ pound dried pasta (small – e.g. orecchiette or small shells)

¼ tsp. ground nutmeg

¼ cup chopped fresh basil leaves, lightly packed

¼ cup half and half

½ cup (generous) grated Parmesan cheese

Extra Parmesan cheese for serving on the side

PREPARATION

Heat 2 tbsp. of olive oil in a large (12-inch) skillet over medium-high heat. Add the ground beef and cook, crumbling with a wooden spoon, for about 10 minutes, or until the meat has lost its pink color and has started to brown. Stir in the garlic, oregano and red pepper flakes and cook for 1 minute. Pour 1 cup of the wine into the skillet and stir to scrape up any browned bits. Add the tomatoes, tomato paste, salt, and pepper, stirring until combined. Bring to a boil, lower the heat and simmer for 10 minutes.

Meanwhile cook the pasta according to package directions, using salted water and a splash of olive oil. Do not overcook pasta!! It should be al dente.

Finish the sauce while the pasta is cooking by adding the nutmeg, basil, half and half and the remaining ¼ cup wine. Simmer for approximately 10 minutes, stirring occasionally, until thickened. Stir the cooked pasta and ½ cup Parmesan gently into the sauce. Serve hot with Parmesan on the side. Serves 4

Serves 2 to 4

I find it difficult to say with accuracy how many people may be served when making any given recipe, which is why a range is often given, and even then I'm not alleging this will always be totally accurate. The reason for this is simple: There are big eaters, there are normal eaters, and there are small eaters.

Big eaters will usually happily accept second helpings, and after finishing the seconds, stare mournfully at their plates in hopes that more might be forthcoming (similar to the look that Clyde gives me every time he finishes a meal).

My definition of a normal eater is someone who, when served a medium-sized serving of food (not too skimpy, not too grand) will finish eating if not everything on their plate, then almost everything, and will almost always decline a second helping if offered one.

A small eater is someone who just doesn't eat that much, and rarely will clean their plate, even if served a small portion. Small eaters can be a blessing when you are entertaining big eaters. What I have a problem with are non-eaters. These people will take minuscule bites of food, claim that it is fantastic, and then proclaim that they just couldn't possibly eat another bite (when, if you added together everything that they consumed, it would probably equal about one bite). Non-eaters don't receive a second invite to my home for a meal.

In closing, if you go on the assumption that the majority of people are normal eaters, then if a recipe says "Serves 2 to 4", you can feel comfortable that it will in fact serve up to 4 people. If you want to really be on the safe side, just double the recipe. I almost always tend toward the philosophy when I'm cooking that too much is better than not enough. Plus, wine and leftovers are my favorite things in my refrigerator.

Manicotti Stuffed with Spinach & Cheeses

INGREDIENTS

Fresh Tomato Sauce with Basil (see p. 167)

1 10-oz. package frozen chopped spinach, completely thawed, excess moisture squeezed out

1 cup crumbled feta cheese

1 cup ricotta cheese

½ cup Parmesan cheese (or mixture of Parmesan and Romano cheeses)

1 egg white

1 tsp. Herbamare® or salt

¼ tsp. nutmeg

8 manicotti pasta shells

1½ cups shredded mozzarella cheese

PREPARATION

Make Fresh Tomato Sauce with Basil (see p. 167), and set aside.

Combine spinach, feta cheese, ricotta cheese, Parmesan (or Parmesan and Romano combination), egg white, Herbamare®, and nutmeg in a medium bowl. Set aside.

Cook manicotti shells according to package instructions, but assure that the shells are *al dente* (tender yet still firm to the bite) and not overcooked. If the shells are too soft, they will be difficult to stuff, and tear apart. Gently spoon the spinach mixture into the cooked shells.

Preheat oven to 350 degrees. Butter a baking dish large enough to hold the pasta shells in a single layer and place the stuffed shells in the baking dish. Pour the tomato sauce over top and bake in the preheated oven for 25 minutes. Remove baking dish from the oven and sprinkle evenly with the mozzarella cheese. Return dish to the oven and continue to bake for an additional 10 minutes. Serves 4

Pasta with Fresh Tomatoes & Thyme

INGREDIENTS

1 lb. dried spiral shaped pasta

3 cups coarsely chopped fresh tomatoes, seeded

5 garlic cloves, minced

2½ tbsp. finely chopped fresh thyme leaves

4 tbsp. balsamic vinegar

6 tbsp. extra-virgin olive oil

1½ cups crumbled feta cheese

PREPARATION

Combine tomatoes, garlic, thyme, vinegar, and olive oil in a large serving bowl. Marinate the tomatoes for 20 minutes.

Cook pasta in salted water according to package directions. Do not overcook! Drain in a colander. While still warm, add pasta to bowl with tomatoes and add one cup of the feta cheese. Toss to combine all ingredients thoroughly (I do this with my hands). Sprinkle remaining ½ cup of feta cheese on top of the bowl. Serves 4 as an entrée, or 8–10 as a side dish

Tomatoes (Fresh)

Fresh tomatoes in grocery stores are frequently not worthy of even being called tomatoes. I do not recommend making recipes that call for fresh tomatoes until they are in season and available from fresh produce stands (or my sister's garden), or food stores specifying that the tomatoes are locally grown.

If a recipe calls for fresh chopped tomatoes and good tomatoes are not available, you are better off substituting canned tomatoes than using those round reddish things that impersonate tomatoes.

"Food is family, tradition, birth, confirmation, marriage, sickness, death - life itself."

Artie Bucco,
"The Sopranos Family Cookbook"

Wild Mushroom, Spinach & Goat Cheese Lasagne

INGREDIENTS

3 6-oz. packages baby leaf spinach, long stems removed and rinsed

⅓ cup extra-virgin olive oil

½ cup finely minced shallots

3 large garlic cloves, finely minced

1 lb. large cremini mushrooms, wiped clean and sliced thinly

½ lb. shiitake mushrooms, stems removed, caps wiped clean and thinly sliced

⅓ cup dry vermouth (or white wine)

2 tbsp. (generous) shredded fresh basil

1 tbsp. chopped fresh thyme leaves

1 cup ricotta cheese

1 tsp. Herbamare® or salt

¼ tsp. pepper

8 oz. mozzarella cheese, grated

10 oz. soft fresh chèvre (goat cheese), crumbled

½ tsp. nutmeg

8 to 12 oz. no-boil lasagna noodles (I like Delallo® Organic Whole Wheat Lasagna)

PREPARATION

Shake the spinach free of excess water and place it in a large pot. Cook over medium heat with the water left clinging to the leaves, stirring frequently, until just wilted and tender, which should take about 5 minutes. Drain the spinach in a fine-mesh sieve or colander, and press with the back of a spoon to remove excess moisture. Coarsely chop the spinach and set aside.

Heat the olive oil in a large saucepan over medium heat. Add the shallots and garlic and sauté until just tender and transparent, not browned. Add the mushrooms, toss to coat with the oil, and sauté, stirring frequently, until they are tender and reduced by half, 5–10 minutes. Add the vermouth (or wine) and simmer until most of the liquid has evaporated. Remove from the heat, stir in the basil, thyme and ricotta and season with ½ tsp. Herbamare® and pepper. Stir in half of the mozzarella and set aside.

In a large bowl combine the spinach with the remaining mozzarella and just over half of the goat cheese. Add the nutmeg and the remaining ½ tsp. Herbamare® and using a fork, stir together gently until creamy.

Preheat the oven to 350 degrees. Lightly butter an 11 x 7-inch baking pan. Spread one third of the mushroom mixture over the bottom of the pan. Top with a layer of the pasta (only use enough noodles to cover in a single layer with very little overlapping). Spread on half of the spinach mixture and top with another layer of pasta. Repeat the layers of mushrooms (one third), pasta and remaining spinach. Finish with a layer of remaining mushrooms and scatter the remaining crumbled goat cheese on top.

Bake, covered with foil, for 45 minutes or until bubbling hot and the noodles are cooked. Allow to rest for several minutes before cutting into serving pieces. Serves 6

Pastitsio *(Baked Pasta With Lamb, Tomatoes & Feta)*
Adapted from Gourmet magazine, Condé Nast Publications

INGREDIENTS

1 lb. ziti or penne (preferably Brown Rice Penne Pasta)

1½ cups (generous) grated Parmesan cheese

½ stick (4 tbsp.) unsalted butter, softened to room temperature

¼ lb. crumbled Feta

White Sauce:

½ stick (4 tbsp.) unsalted butter

¼ cup unbleached flour (all-purpose)

3 cups milk

¼ lb. crumbled Feta cheese

¼ tsp. ground nutmeg

¼ tsp. cinnamon

½ tsp. salt

¼ tsp. black pepper

2 eggs

Tomato Meat Sauce:

2 tbsp. extra-virgin olive oil

1 large sweet onion (yellow or white), finely chopped

4 large garlic cloves, finely chopped

1 bay leaf

1½ tsp. dried oregano

1 lb. ground lamb, very lean

½ cup dry red wine

2 tbsp. tomato paste

1 28-oz. can crushed tomatoes (juice included)

¼ tsp. cinnamon

1½ tsp. salt

¼ tsp. black pepper

⅓ cup minced fresh parsley leaves (preferably Italian flat-leaf)

PREPARATION

Make tomato sauce: In a large pot (or Dutch oven) heat the olive oil over moderately low heat and add the onion, garlic, bay leaf and oregano. Cook while stirring until the onion is softened. Add the lamb and cook the mixture over moderate heat, stirring and breaking up the lumps, until the lamb is no longer pink. Stir in the red wine, tomato paste, crushed tomatoes with juice, cinnamon, salt and pepper. Bring the mixture to a boil, reduce heat and simmer sauce for approx. ½ hour, when it will be thickened. Add the parsley and set aside.

Make white sauce: In a saucepan melt the butter over moderately low heat. Whisk in the flour and cook the mixture (called a roux), whisking, for 3 minutes. Add the milk in a stream, whisking, and bring the mixture to a boil. Add Feta cheese, then reduce heat and simmer the sauce, whisking, for several minutes. Whisk in the nutmeg, cinnamon, salt and pepper. Set sauce aside and let cool for about 5 minutes, then whisk in the eggs.

In a large kettle of boiling salted water, cook the noodles according to the package directions until al dente. Drain the noodles well and transfer to a large bowl. Stir in 1 generous cup of Parmesan cheese, the butter, and the Feta cheese. Spread half of the pasta mixture evenly in a deep 13 x 9 inch baking dish, buttered. Spoon all of the tomato meat sauce evenly over the pasta, and top the meat sauce with the remaining pasta mixture. Pour the white sauce over the pasta, smoothing with a spoon to be sure pasta is covered evenly and completely.

Sprinkle the top with the remaining ½ cup (generous) of Parmesan cheese.

Preheat the oven to 350 degrees and bake the pastitsio for 40–45 minutes, or until the top is golden. Let the casserole stand for approx. 10 minutes until serving. Serves 8

Ziti Al Forno
(Ziti Pasta With Little Meatballs & Sausage)

INGREDIENTS

¾ lb. ziti

1½ cups freshly grated aged Parmesan cheese

1 lb. (16 oz.) ricotta cheese

12 oz. fresh mozzarella cheese, cut into cubes

Sauce (or as Italians say "Gravy"):

2 tbsp. extra-virgin olive oil

1 lb. Italian-style pork sausages

4 garlic cloves, finely chopped

1 6-oz. can of tomato paste

3 28-oz. cans crushed Italian tomatoes

2 cups water

1 tsp. salt

½ tsp. black pepper

¼ cup chopped fresh basil leaves

¼ cup chopped fresh flat-leaf (Italian) parsley leaves

1 tbsp. dried oregano

Meatballs:

1 lb. ground beef (or if preferred, ½ lb. ground beef and ½ lb. ground pork)

½ cup fresh bread crumbs

2 large eggs

2 large cloves garlic, minced

½ cup freshly grated aged Parmesan cheese

2 tbsp. finely chopped fresh flat-leaf (Italian) parsley

1 tsp. salt

½ tsp. black pepper

2 tbsp. extra-virgin olive oil

PREPARATION

Make sauce: Heat the olive oil in a large pot (Dutch oven) and add the sausage, cut into small pieces. Brown well, remove from skillet and set aside. Pour off all but a little fat. Add the garlic to the pot and cook for about a minute over moderately low heat. Do not allow to brown. Add the tomato paste and continue to cook, stirring for another couple minutes. Add the crushed tomatoes to the pot along with the water, salt and pepper. Stir in the cooked sausage pieces, along with the basil, parsley and oregano. Bring the sauce to a simmer and cook, partially covered, over low heat, stirring occasionally for 2 hours.

While the sauce is cooking make the meatballs: Mix all meatball ingredients together in a bowl except for the olive oil (I use my hands). Heat the olive oil in a large heavy skillet over moderate heat until hot. Shape the meat into very small meatballs (about 1 inch in diameter), and cook in heated oil until well browned all over and set aside. You will need to cook the meatballs in batches. After the sauce has simmered for 2 hours, add the meatballs and continue to simmer, partially covered, for an additional 30 minutes. Set aside two cups of the sauce.

Cook the ziti in boiling salted water according to package directions until al dente and drain in a colander. Place ziti in a very large bowl and mix with the gravy (sauce) and 1 cup of the Parmesan cheese until well combined.

Preheat the oven to 350 degrees. Place half of the ziti and sauce mixture on the bottom of a large deep baking dish (a lasagna style pan is good for this recipe). Cover the ziti with the ricotta cheese. Put the mozzarella on top of the ricotta. Spread 1 cup of the reserved sauce over top. Put remaining ziti and sauce mixture on top, cover with the other reserved cup of sauce, and sprinkle top with the remaining ½ cup of Parmesan.

Cover the baking dish with foil and bake for 45 minutes. Remove the foil and continue to bake for an additional 15–20 minutes, or until the center is hot and the sauce is bubbling around the edges. Cover and let stand for 15 minutes before serving.

Note: If desired, you can make this dish ahead and refrigerate for several hours or overnight. Remove from the refrigerator and let stand at room temperature for about 30 minutes before following the baking instructions above. Serves 8–12

Lasagne *I have three words to say about this recipe – "Worth the Trouble"*

INGREDIENTS

½ lb. sweet Italian sausage links

1 tbsp. extra-virgin olive oil

Meatballs:

2 tbsp. extra-virgin olive oil

1 lb. lean ground beef

½ lb. lean ground pork

¼ cup fresh bread crumbs

2 large cloves garlic, minced

¼ cup finely chopped fresh parsley

3 tbsp. Locatelli or Parmesan cheese

1 egg

½ tsp. Herbamare® or salt

¼ tsp. black pepper

Sauce:

½ cup chopped onions

6 large cloves garlic, finely chopped

3 lbs. fresh tomatoes, seeded & chopped

1 6-oz. can tomato paste

1½ tsp. Herbamare® or salt

2 tbsp. finely chopped fresh parsley

2 tbsp. chopped fresh basil

½ tsp. dried oregano

¼ tsp. black pepper

PREPARATION

Make meatballs: Except for the olive oil, place all meatball ingredients in a large bowl and mix well with your hands until everything is thoroughly combined. Heat the olive oil in a large heavy non-stick skillet (the sides of the skillet should be several inches high) over moderate heat. Form the meat mixture into large meatballs and cook until the meatballs are nicely browned on all sides and cooked through. It will take 2 batches to cook all the meatballs. Remove the meatballs with a slotted spoon and place in a bowl and set aside.

While the meatballs are cooking, in a separate small skillet, sauté the sausage in one tbsp. of heated olive oil until it is nicely browned on all sides. Remove from the skillet and cut into bite-size pieces and set aside.

Make sauce: In the large skillet in which the meatballs were cooked (do not wipe or remove any of the oil or browned meatball drippings) add the onion and cook until the onion is softened. Add the remaining sauce ingredients. With hands, crumble cooked meatballs into small pieces and add the crumbled meatballs to the sauce. Also add the sausage pieces to the sauce. Reduce the heat to moderately low and simmer until the sauce is quite thick (approx. 45 minutes to an hour). Remove from heat and set aside.

Béchamel Sauce:

4 tbsp. butter

2 tbsp. flour

½ cup milk

½ cup chicken broth

⅛ tsp. salt

In a small saucepan, melt the butter, add flour & cook, stirring with a whisk, for 1 minute. Slowly add the milk and chicken broth and bring to a boil, continuing to whisk the sauce until it's very thick. Whisk in the salt and remove from the heat and set aside.

Ricotta Filling:

1 egg

½ lb. ricotta cheese

⅓ cup grated Parmesan cheese

⅛ tsp. nutmeg

½ tsp. salt

Beat the egg in a small bowl. Add remaining ingredients and stir well to combine, and set aside.

Cheeses:

1½ cups grated Parmesan cheese

8 oz. sliced mozzarella cheese

5–6 oz. shaved/shredded Grana Padano Parmesan **or** 5–6 oz. shredded Parmigiano Reggiano cheese

½ lb. No Boil Lasagne noodles (preferably 100% Pure Italian Durum Wheat Semolina)

In the following order, layer in a lasagne style deep baking dish (approx. 13 x 9 inches): a little meat sauce, half of the noodles, half of the remaining meat sauce, ½ cup Bechamel, ½ cup Parmesan cheese, half of the mozzarella, half of the Grana Padano (or Parmigiano Reggiano) and half of the ricotta, then the remaining noodles, meat sauce, ½ cup Bechamel, ½ cup Parmesan, the remaining mozzarella, the remaining Grana Padano (or Parmigiano Reggiano) and the remaining ricotta. Top the casserole with the remaining ½ cup of Parmesan. At this point the dish may be covered and refrigerated.

Bring casserole to room temperature and bake in a preheated 400 degree oven for 30 minutes, or until very bubbly. Let stand for 5–10 minutes before cutting into squares and serving. Serves 8

Warm Pasta Salad with Sun-Dried Tomatoes

INGREDIENTS

9 oz. crumbled feta cheese (or approx. 2 cups)

2 tsp. dried basil

2 tsp. dried oregano

2 tsp. dried thyme

¼ tsp. black pepper

1 tbsp. extra-virgin olive oil

8 slices bacon

3 oz. baby leaves of spinach, cut into thin (approx. ½ inch) strips

1 8-oz. jar minced sun-dried tomatoes in herbed oil (L'Esprit de Campagne® is a good choice)

3 cloves of garlic, finely chopped

2 tbsp. capers, drained

½ cup sliced black olives

¾ lb. (12 oz.) fusilli pasta (tri-color if desired)

½ cup extra-virgin olive oil

¼ cup aged balsamic vinegar

1¼ cup Parmigiano Reggiano cheese, grated

PREPARATION

Place crumbled feta in a small bowl, sprinkle with dried herbs and pepper, and drizzle with 1 tbsp. of olive oil. Toss gently to coat cheese evenly with herbs and oil. Set aside.

Fry bacon until crisp. Set aside approx. 1 tbsp. of the bacon drippings. Crumble the bacon and place in a large serving bowl with the spinach, tomatoes, garlic, capers and olives, and toss gently to combine.

Cook pasta according to package directions until al dente. Drain and rinse in a colander. Add hot pasta to the ingredients in the bowl and toss until the spinach is wilted. Top with the herbed feta and toss again.

Whisk together the olive oil, vinegar and reserved tbsp. of bacon drippings. Pour over the salad and toss again. Sprinkle with grated Parmesan and serve. Good warm or at room temperature. Serves 4–6

Happiness is looking in the mirror and loving what you see.

Spaghetti with Tomato Sauce & Meatballs

INGREDIENTS

1 lb. thin spaghetti noodles

Note: I prefer whole wheat noodles, or brown rice spaghetti pasta – more flavor and better for you. If you choose this type of noodle, for planning purposes know that they take longer to cook.

Grated Parmesan cheese – serve on side

Meatballs:

2 tbsp. extra-virgin olive oil

1 lb. very lean ground beef

¼ cup fresh bread crumbs

2 large cloves garlic, minced

¼ cup finely chopped fresh parsley

1 egg

½ tsp. Herbamare® or salt

¼ tsp. black pepper

3 tbsp. Locatelli or Parmesan cheese

Sauce:

2 tbsp. extra-virgin olive oil

2 large sweet yellow onions, chopped

3 medium green bell peppers or 2 large, chopped

1 cup chopped celery

2 large (28-oz) cans diced tomatoes, not drained

4 6-oz. cans tomato paste

8 large garlic cloves, finely chopped

½ tsp. dried basil

½ tsp. dried oregano

½ tsp. dried thyme

2 tsp. salt

1 tsp. black pepper

1 tbsp. sugar

4 bay leaves

1 cup good quality dry red wine

1 lb. mushrooms, washed and ends trimmed, cut into ¼ in thick slices

PREPARATION

Make sauce: Heat olive oil in a large kettle (Dutch oven) over moderate heat and cook the onions, green peppers, and celery, stirring occasionally, until the vegetables are softened. Add all of the remaining ingredients, except for the mushrooms. Simmer uncovered on low heat for 2 hours.

While the sauce is simmering, make the meatballs. Heat olive oil over moderate heat in a large skillet, and put remaining ingredients in a large bowl. Mix well with hands, and then shape mixture into medium-sized meatballs. Place in skillet and cook, turning, until they are well browned on all sides. Do not remove from skillet – remove skillet from heat and set aside.

After the sauce has cooked for 2 hours, add sliced mushrooms and the meatballs – include any liquid that remains in the bottom of the skillet and any brown bits. If you have used very lean ground beef as indicated to make the meatballs, there should not be a lot of grease added to the sauce. Cook for an additional 20 minutes, stirring. The mushrooms will become softened, but will not be mushy.

Cook the spaghetti noodles according to package directions and drain in a colander. Put desired amount of noodles on each serving plate and spoon generous portion of sauce with meatballs over top. Note that the sauce will be very thick! Serve with lots of grated Parmesan cheese on the side. Serves 6

Only humans have sleep disorders. Cats would consider that an oxymoron (with an emphasis on moron).

Five-Cheese Farfalle

INGREDIENTS

4 tbsp. unsalted butter

2 tbsp. all-purpose flour

1½ cups whole milk

1 28-oz. can diced tomatoes in juice

½ tsp. salt

¼ tsp. pepper

1 lb. farfalle (bow-tie pasta)

1 cup grated mozzarella cheese

½ cup grated Parmesan cheese

½ cup crumbled Gorgonzola cheese

½ cup diced Italian Asagio cheese

1 cup freshly finely grated pecorino Romano cheese

½ cup pecorino Romano cheese for sprinkling on top of casserole

½ cup finely chopped fresh flat-leaf parsley

PREPARATION

Melt butter in a large heavy saucepan or Dutch oven over moderately low heat. Add flour and cook, whisking, for 3 minutes. Add milk in a slow stream, whisking, until the mixture starts to thicken. Add juice from the canned tomatoes, whisking, and bring mixture to a boil, continuing to whisk constantly. Stir in the diced tomatoes, salt and pepper and simmer a few more minutes until thickened. Remove from heat.

Cook pasta in a large pot of boiling salted water per package instructions, and drain in a colander. While pasta is cooking, preheat oven to 375 degrees and butter a large shallow baking dish.

Add cooked pasta and all cheeses (except for the ½ cup of pecorino Romano for sprinkling on top) and parsley to the sauce. If the pan that you cooked the sauce in is not big enough to easily stir and combine all these ingredients, put the sauce into a large bowl and then add the rest of the ingredients. Transfer to the buttered gratin baking dish and sprinkle with the remaining ½ cup of pecorino Romano cheese.

Bake in the middle of the oven for approx. ½ hour, or until golden and bubbling. Let stand for 10 minutes before serving.

Serves 6 as a main course, 12 as a side dish

Pesto Alla Genovese with Linguine

INGREDIENTS

2 cups fresh basil leaves

1 cup fresh Italian parsley leaves

1 cup grated Parmigiano Reggiano cheese

½ cup slivered almonds (skins removed)

¼ cup pine nuts (skins removed)

14 walnut halves (skins removed)

2 large cloves garlic

3 tbsp. butter, softened to room temperature in blender or food processor

½ cup extra virgin olive oil

1 tsp. salt

Linguine pasta (9–12 oz.)

Shaved Parmigiano Reggiano cheese for sprinkling on top and to serve on the side

PREPARATION

Place all ingredients in blender or food processor (except for pasta) and blend until smooth. Cook pasta according to package directions until it is al dente. Drain pasta, but reserve approx. 4 tbsp. of the water from the pasta pot. Place linguine in a large serving bowl with pesto and toss well. Add reserved water and toss again.

Sprinkle some of the shaved Parmigiano Reggiano cheese on top of the pasta, and serve additional cheese on the side. Serves 4

Note: Almonds and pine nuts are available in most stores already blanched (with skins removed), which is not normally the case with walnuts. To blanch here's what to do: Heat some water in a small saucepan until boiling. Add the nuts and boil very briefly (approx. 30 seconds). Remove from the pan and drain in a colander. As soon as the nuts are not too hot to handle, rub off the skins and discard them.

Orzo with Roasted Vegetables

Adapted from the Barefoot Contessa Parties Cookbook

INGREDIENTS

1 medium eggplant

2 large red bell peppers

2 large yellow bell peppers

2 large red onions, peeled, halved, and cut into 1-inch chunks

4 large garlic cloves, minced

⅔ cup extra-virgin olive oil

1 tbsp. Kosher salt

1 tsp. black pepper

1 lb. orzo (preferably whole wheat)

½ cup minced scallions (mixture of white and green parts)

½ cup toasted pine nuts

1 lb. feta cheese, cut into ½-inch dice (*not crumbled*)

30 medium-sized fresh basil leaves, torn by hand into pieces

Dressing:

⅔ cup fresh lemon juice

⅔ cup extra-virgin olive oil

2 tsp. Kosher salt

1 tsp. black pepper

PREPARATION

Cut off the ends of the eggplant, peel and cut into 1-inch pieces. Place in a large sheet pan. Core all of the bell peppers, remove inside membranes and seeds, and cut into 1-inch pieces. Add peppers to the baking pan. Peel onions, cut in half, and cut into 1-inch chunks. Add onion to baking pan.

Preheat oven to 425 degrees. Toss vegetables in the baking pan with the garlic, olive oil, salt, and pepper. Assure that the vegetables are as evenly coated as possible. Roast the vegetables in the preheated oven for 25–30 minutes. Turn vegetables with a spatula and continue roasting for an additional 25–30 minutes.

Meanwhile cook the orzo according to the package directions. Drain in a colander and transfer to a very large serving bowl. Add the roasted vegetables to the pasta, scraping all the liquid and seasonings from the roasting pan into the pasta bowl.

Place all dressing ingredients in a small bowl and whisk until well combined. Pour on the pasta and vegetables and toss gently. Allow to cool to room temperature.

When cooled, add the scallions, pine nuts, feta and basil, stirring gently to combine ingredients evenly and thoroughly.

Note: This dish is better if made in advance. Refrigerate until ready to serve. Bring to room temperature before serving, or warm slightly. Serves 12

Lie low, deny everything

Orzo with Roasted Peppers & Chicken

INGREDIENTS

1 medium green bell pepper, halved and seeded (membranes removed)

2 medium red bell peppers, halved and seeded (membranes removed)

¾ cup orzo (rice-shaped pasta)

¾ lb. skinless boneless chicken breasts, cooked and cut into very small pieces

2 tbsp. minced fresh flat-leaf parsley

1 generous tbsp. minced fresh mint leaves

2 tbsp. fresh lemon juice

2 tbsp. extra-virgin olive oil

½ tsp. salt

¼ tsp. black pepper

4 oz. feta cheese, crumbled

PREPARATION

Preheat oven to 400 degrees. Place green and red bell peppers, cut side down, onto a jelly roll or other shallow baking pan. Roast for approx. ½ hour, until the skins are blistered and charred and the peppers are very soft. Remove from oven and set aside until cool enough to handle; then remove skins from the peppers, and cut into thin strips.

While the peppers are roasting, cook orzo according to package directions. Drain in a colander and then place into a large bowl.

Place a vegetable steamer over boiling water in a large pot, add chicken, reduce heat and cover, and steam the chicken for approx. 15 minutes or until firm to the touch. Let sit until cool enough to handle and then cut into small pieces.

Add chicken pieces and roasted peppers to the bowl with the orzo. In a small bowl, whisk together the parsley, mint, lemon juice, olive oil, salt and pepper. When well combined, pour over the orzo mixture and stir gently with a large spoon until well combined. Add feta cheese and stir again to distribute cheese evenly.

Place mixture into a baking dish and bake at 325 degrees just until heated through. Serves 3–4

Orzo with Feta & Cherry Tomatoes

INGREDIENTS

2½ tbsp. extra virgin olive oil

½ cup pine nuts

1 large clove garlic, finely chopped

½ cup packed fresh flat-leaf parsley leaves, chopped

2 tbsp. red wine vinegar

½ tsp. salt

¼ tsp. pepper

1 cup quartered cherry tomatoes

¼ lb. feta cheese

½ lb. orzo

PREPARATION

In a small heavy skillet heat 1 tbsp. olive oil over moderate heat and sauté the pine nuts, sprinkled lightly with salt, until they are golden brown. Note: Pine nuts brown quickly, so stir frequently and keep a watch over them while they are browning. Line a plate with paper towels; remove the nuts from the pan and place on the towels to drain.

In a large bowl, whisk together the garlic, parsley, vinegar, remaining 1½ tbsp. of olive oil, salt and pepper. Add tomatoes and feta and stir gently to combine.

In a large pot, bring water to a boil and cook orzo accordingly to package directions. Put cooked orzo in a large sieve and drain well. Add orzo to tomato mixture and toss gently until just combined. Serve orzo topped with the pine nuts.

Serves 2 as a main course without meat; Serves 3–4 if Middle Eastern Style Meatballs are added

Farfalle with Tomatoes, Cremini Mushrooms & Prosciutto

Adapted from Gourmet magazine, Condé Nast Publications

INGREDIENTS

1 tbsp. extra virgin olive oil

3 tbsp. butter

1⅓ cups finely chopped sweet yellow onions

2 large garlic cloves, minced

¼ tsp. red pepper flakes

2 tsp. chopped fresh basil leaves

½ tsp. dried oregano

10 oz. Baby Bella ("Cremini") mushrooms, stems discarded, caps thinly sliced

2 tbsp. unbleached all-purpose flour

1 cup milk (low-fat is OK)

1 28-oz. can Italian tomatoes, drained and chopped

¼ lb. thinly sliced prosciutto, cut into strips

1 cup grated Italian Fontina cheese

(approx. 4 oz.)

½ cup crumbled Gorgonzola cheese

1 cup finely grated Parmigiano-Reggiano cheese

⅓ cup finely chopped fresh Italian (flat-leaf) parsley

½ lb. (8 oz.) farfalle (bow-tie) pasta

¾ tsp. salt

¼ tsp. black pepper

PREPARATION

Heat the olive oil and 1 tbsp. of the butter in a large skillet over moderately low heat. Add the onions and cook, stirring occasionally, until the onions have softened. Add the garlic, red pepper flakes, basil and oregano and cook, stirring, for about a minute. Add the mushrooms, increase heat to moderate and cook until the mushrooms are tender, about 10 minutes. Transfer the mushroom mixture to a large bowl.

In the same skillet, melt the remaining 2 tbsp. of butter over moderate heat and whisk in the flour. Continue to whisk for about 2–3 minutes to make a roux. Add the milk in a slow stream, whisking constantly, until thickened, which should take several minutes. Pour the thickened sauce over the mushroom mixture, and then stir in the tomatoes, prosciutto, Fontina, Gorgonzola, ¾ cup of the Parmigiano-Reggiano, and the parsley.

Cook the pasta in a large pot of boiling salted water for 5 minutes (pasta will not be completely tender). Drain well in a colander. Add the pasta and salt and pepper to the mushroom mixture and mix gently until pasta is well combined with the sauce. Transfer the mixture to a 2 quart shallow buttered baking dish and sprinkle the top with the remaining ¼ cup of the Parmigiano-Reggiano.

Preheat the oven to 450 degrees and bake the casserole in the middle of the oven for 25 minutes, or until the top is golden and the pasta is tender. Serves 4

"Cats as a class have never completely got over the snootiness caused by the fact that in Ancient Egypt they were worshiped as Gods."

P.G. Wodehouse

Spaghetti, Italian Sausage, Chicken & Peppers

Adapted from Gourmet magazine, Condé Nast Publications

INGREDIENTS

1 lb. sweet or hot Italian sausage links

2 tbsp. extra virgin olive oil

2 large onions, preferably Vidalia, thinly sliced

1 large green bell pepper, cut into thin strips (cored, seeds and membranes removed)

1 large red bell pepper, cut into thin strips (cored, seeds and membranes removed)

4 large garlic cloves, finely chopped

1 lb. skinless boneless chicken breast, cut into small strips (about ½ inch)

1 large (28-oz.) can crushed tomatoes

½ cup dry red wine

1 tsp. oregano

1 tbsp. (generous) finely chopped fresh basil

1 tsp. sugar, preferably organic

1 tsp. Herbamare® or salt

½ tsp. pepper

½ to 1 lb. thin spaghetti noodles

Parmesan cheese for sprinkling on servings and extra to serve on the side

PREPARATION

In a large saucepan or Dutch oven, heat 1 tbsp. of the olive oil over moderate heat. Add the sausages and brown well on all sides. Remove sausages from pan and set aside.

When the sausages are cool enough to handle, cut crosswise into ½ inch thick pieces.

Add the second tbsp. of olive oil to the pan and then add the sliced onions and red and green bell pepper strips. Continue to cook over moderate heat until the onions and peppers are softened. Add chopped garlic and continue to cook for about a minute.

Add the chicken strips and continue to cook, stirring, for a few minutes until the chicken strips turn white. Return the sausage pieces to the pan, and add the crushed tomatoes, wine, oregano, basil, sugar, Herbamare® and pepper and slowly bring to a boil, stirring occasionally, for approx. 15 minutes. The sauce will be very thick.

At this point, you can set the sauce aside until you are ready to serve the meal. At that time, cook the noodles according to package directions. While the noodles are cooking, reheat the sauce over moderate heat until hot. Drain the noodles, put desired amount on each serving plate, and top with a generous helping of the sauce. Sprinkle each portion generously with grated Parmesan cheese, and serve additional cheese on the side. Serves 4–6

Note: The recipe indicates ½ to 1 lb. of noodles. I personally prefer my spaghetti with a minimum amount of noodles and lots of sauce. Make more noodles if you want to go heavier on the noodles.

Chilly winter afternoons, delicious food, cat naps...prodigious purring...

Poultry

I used to shy away from serving chicken (or other types of poultry) to dinner guests because I didn't think it was special enough. The truth is that almost everyone likes poultry, so that makes it normally a safe bet, and there is nothing mediocre, unremarkable or couci-couci (meaning so-so in French) about these recipes.

Ask not what your cat can do for you...

Testimonial

I met Sue Cassidy (who at the time was Sue Welsh, a.k.a. Welshie), when I was looking for a roommate in Washington, DC. A mutual friend made an introduction, and I served curried tuna for dinner. It was a recipe from the Fijian cookbook I had bought while serving as a Peace Corps volunteer in Fiji. We hit it off famously and the rest is history. We have been friends for nearly 40 years, and my tuna curry remains one of the deciding factors in our friendship. It was not very good, but Welshie was tactful and polite (she even requested a second helping!), and we became roommates.

I soon realized Welshie was a stellar cook, way beyond my abilities. We spent whole evenings reading cookbooks and planning new menus. Welshie loved to cook (still does), and I looked forward to the weekends when the aromas from the kitchen drove me to distraction.

Through the years her cooking skills have continued to develop and expand, while her ardor for the activity continues at a fever pitch. What a treat it was for my husband and me to spend a weekend with her and her husband recently and be served gourmet meal after gourmet meal. I can't say enough about her ability in the kitchen.

Susan Flisher Mau
Former Caterer
Tallahassee, FL

Turkey Spiral Loaf

INGREDIENTS

2 eggs

2 lbs. ground turkey meat

1 cup whole wheat bread crumbs

1 tsp. dried Italian seasoning

½ cup V-8 juice

½ cup minced shallots

¾ tsp. dried oregano

¼ tsp. salt

¼ tsp. black pepper

4 oz. Prosciutto ham, cut into small strips

1½ cups shredded Swiss cheese

½ cup minced fresh flat-leaf parsley

3 thin slices (about 3 inches square)
Swiss cheese, cut in half diagonally

Parsley Mayonnaise to Accompany:

1 cup mayonnaise

2 medium garlic cloves, minced

⅔ cup minced fresh flat-leaf parsley

2 tsp. dried oregano

¼ tsp. salt

⅛ tsp. black pepper

PREPARATION

Beat eggs in a large bowl and add turkey, bread crumbs, Italian seasoning, V-8 juice, shallots, oregano, salt and pepper. Mix together well (preferably with hands). On a 12 x 15-inch piece of aluminum foil, pat the meat mixture into a 9 x 13-inch rectangle. Arrange the Prosciutto over the meat, leaving ½ inch margin around the edges. Sprinkle the Swiss cheese and parsley onto the ham. Starting at one of the short ends, carefully roll up the meat, using the foil to lift the meat, and peel off the foil. Pinch the ends of the meat together to seal. Place the roll with the seam side down in a large baking dish.

Preheat the oven to 350 degrees and bake for 1 hour and 15 minutes, or until done. During the last 10 minutes of baking, put the cheese slices on top of the meat loaf. While the meatloaf is baking, prepare the parsley mayonnaise by mixing together all ingredients listed. Spoon the mayonnaise into a serving dish and refrigerate until needed. Serves 6–8.

Baton Rouge, LA, Spring 1989

Sherry "Penney"

Penney has resided with her husband Bob in Baton Rouge for many years – resulting in my making many trips there, and to New Orleans, for happy reunions. Both of those cities are well-known for often elegant and always exceptional locally inspired fare.

However, as marvelous as it is to experience the many superlative restaurants there, it is even better to dine "Chez Penney." She made a fresh crawfish pie for me one time I have never forgotten. And I would fly from DC to Louisiana solely for the experience of imbibing Bob's incomparable rum punches.

When I asked Penney to share a recipe, she provided one of her favorites from her mother's repertoire. She hopes you will enjoy: Turkey Spiral Loaf

Chicken Provençal with Tomatoes & Olives

INGREDIENTS

1 lb. boneless and skinless chicken breast tenders

Herbamare® or salt and black pepper for sprinkling on chicken

¼ cup extra virgin olive oil

1½ cups sweet yellow onion, thinly sliced (1 medium onion)

¼ tsp. Herbamare® or salt

¼ tsp. black pepper

½ cup dry vermouth

½ cup beef broth

½ cup chopped black Kalamata olives

3 large garlic cloves, minced

1 14–15 oz. can diced tomatoes, drained

½ tsp. dried thyme leaves

2 tbsp. small capers (cut in half if large)

¼ cup (generous) chopped fresh basil leaves

Accompaniment – Cheese of choice for sprinkling on top (I like Quattro Formaggio, a blend of Parmesan, Asiago, Fontina and Provolone cheeses

PREPARATION

Season the chicken on both sides with the Herbamare® and pepper. Heat the olive oil in a large skillet over medium heat. When the oil is very hot (but not smoking), add the chicken and cook briefly until browned on both sides (about 5 minutes per side). Remove the chicken from the skillet and set aside on a plate covered with aluminum foil.

Add the onions, salt and pepper to the same skillet and cook over moderate heat for approx. 5 minutes, or until the onions have softened. Add the vermouth and beef broth and cook for 8–10 minutes, which will reduce the liquid slightly. Add the olives, garlic and tomatoes and allow the mixture to cook and reduce for another 10 minutes.

Return the chicken (along with any juices that have accumulated on the plate) to the pan and add the thyme. Cover the skillet and cook for an additional 5 minutes, or until the chicken is just cooked through. Add the capers and basil to the skillet, stirring to combine, just before serving. Serve the cheese on the side. Serves 2–3

Oven-Fried Chicken Drumsticks

INGREDIENTS

1½ cups fresh white or whole wheat bread crumbs (whole wheat preferred)

1½ tsp. salt

¾ tsp. black pepper

4 tbsp. unsalted butter, softened to room temperature in a small bowl

1½ tbsp. Dijon mustard

2 tbsp. mayonnaise

1 tsp. fresh lemon juice

¼ tsp. curry powder

6 large drumsticks (approx. 1–1¼ lbs.)

PREPARATION

Preheat oven to 450 degrees. Place bread crumbs in a shallow baking dish (pie pan is good) and bake in preheated oven for 3 minutes, until dry but not browned. Remove from oven and stir in 1 tsp. of the salt and ½ tsp. of the pepper and set aside. Leave oven on.

Add the mustard, mayonnaise, lemon juice, curry powder, remaining ½ tsp. salt and remaining ¼ tsp. pepper to the softened butter and stir to combine well. Coat each drumstick generously with the butter mixture (a small spoon is good for this, and do them one at a time). Roll each buttered drumstick in the reserved breadcrumbs until well and evenly coated. Place the drumsticks as they are prepared in a shallow baking pan.

Bake the chicken, skin sides up, until very brown and cooked through, which should take approx. 45 minutes. Let chicken stand 10 minutes before serving (do not cover). Serves 2–3

Chicken Breasts with Spicy Cranberry Sauce

INGREDIENTS

1 8-oz. can whole berry jellied cranberry sauce

½ cup medium dry sherry

1½ cups chicken broth

1 tbsp. finely chopped fresh gingerroot

½ tsp. ground nutmeg

½ tsp. ground cloves

¼ tsp. black pepper

2 star anise, whole

½ tsp. dry mustard

2 tsp. prepared spicy brown mustard

2 tbsp. firmly packed dark brown sugar

1 lb. boneless skinless chicken breasts, each breast halved lengthwise

¼ cup flour

1 tsp. salt

⅛ tsp. black pepper

4 tbsp. unsalted butter

PREPARATION

In a medium sized heavy saucepan, combine the cranberry sauce, sherry, chicken broth, gingerroot, nutmeg, cloves, ¼ tsp. black pepper, star anise, dry mustard, prepared mustard, and brown sugar. Cook over medium heat until the sauce begins to simmer. Reduce heat to medium low and cook for 15 minutes, stirring occasionally. Remove from heat and discard the star anise.

Combine the flour with salt and ⅛ tsp. pepper. Heat butter in a large heavy skillet over high heat until it is foamy. Dredge the chicken breasts thoroughly on all sides in the seasoned flour and place in the skillet. Cook on each side for about 1 minute, remove and place in a baking dish. To the skillet (do not wipe out or clean) add the cranberry sauce and cook over moderate heat until the sauce is reduced by about half. The sauce should be thickened, but not thick.

Pour the sauce over the chicken in the baking dish and bake in a preheated 350 degree oven for 15 minutes. The chicken should feel springy to the touch, and the sauce should be bubbling. Remove chicken to serving plates and spoon sauce generously over each serving. Serves 2–3

Turkey Sloppy Joes

INGREDIENTS

1 tbsp. extra-virgin olive oil

1 cup chopped onion

⅓ cup chopped celery

1 cup chopped red bell pepper

3 large garlic cloves, finely chopped

1 lb. ground turkey (Not labeled "all breast meat")

1 tsp. salt

½ tsp. ground black pepper

1 can whole tomatoes in juice (14.5–15 oz.)

¼ cup ketchup

1 tbsp. molasses

1 tbsp. cider vinegar

¾ tbsp. Worcestershire sauce

½ tsp. Tabasco sauce

PREPARATION

Heat oil in a large heavy saucepan over moderate heat until hot and add onion, celery, and bell pepper; sauté vegetables until softened and golden, stirring occasionally. Add garlic and turkey and continue to cook, stirring and breaking up large lumps of turkey with a wooden spoon, until meat is no longer pink. Stir in salt and pepper.

Place tomatoes with juice, ketchup, molasses, vinegar, Worcestershire sauce, and Tabasco in a large bowl. Blend with an immersion blender until smooth. Add to turkey and simmer, uncovered, stirring occasionally, until sauce is thickened, about 20–25 minutes.

Serve on buns of choice. Note: This is so yummy that I usually end up eating it from a bowl and don't bother with the bun. Serves 4

Chicken Curry with Cashews

Adapted from Gourmet magazine, Condé Nast Publications

INGREDIENTS

½ stick (4 tbsp.) unsalted butter

1 large white onion, finely chopped (approx. 2 cups)

3 large garlic cloves, finely chopped

1 generous tbsp. peeled and finely chopped fresh gingerroot

3 tbsp. curry powder (hot or mild, depending on your preference)

1 tsp. ground cumin

1 tsp. salt

½ tsp. cayenne pepper

2 to 2½ lbs. boneless skinned chicken breasts

1 14–15 oz. can diced tomatoes, not drained

¼ cup chopped fresh cilantro

1 cup roasted salted cashew nuts

1½ cups plain whole-milk yogurt (Greek style)

Accompaniment: Cooked rice (brown rice or basmati or jasmine)

PREPARATION

Heat butter in a large heavy pot over moderately low heat until foam subsides. Add onion and cook for about five minutes, or until softened. Add the garlic and gingerroot and cook an additional minute. Add curry powder, cumin, salt and cayenne pepper and cook for another minute or two.

Cut chicken breasts into medium-size strips. Add chicken to the onion mixture and cook, stirring, to coat well. Add the tomatoes with the juice and the cilantro, and bring to a simmer. Cover and cook at a gentle simmer, stirring occasionally, until the chicken is cooked through (approx. ½ hour).

Just before serving pulse the cashews in a mini-food processor until very finely ground, then add to curry along with the yogurt and simmer gently, uncovered, stirring, until the sauce is thickened, about 5 minutes. Serve over rice. Serves 4

Cheesy Chicken

(More kudos to Toni – this extremely easy recipe has always been one of my ultimate favorite ways to prepare chicken. Ti amo, mamma mia.)

INGREDIENTS

4 tbsp. butter

3 large garlic cloves, minced

1 cup fresh whole wheat bread crumbs (or fresh white bread)

½ cup grated Cheddar cheese

¼ cup grated Parmesan cheese

1 tsp. salt

¼ tsp. black pepper

1 lb. boneless and skinless chicken breasts

PREPARATION

Melt the butter in a small pan. Stir in the minced garlic, remove from heat and set aside.

In a mini-food processor, pulse bread to produce crumbs equal to one cup. Process the bread crumbs again, this time with the addition of the 2 cheeses, salt and pepper. Place the bread crumbs on a plate.

Dip each chicken breast in the melted garlic butter to coat well and evenly. Next dredge the chicken pieces on both sides in the crumb mixture, coating well. Place the chicken in a shallow baking pan. The pan should be large enough that the chicken pieces are not touching. Spoon any remaining butter evenly over tops of the chicken.

Preheat the oven to 350 degrees and bake the chicken uncovered for 40–45 minutes, or until tender and nicely browned on top. Serves 3–4

Country Club of York, Spring 1989

Chicken Tenders with White Wine Sauce

This recipe involves a lot of different steps, and is very time-consuming to make. I almost didn't include it in my cookbook for that reason. In fact, it made me tired just entering the thing into my computer. HOWEVER, if you have one of those days when you feel like spending extra time in the kitchen, this dish is totally amazing, and well worth the time and trouble.

INGREDIENTS

2 large red bell peppers

Sun-dried Tomato Pesto (Make Recipe in "Sauces" Section)

Extra-virgin garlic olive oil for dipping chicken pieces (I use Olave® Extra-Virgin Olive Oil (Garlic)

Panko (Japanese bread crumbs) for dipping chicken pieces (approx. 1 cup)

2 tbsp. extra-virgin olive oil

1½ lbs. chicken breast tenders

Herbamare® or salt and pepper for sprinkling on chicken

¼ cup dry vermouth (or white wine)

12 oz. fresh baby leaf spinach

White Wine Butter Sauce:

½ cup dry vermouth (or white wine)

⅓ cup white wine vinegar

3 tbsp. chopped shallots

6 tbsp. butter, well chilled

1 tbsp. sliced scallion (white part only)

¼ tsp. salt

⅛ tsp. white pepper

PREPARATION

Rinse peppers and cut out the stem. Preheat broiler and place peppers in a single layer on a broiler pan lined with foil. Broil peppers approx. 6–8 inches from the heat, turning often, until the peppers are well blackened on all sides and soft. Remove from the oven and cool until they can be handled. With your hands, peel off the blackened skin. The pulp will have some blackened areas remaining after the skin is peeled off, which is the way it should be. Remove the seeds and membranes on the inside of the peppers and cut into strips. Place pepper strips around the perimeter of a 9 x 13 inch baking dish. While the peppers are roasting, make the pesto and set aside.

Cover the bottom of a shallow dish with olive oil, and place panko in a separate dish. Heat 2 tbsp. olive oil in a large heavy non-stick skillet over moderately high heat until very hot. Dip the chicken tenders in the garlic olive oil, letting the excess drip off, and then roll in the panko, covering lightly. You may find it necessary to add more olive oil and/or panko to the dishes to complete the breading process.

Place breaded chicken tenders in the skillet and sprinkle with Herbamare® or salt and pepper. Cook for approx. 5 minutes on each side. Chicken tenders should be lightly browned, but not cooked completely through. As the tenders are cooked, add to the baking dish along with the roasted red peppers. Sprinkle the ¼ cup dry vermouth (or white wine) evenly over the peppers and chicken and set aside.

Make sauce: In a saucepan over medium-high heat, reduce the white wine, white wine vinegar and shallots until there is a generous tbsp. of liquid left. Set aside.

Preheat the oven to 425 degrees. Place the chicken in the oven and bake until the chicken is cooked through, which should take approx. 10–15 minutes.

While the chicken is baking, cook spinach: heat ¼ cup of water over high heat in a large skillet and add spinach leaves. Cook stirring, just until wilted, and set aside.

Finish making the sauce: put the reduced liquid with shallots on a burner over low heat and add the cold butter, one tbsp. at a time, whisking after each addition until incorporated and emulsified. When all the butter has been added, stir in the sliced scallion and salt and white pepper.

When the chicken is done, divide tenders among serving plates, and place roasted peppers along one side of the chicken. On the other side of the chicken divide the spinach among the serving plates. Spoon the reserved pesto generously over top of the chicken tenders. Spoon the white wine butter sauce over the top and sides of the chicken. Serves 4

Hungarian Chicken Breasts

INGREDIENTS

4 small chicken breasts, skinned, boned and split in half

¼ cup (4 tbsp.) butter

3 medium onions coarsely chopped (or to equal approx. 3 cups)

4 garlic cloves, finely chopped

2–3 stalks celery, chopped (or to equal ½ cup)

½ cup (generous) chopped carrots

1 bay leaf

2 tbsp. minced fresh flat-leaf parsley

1 tsp. chopped fresh thyme leaves

2 tbsp. sweet Hungarian paprika

1 tbsp. tomato paste

1 cup chicken broth

1½ tsp. Herbamare® or salt

½ tsp. black pepper

1 generous cup sour cream at room temperature

PREPARATION

Heat 2 tbsp. of the butter in a large skillet until hot and brown the chicken breasts on both sides. Transfer chicken to a plate and cover to keep warm.

Add the remaining butter to the same skillet and cook the onion, garlic, celery, carrots, bay leaf, parsley, thyme, and paprika over moderate heat, stirring occasionally, until the vegetables are softened. Stir in the tomato paste. Add the chicken broth, and stir with a whisk to incorporate well with the seasoned vegetables. Simmer for approx. 5 minutes. Discard the bay leaf and season with Herbamare® and pepper.

Return the chicken to the skillet and cook until the chicken is thoroughly cooked and tender, which should take about 10–15 minutes. Stir in the sour cream and heat until hot but not boiling. Serves 4

Chicken Teriyaki

INGREDIENTS

⅓ cup sunflower oil

⅓ cup soy sauce

2 tbsp. molasses

3 large garlic cloves, minced

2 tbsp. finely chopped fresh gingerroot

2 tsp. dry mustard

1¼ lb.. boneless skinless chicken breasts, cut into thin strips

2 tbsp. sunflower oil

2 large red bell peppers, cut into thin strips (seeds and membranes removed)

2 large green bell peppers, cut into thin strips (seeds and membranes removed)

1 8-oz. can bamboo shoots, drained

½ cup chopped scallions, white part only

½ cup chopped scallions, dark green leaves

Brown rice, cooked according to package directions

PREPARATION

Combine the sunflower oil, soy sauce, molasses, garlic, gingerroot and dry mustard in a medium bowl. Add the chicken strips and stir to coat. Marinate at least one hour or up to one and a half hours at room temperature.

Heat 2 tbsp. of sunflower oil in a large skillet and add red and green pepper strips. Cook over medium heat until the peppers are softened but still firm (not mushy). Remove peppers from skillet with a slotted spoon and set aside. Wipe the residual oil from the skillet with paper towels.

Remove approx. 3 tbsp. of the marinade from the chicken and heat it in the wiped skillet over moderate heat. Add the chicken (with the rest of the marinade) and stir fry for approx. 5 minutes. Return the peppers to the skillet along with the drained bamboo shoots and cook, stirring, for about a minute. Add scallions (white and green parts) and continue to cook, stirring, until the scallions are slightly softened and the chicken is cooked through, which should take approx. 1–2 additional minutes.

Serve over cooked brown rice. Serves 4

Turkey Cheddar Burgers with Sun-Dried Tomato Mayonnaise

INGREDIENTS

2 tbsp. garlic flavored extra-virgin olive oil (good choice is Olave®)

⅓ cup chopped shallots

½ tsp. Herbamare® or salt

¼ tsp. black pepper

⅓ cup chopped Kalamata olives

½ tsp. dried thyme

1 ¼ lb. ground turkey (not labeled "all breast meat")

1 block extra-sharp Cheddar cheese, cut into 4 to 6 half inch slices

Garlic pepper

Additional garlic flavored olive oil for preparing skillet

Hamburger or Kaiser rolls (Optional)

Mayonnaise:

½ cup oil-packed sun-dried tomatoes, drained

2 tbsp. water

2 tbsp. apple cider vinegar

2 tbsp. chopped fresh chives

½ tsp. salt

½ cup mayonnaise

PREPARATION

Heat garlic oil in a small skillet and add shallots. Cook until softened, approx. 3 minutes. Transfer shallots to a bowl and add Herbamare®, pepper, Kalamata olives, thyme and turkey. With hands, mix well to assure all ingredients are incorporated well and evenly into turkey.

On a sheet of wax paper, divide turkey mixture into eight equal mounds. Note: This will make 4 very large burgers. If preferred, divide into 10–12 mounds to make 5 or 6 smaller burgers. Pat mounds into patties of desired thickness and top half of patties with a slice of Cheddar cheese. Place a second patty on top of the cheese and press firmly to seal and form a single patty. Repeat process with remaining burgers.

Rub a non-stick ridged grill/frying pan well with garlic flavored olive oil and heat over moderately high heat until hot but not smoking. Sprinkle one side of burgers with garlic pepper. Place on grill and cook approx. 5 minutes, turn over and sprinkle with more garlic pepper, and continue cooking for another 5 minutes, or until burgers are cooked through (no longer pink). The time it will take to cook the burgers varies depending on how thick and big you choose to make them.

To make mayonnaise: In mini food processor, puree tomatoes with water, vinegar, chives, and salt until well combined. Add mayonnaise and process just until incorporated. Mayonnaise can be made ahead and chilled until ready to serve, or you can make the mayonnaise while the burgers are grilling. Serves 4–6

Dogs will come to you when they're called. Cats take a message and get back to you.

Hungarian Cornish Game Hens

INGREDIENTS

4 Cornish game hens (approx. 1 lb. each)

Herbamare® or salt and black pepper (for sprinkling on hens)

1 tbsp. grapeseed oil

2 tbsp. unsalted butter

1 cup finely chopped onion

3 large garlic cloves, finely chopped

1 tbsp. sweet Hungarian paprika

1 tsp. caraway seed

1½ cups chicken stock or broth

½ cup medium-dry sherry

2 medium fresh tomatoes, seeded and chopped

1 tsp. Herbamare® or salt

½ cup sour cream

PREPARATION

Sprinkle game hens generously on both sides with Herbamare® seasoning and black pepper. In a large flameproof casserole dish (that has a lid), heat the grapeseed oil and one tbsp. of the butter over moderately high heat. Add the hens and brown them on both sides (this should take approx. 3–4 minutes per side). Remove the hens to a plate and pour off most of the fat. Do not wipe out the casserole; about 1 tbsp. of fat should remain.

Add the remaining tbsp. of butter to the casserole. Reduce the heat to moderately low and add the onion, garlic, paprika, and caraway seed. Cook and stir occasionally until the onion is softened. Add the chicken broth and bring to a simmer. Add the hens breast side up to the casserole and braise them covered, in a preheated 350 degree oven for 45 minutes to an hour, or until the juices run clear when the fleshy part of the thigh is pricked with a knife.

Transfer the hens to a plate and cover with aluminum foil to keep warm. Add the sherry and the chopped tomatoes to the casserole, and place over moderately high heat on top of the stove. Reduce the mixture by about half. Reduce the heat to very low, and add 1 tsp. of Herbamare® and the sour cream to the casserole. Stir for a couple minutes to incorporate the sour cream, but do not let the sauce come to a boil. Spoon a generous amount of sauce on each hen before serving, and if desired, serve the remaining sauce on the side. Serves 4

Cornish Hens with Orange Glaze

INGREDIENTS

4 Cornish game hens, split in half

1 generous cup orange marmalade

¼ cup dark brown sugar, firmly packed

4 tbsp. red wine vinegar

2 tsp. Worcestershire sauce

½ tsp. curry powder

2 tbsp. chopped fresh gingerroot

¼ tsp. cayenne pepper

1 tsp. Herbamare® or salt

PREPARATION

Rinse and dry hens, then split in half lengthwise. Line a large baking pan with foil and place the hen halves, skin side down, in the pan.

Combine all remaining ingredients in a small saucepan and heat over moderate heat just to the boiling point. Immediately reduce the heat to low and simmer for a couple minutes, and remove from the heat. Brush the bottom side of the hens with the sauce.

Preheat oven to 350 degrees and bake the hens for 30 minutes. Remove from the oven, turn hens over so that the skin side is up, and brush again with the sauce. Continue to cook for an additional 30–40 minutes, basting with the sauce about every 10 minutes, until the hens are starting to brown on top and are cooked through.

If desired, spoon some of the juices from the roasting pan over each hen half once they are placed on serving plates, or put the juices in a small bowl and serve on the side. Serves 4

Chicken with Sun-Dried Tomato Cream Sauce

Adapted from Gourmet magazine Condé Nast Publications

INGREDIENTS

1¼ lb. boneless skinless chicken breast tenders

Herbamare® or salt & black pepper for sprinkling on chicken

2 tbsp. extra-virgin olive oil

4 large garlic cloves, finely chopped

⅓ cup chopped drained sun-dried tomatoes (packed in oil)

¼ tsp. dried hot red pepper flakes

¼ cup dry vermouth (or white wine)

¾ cup chicken broth

⅓ cup sour cream

¼ cup shredded fresh basil leaves

Shredded basil leaves for garnish

PREPARATION

Pat chicken dry with paper towels and sprinkle both sides generously with Herbamare® and pepper. Heat olive oil in a large heavy non-stick skillet over moderately high heat until hot but not smoking. Cook the chicken pieces, turning once, until they are browned on both sides (approx. 5 minutes per side). At this point the chicken will be almost cooked through. Remove from skillet, put on a plate and cover with foil.

Add garlic, tomatoes, and red pepper flakes to the skillet and sauté, stirring, for approx. 1 minute. Add vermouth and simmer until reduced by about half, which should take no more than 1–2 minutes. Add chicken broth to the skillet and bring to a boil. Simmer uncovered for several minutes.

Pour mixture in the skillet into a bowl and add the sour cream and basil. Blend with a hand mixer (immersion blender) until the sauce is thickened. I prefer that the sauce is not totally smooth. Return the sauce and the chicken (with any reserved juices on the plate) to the skillet and heat over moderate heat for approx. 5 minutes, or until the chicken is just heated through and completely cooked. Serves 3–4

Chicken Curry

INGREDIENTS

2 lbs. chicken breasts, skin & bones included

2½ tsp. salt

6 peppercorns

1 onion studded with 6 whole cloves

1 carrot

2 tbsp. butter

1 cup (generous) chopped red onion

3 tbsp. Madras curry powder

13½ –14½ oz. can unsweetened coconut milk (many good choices – I especially like Native Forest® Organic Coconut Milk)

⅛ tsp. black pepper

3 tbsp. chopped crystallized ginger

¼ tsp. ground cloves

2 tsp. chopped fresh mint leaves

¼ cup fresh lime juice

Brown Rice (cooked according to package directions)

PREPARATION

Place chicken in a large pot/kettle with 3 cups of water, 2 tsp. of the salt, peppercorns, onion with cloves, and carrot. Cover and simmer for 1 hour. Remove chicken from broth and cool until it can be handled. Do not discard the broth.

Melt the butter in a large skillet over moderate heat. Add the onion and sauté until tender. Stir in the curry. Gradually stir in the coconut milk and 1 cup of the reserved chicken cooking broth. Add the pepper, remaining ½ tsp. salt, ginger, cloves and mint. Cover the skillet and cook the sauce over low heat for 30 minutes.

While the sauce is cooking, remove the chicken from the bones and discard all skin. Tear the chicken into small strips (I find it easiest to do by hand), and set aside. After the sauce has cooked for ½ hour, add the chicken to the skillet and reheat (should take about 5 minutes). Just before serving stir the lime juice into the sauce. Serve the curry over cooked rice. Serves 4–6

Poulét Roti *(Classic Roast Chicken)*

INGREDIENTS

1 3 to 3½ lbs. chicken (preferably free-range/organic)

2 tbsp. unsalted butter, softened to room temperature in a small bowl

2 large cloves garlic (approx. 1 tbsp. minced)

½ tsp. salt

1 tsp. finely minced fresh thyme leaves

¼ tsp. black pepper

1 small onion, peeled and cut in half

1 cup dry vermouth (or white wine)

1 cup chicken broth

1 tbsp. cornstarch

PREPARATION

Preheat the oven to 375 degrees. Rinse the inner cavity of the chicken and pat the chicken dry. Place the chicken on a rack in a medium-sized shallow roasting pan. Add the garlic, salt, thyme and pepper to the softened butter and stir to combine well. Using your fingers, rub half of the butter under the skin, over the breast meat of the chicken. Rub the remaining butter over the entire outer surface of the chicken. Place the halved onion in the cavity of the chicken.

Pour the vermouth and ½ cup of the chicken broth into the roasting pan. Roast the chicken in the preheated oven for approx. 1½ hours, or until the juices run clear when a knife is inserted into the thickest portion of the thigh. The chicken skin should be well browned and crispy. Remove the chicken to a platter and remove the rack from the roasting pan and remove the onion from the chicken.

If the roasting pan is flameproof, put on top of the stove and continue. If the pan is not flameproof, pour all of the pan juices from the roasting pan into a saucepan (be sure to scrape the bottom) and continue. Tilt the pan and skim off some of the surface fat with a spoon.

Add the cornstarch to the remaining ½ cup of chicken broth and stir to combine and pour the broth into the saucepan (or roasting dish). Bring the mixture to a boil over medium heat and cook until thickened, which should only take a minute or two. Serve sauce on the side with the chicken. Serves 4

Note: Cooking the chicken on a rack elevated above the wine and chicken broth allows the skin to brown nicely while the steam formed from the liquids in the roasting pan keeps the flesh very moist without the necessity of basting while cooking.

Chicken Piccata with Kalamata Olives

INGREDIENTS

1 lb. thinly sliced chicken breast meat (4 pieces)

Herbamare® or salt and black pepper for sprinkling on chicken breasts

2 tbsp. extra-virgin olive oil

4 tbsp. unsalted butter

¼ cup dry vermouth (or dry white wine)

1 tbsp. fresh lemon juice

¼ cup pitted Kalamata olives, thinly sliced horizontally

1 tbsp. finely chopped fresh flat-leaf (Italian) parsley

PREPARATION

Place each chicken piece (one at a time) between 2 pieces of wax paper and gently pound with a flat metal meat pounder until each chicken piece is approx. ¼ inch thick. Pat the chicken dry, and sprinkle each side with Herbamare® and black pepper.

Heat the oil and 2 tbsp. of the butter in a large heavy skillet over moderately high heat until the foam subsides. Add chicken breast (2 pieces at a time) and cook, turning once, until golden and just cooked through, approx. 1 minute per side. As the chicken is cooked, transfer to a plate and keep warm covered with aluminum foil.

Pour off fat from skillet, but do not wipe or clean skillet. Remove skillet from heat and add vermouth (or wine) to the skillet. Return to heat and bring to a boil, stirring and scraping up any brown bits from the bottom, for 30 seconds. Stir in the lemon juice and remaining 2 tbsp. of butter. Reduce heat to low, and cook, stirring occasionally, just until the butter has melted. Remove pan from heat and stir in the slivered olives and the parsley. Place chicken on serving plates and spoon sauce over. Serves 2–3

Herbs/Seasonings - Fresh vs. Dried

It is generally easy these days to purchase fresh herbs in grocery stores, if you are not so fortunate as to have the ability to grow your own. In many recipes, the difference in taste and quality that results from using fresh herbs is significant. However, there are also many recipes that do not suffer tremendously, if at all, by using dried herbs and spices. In fact, some recipes specify dried herbs as the preferred ingredient choice. If any recipe in this book specifies "fresh," take it to heart, and know by using dried herbs, the flavor will be compromised.

Sometimes you do not have a choice because the fresh herb you need is not available. So here is the scoop on converting fresh to dried: whatever amount is specified for fresh herbs, cut it in half if you are using dried. For example: **1 tbsp. fresh thyme =1½ tsp. dried thyme**

Dried herbs and seasonings do not have an indefinite shelf life. I can't give a specific rule of thumb as to when you should toss that bottle of herbs and replace it with a new one, but in general, if you unscrew the top and you do not get an immediate pleasant aroma that signals the flavor of the herb/seasoning being used, then there's a good chance it is past its prime. Another possible sign that something is past its prime is when you pull it from the shelf and it is covered with a quarter inch of dust.

Chicken Breasts Stuffed with Goat Cheese & Basil

INGREDIENTS

2 boneless skinless chicken breasts (6–8 oz. each)

Chopped fresh basil to equal 2 <u>generous</u> tbsp. (must use fresh basil)

2½ oz. from a log of Chevre (goat cheese)

Herbamare® or salt and black pepper for sprinkling on chicken

1 tbsp. extra-virgin olive oil

3 tbsp. cold salted butter

⅓ cup chicken broth

½ cup dry vermouth

PREPARATION

Cut a 3-inch wide pocket horizontally halfway through the thickness of each breast. Cut toward the thicker side, until the pocket reaches to about ½ inch from the thicker side. Insert one generous tbsp. of chopped fresh basil into the pocket, then 1 ¼ oz. of the Chevre. Tuck the top edge of each pocket inward and fold the tenderloin edge over the pocket like the flap of an envelope. Seal the edges securely with toothpicks. Sprinkle both sides of the breasts with Herbamare® and black pepper.

Heat the olive oil and 1 tbsp. of the butter in a heavy skillet over medium-high heat. When the butter is very hot, add the stuffed breasts, sealed side down, and cook until golden brown, approx. 3 minutes per side. Reduce the heat to low and add the chicken broth. Cover and cook an additional 10 minutes. If you are unsure whether the chicken is thoroughly cooked, carefully make a cut at the thickest portion of the unstuffed top of the breast and assure it is no longer pink. Remove the chicken to a plate and cover with aluminum foil to keep warm.

Increase the heat to moderately high and add the vermouth. Bring to a boil and cook until reduced by about half, approx. 4–5 minutes. Remove from the heat and whisk in the remaining 2 tbsp. of butter (_assure the butter is very cold_) until incorporated. Spoon the sauce over each chicken breast and serve immediately. Serves 2

Chicken Breasts Sautéed with Mushrooms *(my friend Nathalie would say "Blancs de Volaille aux Champignons de Paris")*

INGREDIENTS

2 tbsp. grapeseed oil

2 tbsp. butter

10 oz. white button mushrooms

½ cup chopped shallots

1 lb. boneless skinless chicken tenders

Herbamare® or salt and black pepper for sprinkling on chicken

½ cup chicken broth

½ cup medium-dry sherry

1 tsp. flour

½ cup crème fraîche (or sour cream)

1 tbsp. chopped fresh chives

1 tbsp. chopped fresh tarragon

1 tbsp. chopped fresh Italian flat-leaf parsley

1½ tsp. dried chervil

Brown rice to accompany (cooked according to package directions)

PREPARATION

Heat the oil and butter in a large skillet over medium heat. Cut off the mushroom stems so they are even with the mushroom cap (don't remove the whole stem). Cut the mushrooms into quarters. When the oil and butter are sizzling, add the mushrooms and shallots and sauté until they just begin to soften. Push to the edge of the skillet and add the chicken tenders, which have been generously sprinkled on both sides with Herbamare® and black pepper. Cook until golden brown on both sides, approx. 4 minutes per side.

Reduce the heat to low, add the broth and sherry and stir to mix in the mushrooms and shallots. Cover the skillet and cook the chicken for about 5–10 minutes per side, or until the chicken is cooked through (feels springy to the touch). Remove the chicken from the skillet and put on a plate covered with foil to keep warm.

Whisk the tsp. of flour into the sauce and simmer, stirring occasionally, for several minutes. The sauce should be slightly thickened. Whisk in the crème fraîche, increase the heat to moderately high and continue to cook the sauce for 3–5 additional minutes. The sauce should at this point be thickened a bit more, and slightly reduced.

Add all of the herbs to the sauce and stir to combine. Return the chicken to the skillet and reheat chicken for a minute or two. Place brown rice on serving plates, top with chicken and a very generous amount of the mushroom sauce spooned over each portion. Serves 2–3

Chicken Breasts & Artichoke Hearts

INGREDIENTS

Juice of 1 lemon (approx. 2–3 tbsp.)

1 9-oz. can artichoke hearts, drained and rinsed

2 tbsp. extra-virgin olive oil

2 tbsp. butter (1 of the tbsp. softened separately to room temperature)

1 lb. skinless boneless chicken breast tenders, patted dry with paper towels

Herbamare® or salt and black pepper for sprinkling on chicken tenders

1 cup chopped leeks (white part only) – assure leeks are rinsed well to remove any grit

5 large cloves garlic, finely chopped

¼ cup dry vermouth

½ cup chicken broth

½ cup drained sun-dried tomatoes (packed in olive oil), sliced thin

1 tbsp. unbleached all-purpose flour

2 tbsp. minced fresh basil leaves

PREPARATION

Fill a medium bowl half full of water and add the lemon juice. Trim the end off of each artichoke heart (should only remove about ¼ inch) and cut each one in half. Add the artichokes to the lemon water and set aside.

Heat one tbsp. of the olive oil and one tbsp. butter in a large, heavy, non-stick skillet over moderately high heat until hot but not smoking. Sprinkle both sides of the chicken tenders with Herbamare® and pepper and brown the chicken on both sides (approx. 3-5 minutes per side). Remove tenders from the skillet, put on a plate, and cover with foil to keep warm.

Add the second tbsp. of olive oil to the skillet, reduce heat to low and cook the leeks, stirring, for a couple of minutes, or until just softened. Remove artichoke hearts from the lemon water and pat dry. Push leeks to one side of the skillet and add artichoke hearts, cut side down, and sauté until lightly browned. Add chopped garlic and stir gently to combine all ingredients.

Add the vermouth, chicken broth and sun-dried tomatoes to the skillet and return the chicken to the skillet. Simmer the mixture, covered, for approx. 10–15 minutes, or until the chicken is just cooked through, and springy to the touch. Once again remove chicken from the skillet and return to a plate and cover with foil.

Combine the flour with the softened tbsp. of butter to make a *beurre manié* and whisk it into the sauce and simmer for about 2 minutes. Stir in the basil and spoon sauce over the chicken tenders. Serves 2–3

Salads & Dressings

There are many salad dressings on the market that are extremely tasty. However, making your own salad dressing is pretty easy, and freshly made salad dressing will always be better than something out of a jar or bottle.

An example of something you can do to make a salad more special is to place some stuffed egg halves on the salad serving plate along the sides. Some great recipes for deviled/stuffed eggs appear in the "Appetizer" section. Another idea is to place Goat Cheese Croutons on the sides of the salad plate (see p. 32).

A very important factor when preparing any salad: A terrific salad can be ruined by dousing it with too much dressing. Conversely, there should be enough dressing on the salad so that each bite allows you to enjoy and savor the flavor of the dressing. I have been in some very good restaurants where I had to wonder if they had forgotten to add the salad dressing because it was so sparse. I firmly believe that the best way to get the correct amount of dressing on a salad, and to have it evenly distributed, is to toss the salad gently with your hands. Here's what you do: Wash hands thoroughly. Place all salad ingredients in the bowl (without dressing). Add a small amount of dressing and begin tossing with hands. Continue to add more dressing until you discern that all salad ingredients are coated very LIGHTLY but thoroughly with the dressing. Have salad plates separated and handy. With hands, remove ingredients from salad bowl and put on individual plates. Doing this by hand also allows you to more evenly distribute the ingredients.

Getting massages from Pat in front of the fire! – Priceless!

Testimonial

As a landscape designer, I strive to make my clients' garden spaces a delight for their senses – places to be connected, inspired, and live in the moment. The recipes in Sue's wonderful cookbook do the very same thing.

If you read Sue's stories and prepare the memorable dishes she presents with humor and love, you will also be transported: perhaps to a quaint bistro in Paris, or an off the beaten path that brings you to a Neapolitan restaurant in Italy, or your own mother's kitchen. Wherever you end up, you will be glad that you chose Sue Cassidy as your guide to culinary fun and adventure – where your senses will quiver and tingle.

Bob Busick
Owner and Principal Designer, Bay Haven Landscapes, LLC
Colonial Beach, VA

Spinach Salad with Parmesan Dressing

INGREDIENTS

6-oz. bag fresh spinach, baby leaves

¼ cup thinly sliced red onions

3 bacon strips, cooked and crumbled

1 cup very thinly sliced mushrooms

¼ cup grated Parmesan cheese

Dressing:

⅔ cup extra-virgin olive oil

2 tbsp. fresh lemon juice

½ tsp. salt

⅛ tsp. pepper

1 tbsp. grated Parmesan cheese

⅛ tsp. sugar

⅛ tsp. paprika

¼ tsp. dry mustard

1 clove garlic, minced

PREPARATION

Early in the day (flavor of salad dressing is vastly improved if it sits for at least 8 hours before serving): Mix all dressing ingredients together in small plastic container with lid and whisk until thoroughly combined. Cover and refrigerate until ready to toss salad.

Right before serving, put remaining salad ingredients in a bowl. Toss with about ½ cup of the dressing. Serves 2 to 4

Spinach Salad

INGREDIENTS

4 slices bacon

2 small shallots, chopped coarsely (approx. ⅓ cup)

3 tbsp. olive oil

3 tbsp. red-wine vinegar

¼ tsp. salt

⅛ tsp. black pepper

1 package (6 oz.) baby leaf spinach

½ cup thinly sliced fresh mushrooms

2 hard-boiled large eggs, chopped

PREPARATION

Cook bacon in a medium skillet until crisp and drain well on paper towels. Pour off all but approx. 1 tbsp. of bacon fat in skillet. Add shallots and olive oil to skillet and cook over moderately high heat until shallots are softened and lightly browned, stirring occasionally. Remove skillet from heat and add vinegar, stirring to scrape up any brown bits. Stir in salt and pepper.

Place spinach, fresh mushrooms, bacon (crumbled into small pieces), and chopped eggs in a salad bowl. Pour warm salad dressing from skillet into bowl, toss with hands, and serve immediately. Serves 4

Mediterranean Tuna Salad

INGREDIENTS

⅓ cup mayonnaise

2 tbsp. fresh lemon juice

1 12-oz. can chunk light tuna, packed in water, well drained

½ cup finely chopped drained bottled roasted red peppers

¼ cup chopped Kalamata olives

½ cup chopped celery

3 tbsp. finely chopped red onion

¼ tsp. Herbamare®

⅛ tsp. black pepper

PREPARATION

Combine the mayonnaise and lemon juice until all lemon juice is incorporated. Add remaining ingredients and stir together gently until well combined.

Serve either on bread of choice (pita is good) with lettuce leaves if desired, or serve on bed of lettuce leaves of choice on a plate. Serves 4

Poppy Seed & Red Beet Vinaigrette Salad

Adapted from Gourmet magazine, Condé Nast Publications

INGREDIENTS

1 medium red onion, coarsely chopped

5 medium cooked red beets (canned or fresh)

3 tbsp. water

2 tbsp. red-wine vinegar

1½ tbsp. sugar (preferably organic)

1½ tsp. dry mustard

1 tbsp. poppy seeds

½ tsp. salt

¼ tsp. black pepper

¼ cup olive oil

8 oz. mixed baby leaf lettuces (for example, baby romaine, tango, radicchio)

3 tbsp. toasted pine nuts

3 tbsp. dried cranberries or currants

¾ cup crumbled Gorgonzola cheese

PREPARATION

In a mini-food processor pulse together chopped onion, 3 beets, and water until smooth. Transfer the mixture to a fine-mesh sieve set over a bowl and press on the solids with a spoon to extract as much liquid as possible (it will be thickened). Rub the spoon along the back of the sieve to get any pulp that made its way through the sieve. Discard the solids remaining in the sieve. Add the vinegar, sugar, mustard, poppy seeds, salt and pepper to the beet mixture, whisking until well combined. Add the olive oil, slowly in a stream, continuing to whisk until the oil is incorporated and emulsified.

Slice remaining 2 beets thinly, and cut each slice in half. Place beets, lettuce, pine nuts, cranberries (or currants) and Gorgonzola cheese in a large bowl. Toss gently with enough of the dressing to coat well but lightly. Serves 4

Buttermilk Dressing with Herbs

INGREDIENTS

1 cup well-shaken buttermilk (low-fat OK)

½ cup mayonnaise

2 tbsp. extra-virgin olive oil

2 tbsp. fresh lemon juice

1 large garlic clove

2 tbsp. chopped fresh chives

1 tbsp. chopped fresh flat-leaf parsley

¼ tsp. Herbamare® or salt

¼ tsp. ground white pepper

PREPARATION

Place all ingredients in a mini-food processor or blender and blend until smooth. Dressing will keep, covered and refrigerated, for one week.

Sue's Tips:

When I was working long hours at my full-time job, one of the most rewarding times of my day was when my husband came in the door after his work day ended and emoted, "It smells absolutely fabulous in here! What's for dinner?" When something great is cooking everybody wants to come home. The aromas awaken the olfactory senses, but more important, they silently speak the words, "I care for your well-being by preparing delicious food for you. Sharing this food with you is one of the best ways to demonstrate my love for you."

Creamy Roasted Garlic Vinaigrette

INGREDIENTS

1 cup extra-virgin olive oil

8 garlic cloves, peeled

¼ cup rice vinegar

1 tbsp. Dijon mustard

½ tsp. salt

¼ tsp. white pepper

PREPARATION

Heat the olive oil in a small saucepan over low heat. Add the garlic, making sure the cloves are fully submerged, and cook for 8 to 10 minutes, or until the garlic cloves are soft and begin to turn a light caramel color. *Be careful not to cook the garlic beyond this point, or they will begin to harden and will not be able to be easily and completely mashed to make the dressing.* Remove the oil from the heat and cool to room temperature.

When the garlic and oil have cooled, in a bowl combine the vinegar and Dijon mustard and whisk until blended. Remove the garlic cloves from the oil and add the oil in a thin, steady stream to the vinegar and mustard mixture, whisking continuously, to create an emulsion. Mash the soft garlic cloves into a paste and whisk into the dressing. Season with salt and pepper and chill the dressing until ready to serve.

Note: This dressing is very good on a salad of Bibb lettuce and cherry tomatoes served with goat cheese croutons on the side. (Recipe located in "Bread" Section).

Makes approx. 1½ cups of dressing

Sue always appreciates my help when she's wrapping her Christmas gifts.

Waldorf Salad with Cranberries & Chicken

Toni made this salad frequently because when we were youngsters my sister and I preferred salads that were sweet. This is a very traditional salad, but I've never tasted any that was better than the way it was prepared by mamma mia.

INGREDIENTS

½ cup mayonnaise

¼ cup sour cream

1½ tbsp. fresh lemon juice

3 tbsp. honey

2 apples, unpeeled and cored, cut into small cubes to equal at least 2 cups

1¼ cups chopped celery

½ cup dried cranberries Note: Traditional waldorf salad normally includes raisins – if desired substitute raisins for the cranberries, or use half raisins and half cranberries

½ cup chopped toasted walnuts

2 cups shredded cooked chicken (white/breast meat)

PREPARATION

Place mayonnaise, sour cream, lemon juice and honey in a bowl and stir to combine well. Add the apples, celery, cranberries, nuts and chicken and stir gently to coat evenly with the dressing. Chill for about an hour before serving.

Christmas in York, PA, 1976
Mutual Admiration Society

Blue Cheese Dressing

INGREDIENTS

¼ cup mayonnaise

¼ cup sour cream

4 oz. blue cheese, crumbled

Juice from half a lemon (1½ to 2 tbsp.)

2 tbsp. finely chopped fresh chives

¼ tsp. salt

¼ tsp. black pepper

2 tbsp. milk (low-fat milk is fine if desired)

PREPARATION

Whisk together all ingredients except for the milk in a small bowl. Add all or as much of the milk as you desire to get the dressing to the desired consistency.

Note: This dressing is also great as a dip for raw/fresh vegetables. When using as a dip, I would not add any milk for a thicker consistency. Makes enough dressing for 4 salads

Creamy Basil Dressing

INGREDIENTS

1 cup loosely packed fresh basil leaves

2 tbsp. (generous) chopped shallots

2 tbsp. balsamic vinegar

½ tsp. salt

¼ tsp. black pepper

4 tbsp. mayonnaise

6 tbsp. extra-virgin olive oil

PREPARATION

Rinse basil leaves well and pat with paper towels. Blend basil and all remaining ingredients in a mini-food processor until smooth.

Dressing is especially good on a simple salad of mixed Italian greens, tomatoes, and sliced mushrooms. This amount of dressing is enough for 6–8 salads, depending on the size. Dressing will keep, covered and chilled, for 1 day, so it can be made ahead.

Tuna Salad Sue Chef

INGREDIENTS

½ cup chopped scallions, white part only

2 medium sized ribs of celery, small dice

2 tbsp. minced fresh parsley leaves

1½ tsp. dried dill, crumbled

1 12-oz. can solid white tuna, packed in water, drained

⅓ cup ricotta cheese (low-fat OK)

⅓ cup mayonnaise

1 tbsp. Dijon-style mustard

1 tbsp. small capers, drained

1 generous tbsp. fresh lemon juice

PREPARATION

In a bowl toss together the first four ingredients (a fork works well for better distribution). Add the tuna and toss until tuna is coated well, breaking up the tuna into small pieces. Add the ricotta cheese, mayonnaise, mustard, capers, and lemon juice. Combine ingredients well and chill for at least one hour before serving.

Note: Tuna salad sandwiches were a frequent inclusion in my lunch box when I was in grade school. I loved the way my mother made tuna salad, and it was simpler than my recipe. She combined chopped celery, hard-boiled eggs, tuna, mayonnaise and a little salt and pepper. Yummy

Asparagus Vinaigrette Salad

INGREDIENTS

6 tbsp. extra-virgin olive oil

2 tbsp. fresh lemon juice

1 tsp. Herbamere® or salt

¼ tsp. black pepper

1 large clove garlic, minced

2 tbsp. minced sweet pickles

1 generous tbsp. finely chopped scallions (white part)

2 tbsp. finely chopped sweet yellow bell pepper

1 tbsp. chopped capers

1 tbsp. finely chopped fresh parsley

2 lbs. fresh asparagus, trimmed, washed, steamed until just tender, and chilled

Boston lettuce leaves

PREPARATION

Combine all ingredients above except for the asparagus and the lettuce leaves. Mix well and chill in a covered container.

When ready to serve, place the desired amount of lettuce leaves on each of six salad plates, top with asparagus (evenly divide cooked and chilled asparagus among the plates), and spoon the dressing evenly over each portion. Serves 6

Spinach Salad with Bacon, Dates & Feta Dressing

Adapted from Gourmet magazine, Condé Nast Publications

INGREDIENTS

1 6-oz. bag baby leaf spinach

4 slices bacon, cooked until crisp and crumbled

½ of a small red onion, thinly sliced

⅓ cup chopped dates

Dressing:

½ cup crumbled feta cheese

2 tbsp. fresh lemon juice

1 tbsp. water

2 tbsp. mayonnaise

3 tbsp. extra-virgin olive oil

PREPARATION

In a mini-food processor blend together all dressing ingredients except for the olive oil. Then add the oil and blend until thoroughly incorporated and emulsified.

In a large bowl toss together (preferably by hand) the spinach, crumbled bacon, sliced onions, and dates with the feta dressing. Salad ingredients should be well but lightly coated with the dressing. Serves 4

Romaine Lettuce with Strawberries & Pecans

INGREDIENTS

¼ cup extra-virgin olive oil

¼ cup raspberry vinegar

½ tbsp. sugar (preferably organic)

¼ tsp. hot sauce

¼ tsp. salt

⅛ tsp. black pepper

¼ tsp. cinnamon

1 head romaine lettuce

1½ cup fresh strawberries, stemmed and quartered

½ cup thinly sliced red onion

⅓ cup coarsely chopped toasted pecans

½ avocado, sliced, for garnish (optional)

PREPARATION

Combine the first 7 ingredients and whisk until well combined. Cover and refrigerate for 2 hours.

Separate romaine lettuce leaves and rinse thoroughly. Shake dry and tear by hand into bite-size pieces and place in a salad bowl. Add strawberries, red onion and pecans and toss gently. Pour on a sufficient amount of dressing to coat thoroughly but lightly and toss gently by hand. If desired, arrange slices of avocado on each salad plate as a garnish. Serves 4

Bacon

I don't know a whole lot of people who don't love or at least really like bacon. I was reading a book recently given to me by my beloved niece, Liz, called "eat pray love" by Elizabeth Gilbert – great book – in which she mentions having a friend who is a vegetarian, "except for bacon." That totally cracked me up.

As much as I love bacon, I think it is revolting if undercooked, and served flaccid and greasy. Plus, the more grease and fat that is removed from bacon the more healthful.

Here is how my mother made bacon, and while it takes a bit longer than baking in the oven or zapping in a microwave, it produces the best results. Put bacon in a single layer in a large heavy fry pan. Cook over moderately low heat, turning frequently, until the bacon is totally browned, and NO translucent, fatty portions remain. Remove from skillet and place on a double layer of paper towels in a single layer. IMMEDIATELY blot the bacon very thoroughly (press down hard) with additional paper towels, removing as much grease as possible. You have to do this right away, because if you wait, blotting the bacon will cause it to break into pieces.

Spinach & Bacon Salad

INGREDIENTS

1 medium clove garlic

¼ tsp. salt

2 tbsp. extra-virgin olive oil

2 tbsp. sour cream

2 tbsp. fresh lemon juice

1 tsp. dark brown sugar

5 oz. baby spinach leaves (or 5 oz. mixed baby greens)

3 bacon slices, cooked until crisp and blotted with paper towels to remove excess grease

3 tbsp. (generous) Parmesan cheese

PREPARATION

Mince garlic clove and mash to a paste with the salt. In a small bowl, whisk together the olive oil, sour cream, lemon juice, sugar, and garlic paste. Refrigerate until ready to use.

Place the spinach (or greens) in a large bowl and crumble the bacon over the greens. Add Parmesan and some of the dressing. Toss until the greens are evenly and lightly coated, and add additional dressing as necessary. Serves 4

Vivacious Vinaigrette

INGREDIENTS

¾ cup extra-virgin olive oil

2 tbsp. red wine vinegar

2 tbsp. balsamic vinegar

2 tbsp. fresh lemon juice

1 tbsp. minced garlic cloves

¼ cup shredded fresh basil leaves

2 tbsp. Dijon mustard (grainy or smooth)

¼ tsp. Herbamare® or salt

¼ tsp. black pepper

PREPARATION

Put all ingredients in a blender or mini-food processor and pulse/blend until smooth. Use over whatever ingredients your salad heart desires.

Makes approx. 1 cup

Southwestern Salad

Adapted from Gourmet magazine, Condé Nast Publications

INGREDIENTS

8 oz. mixed soft leaf lettuces (spring mix is a good option or your preference)

1 cup crumbled Feta cheese

1 red bell pepper, roasted, then seeded and cut into thin strips (see p. 213)

2 large garlic cloves, minced in garlic press

1 tsp. anchovy paste

2 tsp. ground cumin

Juice of one lime, or approx. 3 tbsp.

¾ tsp. Tabasco sauce

2 tbsp. mayonnaise

¼ cup extra virgin olive oil

¼ cup peanut oil (plus 1 tbsp. for frying tortilla strips)

Six soft 7 inch corn tortillas, cut into thin strips

PREPARATION

In a small bowl, mash together the garlic, anchovy paste and cumin. Whisk in the lime juice, Tabasco, and mayonnaise. Slowly pour the oils into this mixture, whisking constantly, until the dressing is emulsified and the oils are completely incorporated.

Heat 1 tbsp. peanut oil in a skillet until very hot and add tortilla strips. Fry, stirring frequently, until strips are lightly browned and crispy. Drain well on paper towels and set aside.

In a large bowl combine the lettuces, Feta cheese and roasted bell pepper strips. Toss the salad with the dressing and sprinkle each individual serving liberally with the fried tortilla strips. Serves 6

Olive & Other Oils

When cooking with oil (not counting olive oil) my recipes usually specify grapeseed, sunflower, or safflower oil. All of these oils are refined to withstand high heat. One other popular cooking oil is canola oil, which is made from a European herb plant that produces seeds low in toxic acids and high in monounsaturated fatty acids. If a recipe specifies canola oil, make sure that it is only being used for sautéing at low temperatures. Cooking with canola oil at a high or moderately high temperature produces toxins that are unhealthy to consume. Grapeseed, sunflower and safflower oil can be used interchangeably with no noticeable difference in the end result. Experiment and have fun trying different lighter and healthier options to vegetable oil. Organic oils are always my preference.

Olive oil is probably the most frequently specified oil used in this cookbook, and when a recipe specifies olive oil, use olive oil. The flavor of the recipe will be compromised if a substitute is made. When you buy olive oil, assure it is "extra virgin," preferably cold-pressed. Extra virgin oils come from the first squeezing of the olives, and are pressed without using heat or chemicals, and as a result have a lower acidic content. A lower acidity level is characteristic of superior olive oil. Also, note that when olive oil is designated as being "light" this does not mean that it has fewer calories, just less flavor.

Thousand Island Dressing

INGREDIENTS

⅓ cup mayonnaise

2 tbsp. ketchup

2 tbsp. fresh lemon juice

1½ tbsp. chopped roasted red peppers (bottled OK)

1 tbsp. chopped scallions (white part)

1 tbsp. chopped pickled cucumbers

1 tbsp. minced fresh flat-leaf parsley leaves

¼ tsp. Herbamare® or salt

1 tbsp. water

PREPARATION

Place all ingredients in a mini-food processor (or blender) and blend until smooth. Refrigerate until ready to use. The dressing will keep, covered and chilled, for 1 week.

Note: This dressing is very good served with a lettuce, tomato and cucumber salad with a little chopped hard-boiled egg thrown in, or place some deviled eggs on the side of the salad plate. Makes about 1 cup of dressing.

Spinach Strawberry Salad with Honey Pecan Dressing

INGREDIENTS

6 oz. fresh baby spinach leaves, stems removed

4–5 large fresh strawberries, cored and thinly sliced

2 large fresh mushrooms, cleaned, stems removed, and thinly sliced

4 slices of bacon, cooked until very crisp and crumbled

⅓ cup chopped pecans, lightly toasted

Dressing:

⅓ cup grapeseed oil

3 tbsp. honey

1 tbsp. lemon juice

2 tsp. white wine vinegar

1 tsp. soy sauce

1 tsp. grated lemon rind

1 large garlic clove

PREPARATION

Place all dressing ingredients in a mini-food processor and blend until smooth. Chill thoroughly (at least for 1 hour) until using.

Place all remaining ingredients in a large salad bowl. Toss with dressing, assuring that the salad ingredients are evenly and lightly coated with the dressing. Serves 4

Tomato Salad with Green Goddess Dressing

INGREDIENTS

1 cup mayonnaise

1½ tsp. anchovy paste

1 tbsp. chopped scallions (white part only)

2 tbsp. chopped scallion greens

½ cup chopped fresh flat-leaf (Italian-style) parsley

¼ cup chopped fresh chives

1½ tsp. tarragon vinegar

½ tsp. dried tarragon (or 1 tsp. chopped fresh tarragon)

1 medium clove garlic (whole)

¼ tsp. Herbamare® or salt

¼ tsp. black pepper

Tomatoes

Lettuce of choice

PREPARATION

Combine all ingredients (except for tomatoes and lettuce) in a mini-food processor and blend until smooth and a pale green color. Place lettuce and sliced tomatoes on serving plates, and spoon desired amount of dressing over each serving.

This recipe makes enough salad dressing to serve 6 people

Caesar Salad *Fugetaboutit – this is the real deal*

Croutons:

3 cups sourdough bread cubes (cut into ½ to 1-inch pieces)

¼ cup extra-virgin olive oil

Salt & pepper for sprinkling on croutons

For the Salad:

1 large egg

2 garlic cloves, finely chopped

1 tsp. anchovy paste (**or** several anchovy fillets, drained & chopped)

1 tbsp. fresh lemon juice

1 tbsp. red wine vinegar

1 tsp. Worcestershire sauce

½ tsp. salt

¼ tsp. pepper

⅓ cup extra-virgin olive oil

¾ cup grated Parmigiano-Reggiano cheese

1 head romaine lettuce (about 1 ¼ lbs.), washed, dried, and torn into bite-size pieces, tough stems removed (should equal approx. 12 cups of lettuce)

PREPARATION

Preheat oven to 350 degrees. Place bread cubes on a heavy duty rimmed baking sheet and toss with the olive oil (I find this easiest to do by hand to get equal distribution). Spread cubes evenly and sprinkle croutons lightly with salt and pepper. Bake for 20 to 25 minutes or until the croutons are a deep golden brown color. Remove from oven and set aside.

Place the egg in a small saucepan and cover with cold water. Bring the water to a boil over medium heat. Cook for 1½ minutes. Drain the egg and cool under running water.

In a large bowl combine the garlic and anchovy paste (or chopped anchovies) and mash them together to combine thoroughly and form a paste. Using a whisk beat in the peeled egg, lemon juice, vinegar, Worcestershire, salt and pepper. Gradually whisk in the olive oil and ½ cup of the cheese. At this point if you are not ready to serve the salad, chill the dressing in a covered container.

When ready to serve, toss the lettuce lightly but thoroughly and evenly with the dressing (easiest and most effective if done by hand). Sprinkle with the croutons and remaining ¼ cup of cheese and toss again. Serve immediately. Serves 6

Caesar-Style Salad *Adapted from Gourmet magazine, Condé Nast Publications*

INGREDIENTS

½ cup plain yogurt (Greek-style, not low-fat)

½ tsp. anchovy paste

2 tsp. fresh lemon juice

1 tsp. balsamic vinegar

1 tsp. Dijon mustard

½ tsp. Worcestershire sauce

1 large clove garlic, minced and mashed to a paste with ¼ tsp. sea salt

¼ cup freshly grated Parmesan cheese (plus extra for sprinkling on top)

1 5-oz. package baby romaine soft lettuce leaves

4 tbsp. finely chopped red onion

1 hard-boiled egg, finely chopped

PREPARATION

In a mini food processor, blend together the yogurt, anchovy paste, lemon juice, vinegar, mustard, Worcestershire sauce, garlic paste, and Parmesan cheese. Put dressing in a small bowl, cover and refrigerate until ready to use (at least 1 hour, and up to 2 days).

Right before you are ready to serve, place romaine lettuce in a large bowl. Add dressing gradually, mixing with hands, and add a sufficient amount so that the leaves are well but lightly coated with the dressing. Divide salad evenly onto 4 serving bowls or plates, and sprinkle each serving with 1 tbsp. of red onion, and chopped egg, divided evenly.

Then sprinkle a fairly generous amount of grated Parmesan on top of each serving. Serves 4

Italian Salad Dressing

INGREDIENTS

½ cup extra-virgin olive oil

3 tbsp. minced shallots

2 tbsp. grated Parmesan cheese

1 tsp. salt

¾ tsp. Worcestershire sauce

¾ tsp. dry mustard

¾ tsp. dried basil

¾ tsp. dried oregano

¾ tsp. sugar

¾ tsp. black pepper

¼ cup red-wine vinegar

1 tbsp. fresh lemon juice

PREPARATION

In a mini-processor, combine all ingredients except for the vinegar and lemon juice. Blend for 30 seconds. Add the vinegar and lemon juice and blend for an additional 30 seconds, or until the dressing is well combined. Makes about 1 cup

Versatile Vinaigrette

INGREDIENTS

1 tbsp. Dijon-style mustard

4 tbsp. red wine vinegar

1 tsp. sugar

½ tsp. salt

½ tsp. black pepper

1 tbsp. finely chopped fresh flat-leaf parsley

1 tbsp. finely chopped fresh chives

½ cup extra-virgin olive oil

PREPARATION

Whisk together all dressing ingredients except for the olive oil.

Continue to whisk while slowly dribbling in the olive oil until the mixture thickens. Cover until ready to use. It may be necessary to whisk the dressing again before serving.

Note: This vinaigrette is best if made shortly before it is to be used. Makes approx. 1 cup

Red Leaf Lettuce with Honey-Mustard Dressing & Goat Cheese

INGREDIENTS

5–6 oz. package combination of red leaf and soft leaf lettuces

⅓ cup slivered red onions

¼ cup coarsely chopped glazed pecans

¼ cup crumbled soft mild goat cheese

Dressing:

1½ tbsp. red wine vinegar

1½ tbsp. honey

2 tsp. Dijon-style mustard

2 tbsp. finely minced red onion

⅛ tsp. salt

4 tbsp. extra-virgin olive oil

PREPARATION

For the dressing, combine the vinegar and honey in a small bowl and whisk to blend. Whisk in all of the remaining dressing ingredients and set aside.

Place lettuce and onions in a large salad bowl. Add some of the dressing and gently toss (I use my hands) to assure that the leaves are coated evenly but lightly with the dressing. Add as much dressing as needed, but don't over-dress (my mother used to tell me it was better to be over-dressed than under-dressed, but I never bought that). Add the pecans and goat cheese to the salad and toss again gently to evenly distribute. Serves 4

Taco Salad with Salsa Vinaigrette

INGREDIENTS

2 tbsp. sunflower oil (or canola oil)

1 cup chopped onion

1 large clove garlic, minced

2 tsp. ground cumin

2 tsp. chili powder

1 lb. lean ground beef

2 tbsp. tomato garlic purée (GIA® is good)

¾ tsp. salt

¼ tsp. black pepper

¼ cup canola oil

5 6-inch corn tortillas

2 heads romaine lettuce, thinly sliced crosswise (should equal approx. 8 cups)

3 large tomatoes, cut into small wedges

8 oz. grated extra-sharp Cheddar cheese

⅓ cup sliced scallions (white part)

Vinaigrette:

1 large clove garlic

3 tbsp. red wine vinegar

3 tbsp. fresh lemon juice

½ tsp. cumin

½ tsp. salt

¼ tsp. pepper

½ cup plus 2 tbsp. extra virgin olive oil

1 cup chopped seeded tomatoes

3 tbsp. chopped jalapeño chili (seeded)

½ cup loosely packed fresh cilantro leaves

PREPARATION

Heat the 2 tbsp. of oil in a large heavy skillet over moderately low heat. Add the onions, garlic, cumin, and chili powder and cook, stirring, until the onion is softened, which should take 5–10 minutes. Add ground beef to the onion/spice mixture and cook over moderate heat, breaking up lumps into small pieces, until meat is no longer pink. Remove meat with a slotted spoon to a bowl, and stir in the tomato garlic purée, salt and pepper and set aside.

Wipe out skillet with paper towels and add the ¼ cup canola oil and heat over moderately high heat until very hot. Cut the tortillas into 1-inch strips, and then cut again the other direction so that you will end up with pieces about 1 inch big. Add the tortilla pieces to the hot oil and cook, stirring frequently, until they are a deep golden color and very crispy. Remove from the skillet with a slotted spoon and put on paper towels to drain. Sprinkle the tortilla pieces with salt and set aside.

For the vinaigrette, blend the garlic, vinegar, lemon juice, cumin, salt and pepper in a blender or mini-food processor until smooth. With the motor running add the oil slowly and blend until well combined. Add the tomatoes, jalapeño, and cilantro and blend until smooth.

Place lettuce on six serving plates. Top with the beef mixture. Arrange tomato wedges around the perimeter of the dish. Sprinkle the Cheddar over top of the beef, and then top each serving with the tortilla pieces and scallions. Serve the salad with the dressing on the side, or spoon the dressing over each salad portion. Serves 6 as an entrée

Cats Rule. Dogs Drool.

Curry Chicken Salad with Chutney

INGREDIENTS

1 cup mayonnaise

3 tbsp. mango chutney (chop up any large pieces of mango)

1 tbsp. madras curry powder

1 tbsp. grated lime peel

Juice from 2 limes (to equal approx. ¼ cup)

½ tsp. salt

4 cups diced cooked breast of chicken (approx. 1 ¼ lb.)

2 cups chopped fresh pineapple

2 cups sliced seedless grapes

1½ cup chopped celery

2 tbsp. chopped scallions (white part only)

Toasted slivered almonds (for sprinkling on top)

PREPARATION

Combine mayonnaise, chutney, curry powder, lime peel, lime juice and salt in a large bowl. Toss with remaining ingredients except for almonds. Refrigerate until serving, and then sprinkle each serving generously with some toasted almonds.

Note: This salad tastes best if served the day you make it. Leftover salad will still taste good the following day, but not as good as on day one. Serves 8

Fresh Tomatoes with Vinaigrette Dressing

INGREDIENTS

5 ripe tomatoes

½ cup extra-virgin olive oil

2 tbsp. red wine vinegar

1 tbsp. (generous) chopped fresh basil

1 large garlic clove (minced)

¼ tsp. sugar

½ tsp. Worcestershire sauce

1 tsp. kosher salt

¼ tsp. black pepper

2 tbsp. finely sliced scallions (white part)

1 tbsp. finely chopped fresh Italian (flat-leaf) parsley

PREPARATION

Cut tomatoes into ¼ inch slices and arrange in a shallow serving dish. Whisk together the oil, vinegar, basil, garlic, sugar, Worcestershire, salt and pepper.

Sprinkle the scallions and parsley evenly over top of the tomatoes. Pour the dressing over all and let stand for 30 minutes to one hour before serving. Serves 4

Mozzarella & Tomato Salad

INGREDIENTS

4 large ripe tomatoes, cut into ¼ inch slices

1½ to 2 lbs. fresh mozzarella cheese, cut into ¼ inch slices

¼ cup (generous) shredded fresh basil leaves

¼ cup chopped Italian flat-leaf parsley

½ cup coarsely chopped Kalamata Olives

½ cup Versatile Vinaigrette (see p. 157)

PREPARATION

On a large serving platter, alternate overlapping slices of tomato and mozzarella cheese. Sprinkle basil, parsley and Kalamata olives over all. Spoon the vinaigrette over the salad.

Serve at room temperature. Serves 4–6

Bacon Lettuce & Tomato Salad with Basil

Adapted from Gourmet magazine, Condé Nast Publications

INGREDIENTS

½ lb. lean bacon, cooked until very crisp, drained and crumbled

1 tbsp. canola oil

4 slices sourdough bread, torn into ½ inch pieces

1 tsp. salt

½ tsp. black pepper

1 tbsp. bacon grease/drippings

1 lb. romaine lettuce, torn into bite-size pieces, rinsed and spun dry (or 2 6-oz. packages of pre-washed romaine lettuce leaves)

1 pint cherry tomatoes, halved (quartered if large)

Dressing:

1 tbsp. bacon grease/drippings

½ cup mayonnaise

2 tbsp. red wine vinegar

¼ cup (generous) finely chopped fresh basil leaves

PREPARATION

Fry the bacon until crisp. Remove from skillet to drain, and place one tbsp. of the bacon grease in a small bowl. Retain one additional tbsp. of bacon grease in the skillet and set aside. For the dressing, add remaining dressing ingredients to the bowl and whisk together with the bacon grease. Let the dressing stand, covered, at room temperature.

For croutons: Add the canola oil to the 1 tbsp. of bacon grease in the skillet. Add the bread pieces, salt and pepper. Toss until coated and cook over moderate heat, stirring, until the croutons are golden brown. Set aside on a paper towel until ready to use.

When ready to serve salad, place the romaine, crumbled bacon, tomatoes, and the croutons in a large bowl. Pour the dressing over the salad and toss until well combined. Serves 4

Greek Orzo Salad with Shrimp

Dressing:

6 large cloves of garlic

6 tbsp. dried dill

Juice of 2 lemons (to equal approx. 6 tbsp.)

6 tbsp. extra-virgin olive oil

3 tbsp. red wine vinegar

1 tsp. salt

½ tsp. black pepper

Salad:

1½ cups orzo

1 tbsp. extra-virgin olive oil

2 lbs. shrimp, peeled, deveined and steamed

8 oz. crumbled Feta cheese

2½ cups coarsely chopped and seeded fresh tomatoes

30 small pitted Kalamata olives, chopped

2 tbsp. chopped scallions (white part only)

PREPARATION

For dressing: In a mini-food processor place the whole garlic cloves and dill. Process until the garlic is minced and combined well with the dill. Scrape down the sides and add the lemon juice, olive oil, vinegar, salt and pepper. Pulse for 5 to 10 seconds or until well blended. Refrigerate until needed.

Cook the orzo according to package directions in boiling salted water – be sure not to overcook! – The orzo should be tender but not at all mushy. Place cooked orzo in a colander and rinse with cold water, then place in a large bowl and toss gently with 1 tbsp. of olive oil. Add the remaining salad ingredients to the bowl and toss gently with the dressing until all salad ingredients are as evenly coated as possible.

Cover the bowl and refrigerate until ready to serve. The salad can be prepared 3–6 hours ahead. Serves 8 to 10

Spinach Salad with Gorgonzola Croutons

INGREDIENTS

3 tbsp. crumbled Gorgonzola cheese

1 tbsp. unsalted butter, softened to room temperature

2 large slices (½ inch thick) sourdough bread

1 garlic clove

½ tsp. salt

¼ cup mayonnaise

2 tbsp. extra-virgin olive oil

2 tbsp. red wine vinegar

1 tbsp. honey

1 6-oz. package baby leaf spinach

½ cup very thinly sliced red onion

PREPARATION

Preheat oven to 375 degrees. Mash together Gorgonzola and butter in a small bowl with a fork until well combined. Spread generously and equally on bread slices. Place bread on a baking sheet and place in the lower third of the preheated oven. Bake for 15 minutes, or until golden and crisp. Remove from oven and cut into 1 inch squares.

While the croutons are baking, mince the garlic and mash it in a small bowl with the salt. Place the garlic/salt mixture into a mini-food processor and add the mayonnaise, olive oil, vinegar, and honey. Blend until smooth and set aside.

When ready to serve the salad, toss the spinach in a large bowl with the sliced onions and the warm croutons. Toss with the dressing (I use my hands) until the salad ingredients are thoroughly but very lightly coated with the dressing. Serves 3–4

Thai Beef Salad

INGREDIENTS

¾ lb. beef filet mignon, cut into ¼ inch strips

2 tbsp. grapeseed oil

½ cup finely diced red onion

3 tbsp. soy sauce

2 tbsp. minced jalapeño pepper, veins and seeds removed

3 large garlic cloves, finely chopped

1½ tbsp. finely chopped fresh gingerroot

8-oz. package fresh bean sprouts

¼ cup finely minced fresh cilantro

2 tsp. toasted Oriental sesame oil

2 tbsp. fresh lime juice

¼ tsp. cayenne

1 tbsp. sugar, preferably organic

3-4 oz. fresh baby greens (soft leaf lettuce combination)

PREPARATION

Heat one tbsp. of the oil in a large non-stick heavy skillet over moderately high heat. Add the beef strips and cook, stirring constantly, for about 30 seconds, until lightly browned and still light pink on the inside. Remove meat from skillet and set aside. Pour off liquid from skillet (do not wipe). Reduce heat to moderate and add the second tbsp. of oil, then add the onions, soy sauce, jalapeno pepper, garlic and ginger to the skillet and cook for about 5 minutes, or until the onion is softened. Add bean sprouts, cilantro, sesame oil, lime juice, cayenne and sugar to skillet. Cook for about 1 minute and remove from heat. Return beef strips to skillet and stir gently to combine ingredients well.

Place salad greens on serving plates and spoon beef/bean sprout mixture over the top. Serves 2-3

Why do I wake Sue up at 5am? Because she's there!

Sauces

When I first really got into cooking, in addition to experimenting with recipes and watching what my mother accomplished in her kitchen, I also began reading about cooking methods and processes. I felt that really good cooks rarely if ever took short cuts, especially when making sauces. However, as my career developed and my free time decreased, I changed my tune.

This is particularly true of stock, which is the liquid in which meat, meat bones, seafood, seafood bones or shells, or vegetables have been simmered. Many very good stocks or broths are now available for purchase that I find to be more than acceptable when making sauces.

Most of the sauces included in this cookbook are part of the recipes themselves, so there are a relatively small number of sauce recipes included in this section.

I mentioned before in the "Salads and Salad Dressing" section that freshly made salad dressing will always be better than something out of a jar or bottle, and the same holds true for sauces. As a good example, make your own tartar sauce (outstanding recipe included in this book) and then compare it with any bottled commercial brand, and you will find there is little resemblance between the two.

Sue never gets tired of taking my picture – can you blame her?

Testimonial

Among Sue's innumerable cooking talents, her breakfast muffins stand alone. On a scale of one to ten, the scale should go higher.

Sue started making morning muffins more frequently after Clyde became a member of the family, primarily because of Clyde's early morning wake up calls (usually in the 5AM to 6AM range). It's no secret that Clyde has Sue wrapped around his little paw. It's not enough for her to get up at the crack of dawn and feed him - - he insists upon her companionship while he is consuming his first of many meals for the day. Early hours in the kitchen presented an opportunity to experiment with additional muffin recipes, much to the delight of Sue's husband Pat and any other friends or family who had spent the night.

Our family meets for an annual summer vacation in Bethany Beach, Delaware and we all look forward to Sue's muffins that she always brings for us to enjoy. When Sue asks what kind we want her to bring it is impossible to choose because all her muffins, while very different are equally scrumptious.

Ranking right there with the muffins are Sue's fabulous cookies. The family gathers in York, PA at our home for the Christmas celebration. We always are delighted when the tins of cookies arrive (we're happy to see Sue too). The ginger cream sandwich cookies made with fresh gingerroot stand out as one of our family's all time favorites.

It was no surprise to us that Sue had decided to write a cookbook. We can't wait to host her first book-signing party!

Kristine Gross, her loving sister, & Larry, her favorite brother-in-law
Entrepreneurs (retired), former owners and managers of Cape Horn Country
York, PA

Orange Tomato Cocktail Sauce

INGREDIENTS

⅓ cup (generous) ketchup (preferably organic)

½ tsp. finely grated fresh orange zest

2 tbsp. fresh orange juice

½ tbsp. fresh lemon juice

1 generous tbsp. bottled whipped horseradish

⅛ tsp. hot sauce

PREPARATION

Stir together all ingredients until well combined. This amount of sauce is sufficient for dipping 1 to 1¼ lbs. of steamed shrimp.

Apricot Dipping Sauce

INGREDIENTS

½ cup apricot preserves

1 tbsp. water

1 tbsp. fresh lime juice

1 tbsp. soy sauce

1 tsp. Dijon mustard

1 tsp. finely minced fresh gingerroot

PREPARATION

Place all ingredients in a mini-food processor and pulse until smooth. Serve with Shrimp Tempura. Makes approx. 1 cup

Roasted Tomato-Garlic Sauce *(Adapted from "Vegetable Heaven" by Mollie Katzen)*

INGREDIENTS

3 tbsp. extra-virgin olive oil

3½ lbs. fresh ripe tomatoes (ripe, but not too ripe)

2 garlic bulbs (not small – medium to large)

1 tsp. Herbamare® or salt

1 tbsp. red wine vinegar

½ tsp. black pepper

PREPARATION

Preheat the oven to 375 degrees. Line a shallow baking tray with foil, and brush it with 1 tbsp. of the olive oil.

Cut the tomatoes in half and squeeze out and discard the seeds. Place the tomatoes cut side up on the baking sheet. Slice and discard the tips from the garlic bulbs and stand the bulbs on their bases on the tray. Drizzle the open tomatoes with the remaining 2 tbsp. of olive oil and place the tray in the oven.

Bake the tomatoes and garlic for 30 minutes. Remove from the oven and turn the tomatoes over. Carefully pour off the juices into a large bowl. Return the tray to the oven and bake an additional 30 minutes.

Cool the tomatoes to room temperature, then pull off and discard the tomato skins. Place the tomatoes in the bowl with the reserved tomato juice. Break the garlic bulbs up into cloves and squeeze the pulp from each clove into the bowl with the tomatoes. Use an immersion blender to purée the ingredients together until smooth. Add Herbamare®, vinegar and pepper. Cover and refrigerate until ready to use.

Note: This sauce keeps for up to two weeks if tightly covered and refrigerated.

I love it when a catnip toy can double as a body pillow.

Fresh Tomato Sauce with Thyme

INGREDIENTS

4 tbsp. extra-virgin olive oil

¼ lb. (8 tbsp.) butter

3 cups finely chopped onion

4 large cloves garlic, finely chopped

2 tsp. chopped fresh thyme leaves

2 tsp. sugar, preferably organic

2 bay leaves

1 tsp. Herbamare® or salt

½ tsp. black pepper

4 cups seeded chopped fresh tomatoes

12 tbsp. tomato paste Note: I prefer using "Double Concentrated Tomato Paste" that you buy in a tube – a very good brand is Amore®

PREPARATION

Heat the olive oil and 4 tbsp. of the butter in a large saucepan, add the onion and garlic and cook over low heat, stirring occasionally, until the onion is softened. Add all remaining ingredients (except for the remaining 4 tbsp. of butter) and simmer, stirring occasionally, for 20–30 minutes. Set aside until ready to use.

Right before serving, return the sauce to the heat and add the remaining 4 tbsp. of butter. Cook until the sauce is reheated and the butter is melted. Makes about 4 cups

---

Pesto

INGREDIENTS

2 tsp. extra-virgin olive oil

¼ cup pine nuts

1 cup coarsely chopped fresh basil leaves

⅓ cup grated Parmigiano-Reggiano cheese

2 large garlic cloves, finely chopped (to equal approx. 1 tbsp.)

1 tbsp. water

¼ tsp. salt

⅛ tsp. black pepper

¼ cup extra-virgin olive oil

PREPARATION

Heat 2 tsp. of olive oil in a small skillet over moderate heat. Add pine nuts and cook, stirring, until nicely browned. Pine nuts tend to brown quickly, so keep a close watch to assure they do not burn. Set aside.

Place basil, pine nuts (removed from skillet with a slotted spoon), Parmesan, chopped garlic, water, salt and pepper in a mini-food processor and pulse until finely chopped and well blended. With the motor running, add the olive oil in a slow stream and blend until combined well.

Note: If refrigerated, bring to room temperature before serving.

Béchamel Sauce

INGREDIENTS

3 tbsp. unsalted butter

2 tbsp. unbleached all-purpose flour

1 cup whole milk

½ tsp. salt

¼ tsp. white pepper

⅛ tsp. ground nutmeg

PREPARATION

Melt the butter in a small heavy saucepan. Sprinkle in the flour and cook over low heat, whisking constantly, for 5 minutes. Do not allow to brown!

Meanwhile, bring the milk to a boil in a separate small saucepan, and when it reaches a boil, remove the butter and flour mixture from the heat and pour in the boiling milk all at once. As the mixture boils and bubbles beat it with a whisk until the bubbling stops.

At this point, return the pan to the stove and cook over medium heat until the sauce again comes to a boil, stirring constantly, for 5 minutes. Whisk in the salt, white pepper and nutmeg. If not using right away, place in a covered container and refrigerate. Makes approx. 1 cup of thick sauce

Sun-Dried Tomato Pesto

INGREDIENTS

¼ cup sun-dried tomatoes, packed in oil, lightly drained

¼ cup + 2 tbsp. chopped fresh Italian (flat-leaf) parsley

3 tbsp. sliced pitted Kalamata olives

1½ tsp. red wine vinegar

2 cloves garlic, peeled and cut in half

1 medium shallot peeled and cut in quarters

¼ tsp. salt

1½ tsp. black pepper

1 tbsp. extra-virgin olive oil

PREPARATION

Place all ingredients except for olive oil in a mini-food processor and pulse until all ingredients are smooth and well combined. Add olive oil and continue to process until the oil is incorporated.

Note: This pesto is used as an ingredient in Pesto Deviled Eggs.

Eggplant & Sausage Sauce
Adapted from Gourmet magazine, Condé Nast Publications

INGREDIENTS

1 1-lb eggplant

1 tsp. salt

¼ cup extra-virgin olive oil

3 cups chopped sweet yellow onions

¾ lb. Italian spicy hot sausage (pork or chicken)

1 large red bell pepper, chopped

2 lbs. tomatoes, seeded and chopped

1 cup chicken broth

½ cup dry vermouth, or other white wine

1½ tsp. dried oregano

½ tsp. salt

⅓ cup (generous) minced fresh Italian-style (flat-leaf) parsley

5 large garlic cloves, finely chopped

½ tsp. black pepper

½ to 1 lb. of pasta (your choice – I like to serve this sauce with extra-thin spaghetti noodles or angel hair pasta

Parmesan cheese (grated) for sprinkling generously on top of each serving

PREPARATION

Peel and trim the ends off the eggplant, and cut it into ½ inch cubes. Place in a colander and sprinkle with the tsp. of salt. After the eggplant has been in the colander for about 15 minutes and starts to soften, toss with your hands well to more evenly distribute the salt. Continue to drain in the colander for at least another 45 minutes.

In a large deep-sided skillet heat the olive oil over moderate heat and cook the onions, stirring occasionally, until they are softened and golden. Remove the casings from the sausage and tear the sausage meat into small pieces. Add the sausage to the skillet and cook over moderately high heat, breaking up the sausage into even smaller pieces as it cooks, until the sausage is lightly browned.

Remove the eggplant from the colander and place on layers of paper towels. Blot all over with additional paper towels to remove excess moisture. Add eggplant and the red pepper to the skillet and cook for about 5 minutes. Add the tomatoes, chicken broth, vermouth, oregano, and ½ tsp. salt and cook the mixture, covered, over moderately low heat for 30 minutes. Add the parsley, garlic and pepper and continue to cook the mixture, uncovered, for an additional 10–15 minutes. The mixture should be very thick.

Serve the sauce with pasta and Parmesan cheese on the side. Makes approx. 2½ to 3 cups

Fresh Tomato Sauce with Basil

INGREDIENTS

4 to 6 large ripe tomatoes (approx. 3 lbs.)

2 tbsp. extra-virgin olive oil

4 large garlic cloves, thinly sliced

1 tsp. sugar

1 tsp. Herbamare® or salt

1 tbsp. finely minced fresh Italian (flat-leaf) parsley

¼ cup dry red wine

1 tbsp. (generous) chopped fresh basil

PREPARATION

Remove cores from tomatoes and halve crosswise. With thumbs, gently remove seeds. Coarsely chop tomatoes and set aside in a bowl.

Heat the oil in a large saucepan over moderately high heat until hot but not smoking. Add garlic and cook, stirring, for about 1 minute, or just until golden. Reduce heat to moderately low and add tomatoes (with any juices that have accumulated), sugar, ½ tsp. Herbamare®, parsley, and red wine. Bring to a simmer and simmer, uncovered, stirring occasionally, for approx. 45 minutes to one hour, or until thickened.

Stir in basil and remaining ½ tsp. Herbamare and cook for an additional minute or two.

Makes approx. 2½ cups

Cooking with Wine

It is a myth that you shouldn't cook with cheap wine. If you use more expensive wine in your cooking, there will be a difference in taste, but like everything in life, individual tastes will dictate a preference as to which taste is the more pleasing. My own premise is simple: I cook with more expensive wines, because I'll be happier finishing the opened bottle.

Lots of my recipes specify "dry vermouth" as an ingredient. Whenever dry vermouth is specified, white wine can always be substituted. I specify vermouth for two reasons: I like the flavor of vermouth as a cooking ingredient and I always keep a bottle of vermouth chilled in the refrigerator (who knows when a guest will request a martini?). This means that when I need white wine for a recipe, it's readily available, and it's not necessary to open a bottle of white wine if one is not available (as if).

Green Goddess Sauce

INGREDIENTS

½ cup mayonnaise

1 clove garlic, minced

½ tsp. anchovy paste

¼ cup chopped scallion greens

¼ cup chopped fresh chives

¼ cup chopped fresh parsley (preferably flat-leaf Italian)

1 tbsp. fresh lemon juice

½ tbsp. tarragon vinegar

¼ tsp. salt

⅛ tsp. black pepper

¼ cup sour cream

PREPARATION

Blend all ingredients well. Serve with fish as an alternative to tartar sauce. Makes approx. 1 cup

Parsley & Chives

Lots of my recipes include fresh parsley. You can save a lot of time when a recipe calls for parsley by doing the following:

Buy a large bunch of fresh parsley (I almost always use the Italian flat-leaf variety), and rinse thoroughly in a colander. Pull off all of the larger stems. At this point, leave the parsley in the colander for a while until a lot of the water has evaporated. Then blot the parsley gently between paper towels until you have removed as much of the moisture as possible. In batches, mince parsley in a mini-food processor. Transfer the parsley to a freezer-proof plastic container and place in the freezer. Whenever a recipe calls for fresh parsley, pull out the container, remove the appropriate amount, and immediately stick the container back in the freezer.

The above procedure for freeze drying parsley also works beautifully for fresh chives. Fresh chives are long and thin. After rinsing and drying, you can line up a lot of them and cut horizontally all at once. Use a sharp knife and cut about 1/16th of an inch thick. You will get cute little circles by doing this. As with the parsley, immediately transfer to a freezer-proof container and place in the freezer.

Did you know that chomping on a piece of parsley is a natural breath deodorizer, and has been referred to as "nature's mouthwash?" Good to know when you've eaten a lot of garlic, which is a regular occurrence in my life.

Cilantro Mayonnaise

INGREDIENTS

1 cup mayonnaise

1 to 1¼ cups loosely packed cilantro leaves

Juice from a small lime (to equal 1½ to 2 tbsp. fresh lime juice)

2 tsp. soy sauce

1 large clove garlic

PREPARATION

Place all ingredients in a mini-food processor and blend until smooth.

Note: This is especially good on a turkey sandwich – Use toasted whole grain bread, sliced deli-style roasted turkey (smoked if desired) with lettuce and tomato – and a <u>generous</u> amount of the cilantro mayonnaise – YUM!!

Rémoulade Sauce

INGREDIENTS

⅓ cup finely chopped dill pickles (not sweet)

½ cup mayonnaise

¼ cup sour cream

3 tbsp. finely chopped fresh Italian (flat-leaf) parsley

2 tbsp. (generous) finely chopped shallots

2 tbsp. ketchup

1 tsp. Tabasco sauce

1½ to 2 tbsp. fresh lemon juice (approx. the juice of ½ lemon)

½ tsp. Herbamare® or salt

PREPARATION

Whisk together all ingredients and refrigerate until ready to use. Serve with Cajun Catfish.

Tartar Sauce

INGREDIENTS

1 cup mayonnaise

1 large clove garlic, finely chopped

¼ cup finely chopped scallions, white part only

2 tbsp. chopped sour pickle

1 tbsp. chopped capers

2 tbsp. finely chopped fresh parsley

2 tbsp. chopped fresh chives

1 tsp. Dijon mustard

1 tsp. dried tarragon (or 2 tsp. chopped fresh tarragon leaves)

1 tbsp. fresh lemon juice

¼ tsp. white pepper

PREPARATION

Combine all ingredients and chill until ready to serve. Yield: Approx. 1¼ cups.

Mustard Herb Sauce

INGREDIENTS

½ cup mayonnaise

¼ cup sour cream

1 tbsp. Dijon Mustard

½ tbsp. spicy brown or whole-grain mustard

1½ tbsp. dried dill weed

¾ tsp. dried tarragon (or 1½ tsp. fresh tarragon, finely chopped)

1 tsp. (generous) freshly grated lemon zest

PREPARATION

Stir together all ingredients and combine well. Chill until ready to serve. Serve with either poached or broiled or sautéed fish (salmon is a good choice). Makes approx. 1 cup

Sue's Tips:

If cooking is equated with having fun, as with everything in life it's all about attitude. Attitude is a choice. Scott Hamilton's victory over cancer was aided significantly by his credo: "The only true disability in life is a bad attitude."

We've all heard the phrase "slaving over a hot stove," which is nothing but a frame of mind. The care and feeding of those you love can be approached with happiness and creativity if you choose this path. I have a vision of a new generation of cooks who embrace the notion that cooking is normal and a positive experience, and that take out and fast food is not the norm.

Consider the long range beneficial effects of cooking your own meals: nurturing environment, cost benefits and better health.

Seafood

If a recipe for a fish entrée looks appealing to you but you don't like the type of fish specified, have fun, be creative, and experiment: make the recipe using fish that is more preferable. Also, you may think you do not like this type of fish because you once had it and it was prepared abominably. The first time I made my "Spicy Blackened Catfish" for my husband, Pat, after he came up for air, he asked me what kind of fish I had served, and couldn't believe when I told him it was catfish, which he previously thought was loathsome. See p.185 for more general comments about seafood.

Dogs have masters. Cats have staff.

Testimonial

Visiting D.C., my husband and I got the chance to sample many popular restaurants but no meal was as memorable as dining with Sue, her husband and Clyde. I normally control my portions with ease but with each mouthful of Sue's lasagna, I found myself savoring the taste and wanting just one more bite. I know "Cooking With Clyde" will be my most valued cookbook.

Meg Mathisen
Professional Writer
Burbank, CA

Catfish with Lemon Aioli

INGREDIENTS

¾ to 1 lb. catfish

Extra-virgin olive oil (approx. 1 tbsp.)

1 tsp. dried thyme

⅛ tsp. cayenne pepper

¼ cup mayonnaise

2 tsp. fresh lemon juice

1 medium garlic clove, minced

1 tbsp. finely chopped fresh parsley

PREPARATION

Preheat oven broiler. Lightly rub the tops of the catfish fillets with olive oil. Sprinkle thyme and cayenne on top. Broil until done (approx. 8 minutes, 6–8 inches from heat). Fish is done when it flakes easily when tested with a fork.

While fish is broiling, combine mayonnaise, lemon juice, garlic and parsley in a small serving bowl to make aioli. When fish is done, remove from broiling pan to plates for serving. Spoon a generous amount of aioli on each piece of fish, and serve the remaining sauce on the side. Serves 2–3

Salmon with Teriyaki Sauce

INGREDIENTS

1 lb. salmon fillets

3 tbsp. sherry (medium dry)

3 tbsp. light brown sugar

2 tbsp. water

2 tbsp. soy sauce

2 tbsp. sunflower oil

1½ tbsp. fresh gingerroot, minced

4 crushed garlic cloves

1 tbsp. sesame seeds

PREPARATION

In a small saucepan, combine sherry, brown sugar, water, soy sauce, oil, gingerroot, and garlic. Bring to a simmer and simmer for approx. 10 minutes, or until slightly reduced.

Preheat oven to 425 degrees. Put salmon in baking dish, and pour sauce over fish. Sprinkle sesame seeds on top of fish. Bake for 10 to 15 minutes or until fish flakes easily when tested with a fork. Serves 2–3

Swordfish with Niçoise Vinaigrette

Adapted from Gourmet magazine, Condé Nast Publications

INGREDIENTS

¼ cup finely chopped pitted Kalamata black olives

¼ cup finely chopped drained bottled roasted red pepper

3 tbsp. finely chopped fresh parsley leaves

1 tbsp. capers, chopped fine

1 tsp. anchovy paste

1 large garlic clove, finely chopped

¼ tsp. salt

2 tbsp. minced scallion, white part only

1½ tbsp. balsamic vinegar

5 tbsp. extra-virgin olive oil

2 1-inch thick swordfish steaks (about ½ lb. each)

PREPARATION

In a small serving bowl stir together the olives, roasted red pepper, parsley, capers, anchovy paste, garlic, salt, scallions, vinegar, and 3½ tbsp. olive oil. Set aside.

In a heavy non-stick skillet, heat the remaining 1½ tbsp. of the olive oil over moderately high heat until the oil is very hot but not smoking. Pat the swordfish steaks dry with paper towels, and sauté fish in the hot oil for 4–5 minutes on each side, or until they are just cooked through.

Transfer fish to plates and spoon some of the sauce over each serving. Serve the remaining sauce on the side. Serves 2–3

Glazed Salmon Fillets with Dill Mustard Sauce

Adapted from Gourmet magazine, Condé Nast Publications

INGREDIENTS

4 tbsp. white wine vinegar

¼ cup Dijon mustard

3 tbsp. firmly packed light brown sugar

½ cup grapeseed oil

1 tbsp. plus 1 tsp. soy sauce

1 generous tbsp. dried dill

1 lb. salmon fillets

PREPARATION

In a small bowl, whisk together the vinegar, mustard and brown sugar. In a slow stream, pour oil from measuring cup into this mixture, whisking continuously, until the oil is completely incorporated (emulsified).

Remove ¼ cup of this mixture to another small bowl and stir in 1 tbsp. of the soy sauce to make a glaze. Whisk dill and 1 tsp. of soy sauce into the remaining mixture to make a sauce and set aside at room temperature until ready to serve.

Preheat broiler. Rinse salmon fillets and pat dry. Arrange the fillets, skin side down, on a broiler pan or shallow broiler-safe baking dish. Spoon the glaze evenly over top of fish. Broil the salmon 4–6 inches from the heat for approx. 10 minutes, or until just cooked through. Serve the salmon with the sauce on the side. Serves 2–3

Mushroom Broiled Halibut

(Or Sea Bass) | Recipe Contributed By Nathalie Cadot, Falls Church, Va

INGREDIENTS

2 cups thinly sliced cremini mushrooms

2 tbsp. finely chopped shallots

⅓ cup mayonnaise

2 tbsp. chopped fresh parsley

1 tbsp. fresh lemon juice

1 tbsp. grated fresh gingerroot

¼ tsp. each salt and pepper

4 halibut steaks or fillets (approx. 1 to 1½ lbs.)

PREPARATION

In a bowl, mix together all ingredients except for the fish and set aside.

Place the fish skin side up on a greased rimmed broiler-safe baking dish and broil the fish for 5 minutes. Turn the fish over with a spatula, and spread the mushroom mixture evenly over the fish. Continue to broil until the mushroom mixture is golden brown and the fish flakes easily when tested with a fork, which should take an additional 5–8 minutes. Serves 3–4

Special note from Nathalie: Pouilly Fumé (a white wine) goes very well with this dish!

Baked Catfish Oriental

Adapted from Gourmet magazine, Condé Nast Publications

INGREDIENTS

3 tbsp. unsalted butter

2 tbsp. freshly grated gingerroot

3 tbsp. fresh lemon juice (or juice from half of a large lemon)

1 tsp. Oriental sesame oil

1 tsp. Dijon-style mustard

½ tsp. soy sauce

¼ tsp. cayenne pepper

¼ tsp. salt

1 lb. catfish fillets

8 scallions, sliced thinly on the diagonal, white and light green part only

2 tbsp. toasted sesame seeds (sesame seeds can be purchased already toasted)

Japanese Oriental style noodles (Somen or Soba) to accompany – 4 oz.

PREPARATION

In a small heavy skillet, cook the gingerroot in 2 tbsp. of the butter over low heat, stirring until golden (about 1 minute). Add the remaining 1 tbsp. butter and the lemon juice and cook, stirring, until the butter is melted. Stir in the sesame oil, the mustard, soy sauce, cayenne, and salt. Remove skillet from heat.

Arrange fish in a baking dish just large enough to hold in one layer. Pour sauce over the fish and sprinkle with the sliced scallions.

Preheat oven to 425 degrees. Cover baking dish loosely with aluminum foil and bake for 12-15 minutes, or until fish fillets just flake when tested with a fork. Sprinkle with sesame seeds before serving. Place each fish serving portion over noodles, cooked per package instructions. Serves 2–3

Shrimp in Malaysian Spicy Coconut Milk Sauce

Adapted from Gourmet magazine, Condé Nast Publications

INGREDIENTS

1½ tbsp. grated fresh gingerroot

1½ tsp. dried hot red pepper flakes

6 medium garlic cloves

2 tbsp. cashew nut pieces (unsalted)

1½ tsp. ground cumin

½ tsp. tumeric

1½ lbs. large shrimp

1 large red onion

2 tbsp. grapeseed oil

1 cup canned unsweetened coconut milk (good choice is Native Forest® Organic Coconut Milk)

1 tbsp. packed light brown sugar

1 tbsp. salt

2 tbsp. fresh lime juice

Brown Rice, prepared per the package directions

PREPARATION

In a mini-food processor, grate enough fresh gingerroot to measure 1½ tbsp. Keep gingerroot in the processor, and add to food processor red pepper flakes, garlic cloves, cashew nuts, cumin and tumeric. Process mixture until it is totally combined and resembles a paste.

Shell shrimp and devein; rinse in a colander, drain well and set aside. Halve the onion lengthwise, then cut halves lengthwise into julienne (thin) strips.

Heat the oil in a large heavy skillet over moderately low heat until hot. Cook the paste mixture in oil, stirring, until fragrant, for several minutes. Add the onions and cook, stirring, until they are softened. Stir in coconut milk, brown sugar and salt and bring to a low boil. Add shrimp and lime juice and cook over moderate heat, stirring occasionally, until the shrimp are just cooked through, about 5 minutes. DO NOT OVERCOOK THE SHRIMP. Serve the shrimp and sauce over brown rice. Serves 4

Trout with Lemon Caper Butter

INGREDIENTS

4 tbsp. butter, melted

Juice from half a lemon (approx. 2 tbsp.)

1 tsp. freshly grated lemon zest

1½ tbsp. capers, drained

1 lb. trout fillets, with skin

1 tbsp. grapeseed oil, plus extra for rubbing or brushing on fish

Salt (or Herbamare®), white pepper and paprika for sprinkling on fish

PREPARATION

Melt butter in very small saucepan. Remove from heat and add lemon juice and capers. Stir until smooth.

Rinse trout under cold water and pat dry thoroughly with paper towels. Brush (or rub lightly with fingers) with a small amount of grapeseed oil and sprinkle lightly with salt (or Herbamare®), pepper and paprika.

Heat the oil in a large non-stick skillet until very hot but not smoking. Add trout, skin side down, and cook for 3–5 minutes. Turn fish and cook 1 minute longer. Remove from pan, top with sauce and serve hot. Serves 2–3

Note: This recipe is good with almost any variety of fish.

If your tail stays straight for more than 8 hours, call your vet.

Shrimp Curry

INGREDIENTS

3 tbsp. butter

3 cups chopped red onions

4 large cloves garlic, finely chopped

1½ cups seeded chopped fresh tomatoes

1 large apple, peeled, cored and chopped

½ cup chopped celery

1 tbsp. unsweetened coconut

2 tbsp. chopped fresh gingerroot

13½ to 14½-oz. can of coconut milk

1 tsp. sugar, preferably organic

2 tbsp. curry powder

1½ tsp. salt

¼ tsp. black pepper

1½ lbs. medium raw shrimp, shelled and deveined

Brown rice as an accompaniment (cook according to package directions)

PREPARATION

In a large skillet heat the butter over moderate heat, add the onions and cook until softened and lightly browned. Add the garlic, tomatoes, apple, celery, coconut and fresh gingerroot and cook for another minute or two. Add the coconut milk and bring slowly to a boil.

Blend the sugar, curry powder, salt and pepper with one tbsp. of water to make a paste. Add gradually, stirring, to the boiling mixture. Reduce heat and simmer, partially covered, stirring occasionally, until the vegetables are very tender, which should take 30–45 minutes.

Remove the lid and add the raw shrimp. Cook an additional five minutes, stirring occasionally, until the shrimp are pink and just cooked through. Serve the curry over brown rice. Serves 4

Crab Cakes with Red & Green Bell Peppers

INGREDIENTS

¼ cup finely chopped red bell pepper

¼ cup finely chopped green bell pepper

3 tbsp. unsalted butter

1 large garlic clove, finely chopped

¼ cup crushed saltine crackers

1 large egg

2 tbsp. minced scallions, white part

1 tbsp. fresh lemon juice

1 tsp. Worcestershire sauce

⅛ tsp. cayenne pepper

1 tbsp. mayonnaise

½ lb. lump crab meat, picked over to remove any shells (best done by hand)

1 tbsp. grapeseed oil

2 tbsp. finely ground saltine crackers (preferably Multi Grain)

Tartar sauce as an accompaniment

PREPARATION

In a small skillet cook the bell peppers in 2 tbsp. of the butter over low heat, stirring occasionally, until peppers are softened, but not mushy. Turn off heat and stir in garlic. Transfer the mixture to a bowl, add the ¼ cup of crushed saltines, the egg, scallions, lemon juice, Worcestershire sauce, the cayenne, and the mayonnaise and combine the mixture well. Add the crab meat and stir gently, until the mixture is just combined.

Cover the mixture and let it stand for 10 minutes. In a large heavy non-stick skillet, heat the oil and the remaining 1 tbsp. of butter over moderately high heat until very hot and the foam from the butter has subsided. When the butter and oil have reached the right temperature, form the mixture into four crab cakes and coat lightly with the remaining 2 tbsp. finely ground saltines. Note: Do not be concerned that the crab cakes do not appear to be holding together very well as you form them. This is because they do not have a lot of "filler" stuff, which is a good thing. Form the cakes one at a time with your hands, coat with the ground saltines, and immediately put each crab cake into heated skillet. Once they start to cook, they will hold together fine.

Cook crab cakes until deep golden brown on bottom side (approx. 5 minutes), then very carefully turn crab cakes with a spatula and continue to cook until nicely browned on the other side. Serve the crab cakes with tartar sauce (see p. 169). Serves 2–3

Salmon with Red Wine & Orange Butter Sauce

Adapted from Gourmet magazine, Condé Nast Publications

INGREDIENTS

Juice squeezed from 1 orange (or ¼ cup)

½ cup full-bodied dry red wine

¼ cup chopped shallots

2 tbsp. balsamic vinegar

1 tsp. tomato paste

1 Turkish bay leaf

1 generous tbsp. grated orange rind

4 tbsp. unsalted butter, softened

½ tsp. salt

1 lb. salmon fillets

Olive oil

PREPARATION

Combine orange juice, wine, shallots, vinegar, tomato paste and bay leaf in a small heavy saucepan. Slowly bring mixture to a boil over moderate heat and then boil for 20–30 minutes, or until mixture is reduced to approx. ⅓ cup. Remove from heat and discard bay leaf. With a whisk, incorporate orange rind, butter and salt. Set sauce aside until you are ready to broil the fish.

Preheat broiler: Place fish in foil-lined broiler pan or broiler-proof shallow baking dish. Rub top of salmon all over gently with olive oil. Broil fish approx. 6–8 inches from the heat until just cooked through and lightly browned on top, approx. 10 minutes. Spoon the sauce on salmon before serving. Serves 2–3

Salmon Cakes

INGREDIENTS

1 salmon fillet (¾ lb.)

2 tsp. grapeseed oil

Herbamare® or salt and black pepper for sprinkling on salmon

4 tbsp. unsalted butter

1½ tbsp. finely chopped fresh gingerroot

½ cup diced sweet yellow onion

½ cup finely diced celery

½ cup finely diced red bell pepper

½ cup mayonnaise

1 tbsp. fresh lemon juice

¼ tsp. cayenne pepper

1 tsp. minced fresh thyme leaves

1 tbsp. snipped fresh chives

1½ tbsp. minced fresh flat-leaf parsley

2 tbsp. grapeseed oil

¾ cup panko (Japanese bread crumbs) – I like Sushi Chef® made by Baycliff Company

PREPARATION

Preheat the oven to 250 degrees. Place the salmon in a shallow baking dish, rub the salmon all over with the grapeseed oil, and sprinkle Herbamare® and pepper on the salmon to season. Bake the fish until the fat between the layers turns opaque, and the fish flakes when pierced with a knife, which should take no more than 20 to 25 minutes. Remove from the oven and set aside to cool.

In a nonstick skillet melt 2 tbsp. of the butter over moderate heat. Add the gingerroot, onion, celery and red bell pepper and sauté, stirring frequently, until the vegetables are softened but not browned. Add ½ tsp. Herbamare® (or salt) and ⅛ tsp. of pepper to the vegetables and set aside to cool.

In a mixing bowl, combine the mayonnaise, lemon juice, cayenne pepper, thyme, chives and parsley and stir to blend. Using a fork or your fingers (which is my preference) remove the salmon from the skin and break it into medium-sized pieces. Be sure to remove any bones that may be present. Add the salmon to the mixing bowl, and add the cooked vegetables. Mix the ingredients together very gently, being careful to not mash the salmon. Refrigerate the salmon mixture for at least 45 minutes or up to 8 hours.

When ready to serve, heat the remaining 2 tbsp. butter and the 2 tbsp. grapeseed oil in a large heavy non-stick skillet over moderate heat. Form the salmon mixture into four cakes, rolling each one completely in the panko. Cook until the salmon cakes are a deep golden brown on each side. Serves 2

Greek-Style Halibut with Cherry Tomatoes & Herbs

INGREDIENTS

1 lb. pieces halibut fillet (approx. 1 inch thick)

Herbamare® or salt and black pepper

¼ cup mayonnaise

2 tbsp. crumbled feta cheese

1½ tbsp. chopped fresh mint leaves

1½ tsp. dried dill (or 1 tbsp. chopped fresh dill)

1 tsp. (generous) fresh lemon juice

Sautéed Cherry Tomatoes with Garlic and Herbs to accompany (see p. 221)

PREPARATION

Line a broiler pan or broiler-safe shallow baking dish with foil. Place fish, skin sides down, on pan in a single layer and sprinkle lightly with Herbamare® and black pepper.

Whisk together the mayonnaise, feta, mint, dill and lemon juice. Spread evenly over top of fish. Preheat broiler and broil fish 8–10 inches from the heat until just cooked through, which should take approx. 10–12 minutes. The topping will be a dark brown color. If the topping appears to be browning too quickly, cover the fish loosely with foil until the fish is cooked.

Place fish on serving plates and spoon Sautéed Cherry Tomatoes with Garlic and Herbs around the sides of the fish. Serves 2–3

Shrimp & Scallops in Thai Green Curry Sauce with Noodles

Adapted from Gourmet magazine, Condé Nast Publications

INGREDIENTS

2 tbsp. sunflower oil

2 4-inch long hot red chili peppers, thinly sliced crosswise, seeds and membranes removed

5 tbsp. chopped scallions, white part only

4 tbsp. sliced scallion greens

1 lb. large shrimp, shelled and deveined

1 lb. sea scallops

Herbamare® or sea salt for sprinkling on seafood

13½ –14½ oz. can unsweetened coconut milk (Native Forest® Organic great choice)

1 tbsp. Thai green curry paste

¼ cup chicken broth

1 tbsp. packed light brown sugar

1½ tbsp. Asian fish sauce

2 tbsp. fresh lime juice

8–9 oz. thin noodles (e.g. linguine) – (I like Eden® Brown Rice Udon – Wheat Pasta with Brown Rice)

⅓ cup chopped fresh cilantro

PREPARATION

Heat one tbsp. of the sunflower oil in a large heavy non-stick skillet over moderately high heat. Add the sliced chilies and white part of the scallions and cook, stirring, until the scallions are lightly browned. Transfer with a slotted spoon to a small bowl and set aside. Place the scallion greens in a separate small bowl and set aside.

Pat the scallops and shrimp very well with paper towels to remove as much moisture as possible and sprinkle with Herbamare® or sea salt. Add the second tbsp. of sunflower oil to the skillet and heat until very hot but not smoking. Add the shrimp to the skillet and cook for approx. 1½ minutes on each side and remove with a slotted spoon to a bowl. Then add the scallops to the skillet and cook for about 1½ minutes on each side, remove with a slotted spoon and place in the bowl with the shrimp. At this point the shrimp and scallops will be almost completely cooked through.

Pour off all liquid in the skillet, reduce heat to moderate and add the coconut milk, curry paste, chicken broth, brown sugar, fish sauce and lime juice and simmer, stirring occasionally, for 5 minutes. Meanwhile, cook the noodles according to package directions in boiling salted water until just tender, not overcooked, and drain in a colander. Add the noodles and chopped cilantro to the sauce, stirring until well combined. Add the shrimp and scallops along with any juice that has accumulated in the bowl to the sauce mixture. Cook for an additional minute or so, or until the shrimp and scallops are heated and completely cooked.

Divide the mixture among 4 pasta bowls. Sprinkle reserved red chili and scallion mixture plus the green scallions equally over each serving bowl. Serves 4

Steaming Shrimp

Steaming shrimp is really easy because they hardly take any time at all, and it is very easy to judge when they are ready. Remove the shells from the shrimp and devein them. I don't think devein is a real word, but what it means is to run a sharp knife along the back of the shrimp, and remove any material that has collected inside the surface of the shrimp. You'll quickly understand why you're doing this because some of the stuff that you remove looks pretty disgusting. Steam in a vegetable steamer for no more than 3–5 minutes, depending on the size of the shrimp. The shrimp will turn pink and feel firm to the touch.

Cod with Almonds & Lemon Butter Sauce

INGREDIENTS

3 tbsp. butter

1 tbsp. lemon-dill herb mix

2 tbsp. fresh lemon juice (approx. the juice from half a lemon)

2 large cloves garlic, minced

¼ cup sliced almonds

1 lb. cod fillets

PREPARATION

Melt 2 tbsp. butter in small saucepan and remove from heat. When butter has cooled for a couple minutes, add lemon-dill mix, lemon juice, and garlic. In separate small skillet, sauté almonds in the remaining 1 tbsp. butter until both the almonds and the butter are a nutty brown color. Set aside.

Preheat oven to 425 degrees. Place fish in non-stick baking dish (or rub dish lightly with butter before adding fish). Spoon the lemon butter sauce evenly over each fish fillet. Bake 10–12 minutes, or until the fish flakes easily when tested with a fork. Sprinkle with toasted almonds before serving. Serves 2–3

Sesame-Crusted Halibut

INGREDIENTS

¼ cup flour

½ tsp. salt

¼ tsp. white pepper

1 large egg, lightly beaten

¼ cup sesame seeds

1 lb. halibut fillets

¼ cup safflower oil

PREPARATION

Combine first three ingredients in a shallow dish. Place egg in another shallow dish and beat lightly. Place sesame seeds in another shallow dish. Dredge fish in flour mixture on all sides; dip in egg, and immediately press one side (not the skin side) of the fish into the sesame seeds, coating heavily.

Heat oil in a large non-stick skillet over medium-high heat. Cook fish, seed side up, for approx. 5 minutes, or until lightly browned. Turn and cook an additional 5 minutes, or until the fish flakes easily with a fork and sesame seeds are browned. Serve with tartar sauce or Green Goddess Sauce (see p. 167). Serves 2–3

Spicy Blackened Catfish

INGREDIENTS

½ tsp. dried oregano

½ tsp. dried thyme

2 tsp. Hungarian (sweet) paprika

¼ tsp. cayenne pepper

½ tsp. organic sugar

½ tsp. salt

¼ tsp. black pepper, coarsely ground

1 lb. catfish fillets

1 tbsp. garlic oil (a great choice is Olave® Extra Virgin Olive Oil - Garlic)

1 tbsp. unsalted butter

PREPARATION

In a small bowl combine the oregano, thyme, paprika, cayenne, sugar, salt, and pepper. Pat the catfish dry and sprinkle half of the spice mixture on one side of the fish fillets.

In a large skillet, heat the garlic oil and butter together over moderately high heat until the butter foam subsides. Add catfish to skillet. The side that has the spice mixture on it should be facing down. As soon as the fish is in the skillet, sprinkle the remaining spice mixture on the other side. Saute for approx. 5–6 minutes on the first side before turning. Note: when you turn the fish, it should have a very dark, blackened appearance. Do not worry – it will not taste burned. Continue cooking on the other side for an additional 5–6 minutes, or until cooked through.

Transfer fish to serving plates and spoon whatever is left in the pan over top of the fish. Serves 2–3

Catfish & Vegetables with Pecan Sauce

Adapted from Gourmet magazine, Condé Nast Publications

INGREDIENTS

2½ cups frozen okra, cut (thawed in a colander and thoroughly rinsed)

2 cups grape tomatoes

4 tbsp. sunflower oil

1 tsp. Herbamare® or salt

½ tsp. pepper

2 cups frozen corn, thawed, or 1 14–15 oz. can sweet corn, thoroughly drained

3 tbsp. unsalted butter

⅓ cup coarsely chopped pecans

½ tsp. Blackened Creole Seasoning (e.g. Frontier™ blackened Creole blend)

2 tsp. fresh lemon juice

1 lb. catfish fillets, patted dry with paper towels

Additional Blackened Creole Seasoning for sprinkling on fish

PREPARATION

Put an oven rack in the lower third of the oven and preheat to 500 degrees. Toss okra and tomatoes with 2 tbsp. sunflower oil, Herbamare® and pepper in a bowl. Spread in a large shallow greased baking pan and roast in the lower third of the oven until the tomato skins begin to burst, or approx. 10–15 minutes. Remove vegetables from oven and add corn, stirring gently to combine with okra and tomatoes. Continue to roast vegetables in lower third of oven for another 10–15 minutes.

While vegetables are roasting, in a small skillet melt butter over moderate heat. Add the pecans and ½ tsp. blackened Creole seasoning and cook, stirring occasionally, until both the nuts and the butter are a deep golden brown. Remove from the heat and cool for several minutes before stirring in the lemon juice. Set aside.

Sprinkle fish fillets on both sides generously with the Blackened Creole Seasoning. Heat remaining 2 tbsp. sunflower oil in a heavy non-stick skillet over moderately high heat until oil is very hot but not smoking. Add fish and sauté on one side for approx. 5 minutes; turn and finish cooking until fish is done (flakes easily when tested with a fork), which will take approx. 5 more minutes. The fish should be a very deep brown color on both sides. Remove from heat.

Spoon a generous amount of the roasted vegetables on each plate, and top with a piece of fish. Spoon pecan butter generously on top of fish and serve. Serves 2–3

Honey-Mustard Salmon

INGREDIENTS

¼ cup extra-virgin olive oil

1 tbsp. honey

2 tbsp. Dijon mustard

3 large cloves garlic, minced

½ tsp. cayenne pepper

½ tsp. ground coriander

2 tbsp. fresh lemon juice

1 lb. salmon fillets

PREPARATION

Combine all ingredients except for salmon in a small saucepan and whisk together thoroughly. Cook on low heat for 5 minutes.

Place salmon, skin side down, in a foil-lined baking dish, safe for use under the broiler. Spoon a generous amount of the sauce evenly on top of the salmon. Broil approx. 10 minutes, or until top of salmon is lightly blackened, and fish flakes easily when tested with a fork. Top salmon with remaining sauce before serving. Serves 2

Seared Tilapia with Lime Butter

Adapted from Gourmet magazine, Condé Nast Publications

INGREDIENTS

3 tbsp. unsalted butter, softened to room temperature

1 tbsp. finely chopped shallots

1 tsp. finely grated fresh lime zest

Juice of ½ small fresh lime (approx. 2 tsp.)

¼ tsp. cayenne pepper

½ tsp. salt

2 tbsp. grapeseed oil

1 lb. tilapia fillet

Blackened bottled seasoning (lots of good choices – I like Frontier™ blackened creole blend)

PREPARATION

To make lime butter: In a small bowl with a spoon stir well the softened butter, shallots, lime zest, lime juice, cayenne and salt. Stir until the lime juice is fully incorporated.

Heat oil in a large non-stick skillet until very hot and sprinkle fish fillets on both sides with blackened seasoning. Sauté fish turning once until lightly blackened and just cooked through, approx. 2–3 minutes per side. If done in batches, remove fish to a plate and cover with foil to keep warm while second batch is cooking.

Place a generous dollop of lime butter on each fish fillet before serving. Serves 2–3

Cajun Catfish with Rémoulade Sauce

INGREDIENTS

1 lb. catfish fillets (or tilapia fillets)

2 tbsp. extra-virgin olive oil

Cajun Seasoning spice blend (McCormick® brand is very good)

Rémoulade Sauce (See p. 169)

PREPARATION

Rub fish fillets well with approx. ½ tbsp. of the olive oil on both sides. Sprinkle both sides of fish liberally with the Cajun Seasoning. Heat the remaining oil in a large heavy skillet until very hot, but not smoking. Sauté the fish for approx. 5 minutes on each side, or until fish is well browned and flakes easily.

Serve the fish with Rémoulade Sauce on the side. Serves 2

If you think you don't like catfish, try Sue's recipes. If you think you don't like cats, try me!

Shrimp & Scallop Gratin

INGREDIENTS

½ lb. raw shrimp, shelled and deveined

½ lb. raw sea scallops, cut in half

2 tbsp. medium-dry Sherry wine

¼ cup chopped parsley

2 large garlic cloves

2 tbsp. chopped shallots

¼ tsp. dried oregano

¼ tsp. salt

⅛ tsp. cayenne pepper

⅛ tsp. black pepper

1 ¼ cups fresh bread crumbs

4 tbsp. butter

PREPARATION

Place the shrimp and the scallops in a shallow baking (gratin) dish. Sprinkle the seafood with the Sherry.

In a mini-food processor, place the garlic cloves and the chopped parsley. Process until the garlic is chopped and the mixture is well combined. Transfer to a small bowl and stir in the shallots, oregano, salt, cayenne, black pepper, and bread crumbs.

Melt the butter in a skillet over low heat and add the bread crumb mixture. Cook stirring gently for a couple minutes. Remove from the heat and spoon crumb mixture evenly over the shrimp and scallops.

Place the baking dish in a preheated 400 degree oven and bake in the upper third of the oven for approx. 12 to 14 minutes, or until the topping is a deep golden brown. Serves 2–4

Cheesy Broiled Flounder

INGREDIENTS

1 lb. flounder fillets

½ of a lemon

2 tbsp. butter, softened

1 tbsp. mayonnaise

¼ cup grated Parmesan cheese

2 tbsp. grated Cheddar cheese

2 tbsp. chopped shallots

¼ tsp. salt

½ tsp. dried parsley

¼ tsp. Tabasco sauce

PREPARATION

Place aluminum foil in bottom of shallow broiler-safe baking dish. Put fish fillets in dish, assuring they are not overlapping. Cut lemon in half and squeeze half of the lemon over the fish.

Combine remaining ingredients well in a small bowl and set aside.

Broil fish approx. 6–8 inches from the flame for about 3–4 minutes, or until fish is almost done. Remove from oven and spread topping evenly over fillets. Return fish to the oven and broil until the topping is a deep nutty brown color and is bubbling. This will not take very long, only about 30 seconds to a minute. Monitor the final step closely to be sure the topping doesn't burn. Remove from oven and serve. Serves 2–3

Cats are like delicate plants that need constant tending and nurturing...and meals served on demand.

Deviled Crab Cakes

INGREDIENTS

½ cup chopped shallots

¼ cup chopped red bell pepper

¼ cup chopped orange bell pepper

6 tbsp. chopped celery

3 tbsp. butter

2 large eggs

2 tbsp. sour cream

1 tsp. dry mustard

1 tsp. Worcestershire sauce

¼ tsp. cayenne pepper

¼ tsp. salt

4 tbsp. thinly sliced scallion greens (reserve white part for another use)

½ cup finely ground saltines, plus 4 additional tbsp. for coating crab cakes

1 lb. lump crabmeat, picked over well to remove all shells (preferably by hand)

1 tbsp. grapeseed oil

Accompaniment – Tartar sauce (see p. 169)

PREPARATION

Cook shallots, peppers and celery in 2 tbsp. of butter in a 10 inch nonstick skillet over moderately low heat, stirring occasionally, until vegetables are softened.

In a large bowl, whisk together the eggs, sour cream, dry mustard, Worcestershire sauce, cayenne and salt. When well combined, stir in scallions, cooked vegetables, and ½ cup saltine crumbs. Gently stir in crabmeat.

Heat the remaining 1 tbsp. butter and the grapeseed oil in a large non-stick skillet over moderate heat. With hands, form mixture into 6 to 8 crab cakes, depending on the size you desire. Dredge the cakes lightly in the 4 tbsp. remaining ground saltine crumbs. Note: It is much easier to do this one at a time, and as soon as each cake is coated with the crumbs, place it in the heated skillet. Cook crab cakes, until golden brown (approx. 5 minutes), then turn and cook on other side until golden brown. Serves 4

Broiled Sole with Almonds

INGREDIENTS

1 lb. fillets of sole

2 tbsp. melted butter

¼ tsp. salt

¼ tsp. garlic salt

¼ tsp. paprika

Several shakes of pepper

Sauce:

3 tbsp. butter

¼ cup slivered almonds

1 tbsp. lemon juice

1 tbsp. chopped fresh parsley

PREPARATION

Line a shallow broiler-proof baking dish with aluminum foil and brush the foil with a small amount of the melted butter. Lay fish on buttered foil, skin side down. Sprinkle with seasonings and dribble the remaining melted butter evenly over the fish. Preheat the broiler, and broil fish about six inches from the heat for approx. 10 minutes, or until fish is done (flakes easily when tested with a fork).

While the fish is broiling, melt butter in a small saucepan over moderate heat. Add almonds and sauté until both the almonds and the butter are a nutty brown color. Set aside. When fish is cooked and ready to be served, add lemon juice and parsley to the almond butter and pour spoonfuls evenly over each fish serving. Serves 2

Indonesian Roasted Salmon

INGREDIENTS

3 tbsp. unsalted butter

¼ tsp. red pepper flakes

1 large clove garlic, finely chopped

2 tbsp. firmly packed light brown sugar

2 tbsp. fresh lime juice

2 tbsp. soy sauce

½ tsp. cornstarch dissolved in ½ tsp. water

1 lb. salmon fillets (2 pieces, ½ lb. each)

Garlic pepper

Kosher or sea salt

PREPARATION

In a small saucepan, melt 2 tbsp. of the butter over medium heat. Add the red pepper flakes and garlic and stir about a minute, just until fragrant. Add the sugar, lime juice, and soy sauce and bring to a boil. Immediately reduce heat to moderately low and simmer, stirring frequently, until the sugar is dissolved, about 3 minutes. Add the cornstarch mixture and continue to cook until the sauce is slightly thickened, about 1–2 more minutes. Set aside.

Preheat oven to 400 degrees. Sprinkle the salmon with garlic pepper and kosher salt. In a heavy non-stick ovenproof skillet, melt the remaining tbsp. of butter over high heat. Swirl to coat the pan evenly, and add the salmon, skin side up. Sear the salmon for approx. 2 minutes, then turn over and sear the other side (flesh side up), for another 2 minutes. Spoon about 1 tbsp. of the sauce over each fish fillet, and place in the oven. Roast the salmon until opaque throughout, approx. 5–10 minutes.

Place salmon on serving plates, and spoon remaining sauce evenly over each portion. It is desirable to remove the skin from the fish before serving, which should be very easy to do with a spatula. Serves 2

Note: This is good served with sautéed spinach on the side as a vegetable accompaniment.

Scallops with Tarragon & Chives

Adapted from Gourmet's In Short Order (1993), Condé Nast Publications

INGREDIENTS

3½ tbsp. unsalted butter

1 lb. large sea scallops, rinsed and patted dry

2 large garlic cloves, finely chopped

1 large shallot, finely chopped (5–6 tbsp.)

2 tbsp. minced fresh chives

1 tbsp. minced fresh tarragon leaves (using fresh tarragon is important)

1 tbsp. fresh lemon juice

½ tsp. salt

¼ tsp. pepper

1 package (6–8 oz.) fresh baby spinach leaves

PREPARATION

In a heavy large non-stick skillet, heat 1½ tbsp. of the butter over moderately high heat until the foam subsides; add the scallops and sauté for approx. 1 to 1½ minutes on each side. The scallops should be lightly browned. Transfer scallops to a plate.

Add another 1½ tbsp. of butter to the skillet, reduce heat to moderately low, and cook the garlic and shallots, stirring, until the shallots are softened. Add the chives, tarragon, lemon juice, salt and pepper and stir to combine. Return the scallops to the skillet with any juices that collected on the plate and cook until they are heated through,

Heat a small amount of water (approx. ¼ cup) to the boiling point in a separate skillet with tall sides. Add the spinach and cook briefly, stirring, just until the spinach leaves are wilted. Drain the spinach in a colander. Add remaining ½ tbsp. butter in this skillet and return spinach to skillet; stir gently to coat evenly with butter.

Arrange spinach in the middle of 2 serving plates, and top with equal amount of scallops and butter sauce. Serves 2

Fish & Other Fresh Seafood

When deciding how much fish to buy, a good rule of thumb is ½ lb. per person. If you're a light eater, this will probably be too much, but I like to err on the side of excess unless I'm well acquainted with someone's eating habits.

Any seafood recipe will be compromised or ruined by buying seafood that is not really fresh. When fish is purchased it should not have a strong fishy odor. Most fish that is really fresh doesn't even smell like fish; when you put your nose right up next to it there is practically no odor at all. Only buy fish at seafood markets or food stores with a reputation for selling really fresh fish. Also, once you purchase seafood, use it the same day preferably, but no later than the next day.

I normally purchase fish listed as "Best Choices" and "Good Alternatives" in the Seafood Watch® Seafood Guide, which is a great way to take some responsibility for enhancing and maintaining the health of the oceans. The threat of dangerous oceanic change and how we can help to reverse this trend is explored in the extremely wise and insightful book "The World Is Blue" by Sylvia A. Earle.

Fillet of Sole Meunière

INGREDIENTS

1 lb. fillet of sole

Milk to cover fillets

2 tbsp. grapeseed oil

¼ cup flour

¼ tsp. salt

⅛ tsp. black pepper

3 tbsp. butter

3 generous tbsp. lemon juice, at room temperature

2 tbsp. chopped fresh flat-leaf (Italian) parsley

Capers (Optional – if large capers, cut in half)

PREPARATION

Place fish in a shallow baking dish and pour enough milk over the fillets to cover them. Set aside. Heat the oil in a large non-stick skillet over moderately high heat until hot but not smoking.

While oil is heating, blend the flour with the salt and pepper on a plate. Drain the fillets (one at a time) but do not dry. Roll both sides of each fillet in the seasoned flour until evenly coated, then place in heated oil and cook for approx. 5 minutes, or until fish is golden brown. Turn onto the other side and continue cooking for an additional five minutes. Transfer fish to a plate and cover with foil to keep warm.

Wipe out the skillet with a paper towel. Add the butter to the skillet and heat over moderate heat until it is browned. Remove from the heat and add the lemon juice and the parsley, stirring to combine well. Place fish on serving plates and spoon sauce evenly over each portion.

Note: If desired, sprinkle approx. 1 tbsp. of drained capers over each serving. Serves 2

Oven-Fried Cod or Haddock Fillets

INGREDIENTS

½ tbsp. salt

½ cup milk

1 lb. fish fillets, cut into serving pieces

½ cup fresh bread crumbs, very finely crumbled

¼ cup grated Parmesan cheese

¼ tsp. thyme

⅛ tsp. paprika

2 tbsp. melted butter

Lemon wedges

PREPARATION

Preheat the oven to 525 degrees (very hot). Add the salt to the milk in a shallow dish.

Process bread of choice in a mini-food processor until there is enough to measure ½ cup. Add the Parmesan cheese to the half cup of bread crumbs in the processor with the thyme and paprika. Process the crumb mixture until well combined and place on a plate.

Dip the fish fillets first in the salted milk and then in the crumb mixture, coating very well. Put the fish in a shallow, well buttered baking dish. Pour the melted butter over the fish evenly. Bake on the top shelf of the oven for about 10–12 minutes. Crumbs will be well browned. Check fish during last several minutes of baking to assure the crumbs are not burning.

Serve with lemon wedges, and if desired, serve Tartar Sauce or Green Goddess Sauce on the side (see p. 167). Serves 2–3

Fillets of Sole with Glazed Bananas
(Sole West Indies)

INGREDIENTS

¼ cup flour

1 tsp. paprika (not Hungarian)

1 tsp. salt

¼ tsp. white pepper

¾ lbs. fillets of sole

¼ cup (4 tbsp.) butter

½ cup dry vermouth

½ tsp. ground ginger

Juice of ½ a fresh lemon (2 tbsp.)

2 tbsp. firmly packed dark brown sugar

2 bananas (ripened but still firm) – Peeled, cut lengthwise, then cut in half

Toasted thinly sliced almonds for sprinkling on top

PREPARATION

On a plate, mix together the flour, paprika, salt and white pepper. Melt the butter in a large heavy non-stick skillet over medium heat. Thoroughly dredge each fish fillet in the flour mixture, and brown the fish for 2–3 minutes on each side. The fish should be a nice nutty brown color. Remove fish to a dish and cover with foil to keep warm.

To the skillet add the wine, ginger, lemon juice and brown sugar. Combine thoroughly and then add bananas cut side down. Cook over medium heat until the sauce thickens and the bananas are very soft, which should take about 5–10 minutes.

To serve, cover the fillets with the bananas and sauce, and sprinkle each portion liberally with toasted almonds. Serves 2

> ## Sue's Tips:
>
> "Life, including Fine Dining, is not meant to be taken too seriously."
>
> - Zen, and the Art of Fine Dining

Shrimp Tempura

INGREDIENTS

½ cup all-purpose flour

¼ tsp. nutmeg

⅛ tsp. cayenne pepper

¼ tsp. Herbamare® or salt

1 egg, separated

⅔ cup milk (low-fat if desired)

¼ cup safflower oil

1 to 1½ lbs. uncooked large or jumbo shrimp, shelled and deveined

PREPARATION

Place the flour, nutmeg, cayenne and Herbamare® in a bowl. Add the egg yolk and gradually add the milk, stirring, until very well combined.

Beat the egg white in a separate bowl with an electric mixer until very stiff and gently fold the egg white into the batter.

Heat the oil in a large non-stick heavy skillet until very hot but not smoking. Dip shrimp in batter allowing some of the excess to drip off and drop into the skillet, assuring that the shrimp are not touching each other. When the shrimp are well browned on one side (approx. 2–3 minutes), turn with a fork and brown on the other side. Drain the shrimp on paper towels. Shrimp can be kept warm in the oven (at 200 degrees), but should be served as soon as possible (preferably no more than 5–10 minutes after removing from frying pan). Serve with Apricot Dipping Sauce (see p. 164). Serves 2–4

Broiled Fish Fillets with Bacon, Onions & Raisins

Adapted from Gourmet magazine, Condé Nast Publications

INGREDIENTS

2 medium thick bacon slices

1 tbsp. extra-virgin olive oil, plus extra for rubbing on the fish

1¼ cup coarsely chopped red onion

¼ cup golden raisins

¼ cup red-wine vinegar

1 tsp. sugar

1 lb. fish fillets (e.g. trout, fillet of sole)

Herbamare® or salt and black pepper for sprinkling on fish

PREPARATION

Cook bacon in a medium heavy skillet over medium heat until browned and crisp and drain well on paper towels. There should be approx. 1 tbsp. of bacon fat left in the skillet. If there is more, pour off the extra fat. Add the olive oil to the skillet and heat. Add the onions to the skillet and cook over moderate heat, stirring occasionally, until the onion is softened and beginning to brown on the edges.

Crumble the bacon into very small pieces and add to the onions along with the raisins, vinegar and sugar. Cook over moderate heat until almost all of the liquid is evaporated. Remove from the heat and cover to keep warm.

Arrange the fish fillets in a broiler-proof baking dish in one layer and preheat the broiler. Lightly rub or brush the fish with olive oil and sprinkle with Herbamare® and black pepper. Broil fish approx. 6 inches from the heat for approx. 3–5 minutes, or until the fish is just cooked through.

Place fish on serving plates and spoon the onion mixture over top. Serves 2–3

Shrimp Capri

INGREDIENTS

⅓ cup extra virgin olive oil

½ tsp. crushed red pepper flakes

3 large garlic cloves, minced

2 tbsp. capers, drained

12 pitted Kalamata olives, halved

20 cherry tomatoes, halved

1 lb. large shrimp, shelled and deveined

½ cup dry vermouth or dry white wine

1 tbsp. fresh lemon juice

2 tbsp. chopped fresh flat-leaf (Italian) parsley

1 tsp. salt

½ tsp. black pepper

3 tbsp. unsalted butter

Brown rice to accompany, cooked according to package directions

PREPARATION

Heat olive oil in a large skillet over moderate heat until hot, and add the pepper flakes and garlic. Cook for approx. 30 seconds and then add the capers, olives and cherry tomatoes. Continue to cook for several more minutes, or until the tomatoes are softened but still hold their shape.

Add the shrimp to the skillet and cook, stirring for one minute. Add the wine, lemon juice, parsley, salt and pepper. When the liquid reaches a slow boil, add the butter, one tbsp. at a time, and stir until the butter is melted and well blended.

Spoon shrimp over rice and serve immediately. Serves 3–4

Shrimp with Garlic Panko & Almonds

INGREDIENTS

1 lb. raw shrimp, peeled and deveined

6 tbsp. unsalted butter, softened to room temperature in a small bowl

3 large garlic cloves, minced

½ tsp. salt

1½ tbsp. dry or medium-dry sherry

½ cup panko (Japanese bread crumbs – Sushi Chef® is a good choice)

2 tbsp. chopped fresh flat-leaf parsley

⅛ tsp. black pepper

¼ cup sliced almonds, lightly toasted

PREPARATION

Preheat oven to 400 degrees. Pat shrimp dry and arrange in one layer in a buttered shallow baking dish.

Add garlic, salt, and sherry to butter and cream together until sherry is incorporated and the mixture is well blended. Stir in the panko, parsley, and pepper. Dot shrimp evenly with the crumb mixture and sprinkle the toasted almonds over the crumb mixture.

Bake in preheated oven just until the shrimp are cooked through and the topping is lightly browned, approx. 15 minutes.

Serves 2–3

I've been overserved...

Scallops with Shallots & Tomatoes

INGREDIENTS

3 tbsp. unsalted butter

¾ lb. sea scallops, rinsed and patted dry

½ tsp. Worcestershire sauce

2 large garlic cloves, finely chopped

⅓ cup finely chopped shallots

¼ cup minced fresh parsley leaves

1 tbsp. fresh lemon juice

½ cup chopped fresh tomatoes, seeded

½ tsp. Herbamare® or salt

¼ tsp. black pepper

PREPARATION

In a heavy skillet, heat 1½ tbsp. of the butter over moderately high heat until the foam subsides, and the butter is very lightly browned. Add the scallops and sauté for approx. 1 minute on each side, and transfer to a plate with a slotted spoon. Scallops should be very lightly browned.

Reduce the heat to low, and add the remaining 1½ tbsp. butter to the skillet. When the butter is melted, add the Worcestershire sauce, garlic, shallots, and parsley, and cook for approx. 5 minutes, or until the shallots are softened. Add the lemon juice, tomatoes, Herbamare® and pepper to the pan, and stir gently to combine. Return scallops to the skillet and cook just until scallops are reheated and tomatoes are slightly softened, approx. 3–5 minutes. Serve scallops with shallot and tomato sauce spooned evenly over each portion. Serves 2

Shrimp with Tomatoes & Feta Cheese
Adapted from Gourmet magazine, Condé Nast Publications

INGREDIENTS

2 tbsp. butter

2 tbsp. extra-virgin olive oil

1 cup chopped shallots

2 tbsp. finely chopped garlic

4 cups seeded chopped tomatoes

1 tbsp. dried dill

2 tbsp. minced fresh basil leaves

1 tsp. sugar

2 tsp. dry mustard

1 lb. shrimp, shelled and deveined

½ cup chopped fresh flat-leaf (Italian) parsley

3 tbsp. dry vermouth

1 tsp. black pepper

½ tsp. salt

4 oz. crumbled Feta cheese

PREPARATION

In a large heavy non-stick skillet, heat the butter and olive oil over moderate heat. Add the shallots and garlic and cook for several minutes, until the shallots are softened. Add the tomatoes, dill, basil, sugar, and dry mustard and cook the mixture for 10–15 minutes, or until the mixture is reduced by about one third. Add the shrimp, parsley, vermouth, pepper and salt and cook, stirring, for 2–3 minutes, until the shrimp is pink on all sides, but not completely cooked through.

Preheat the oven to 450 degrees. Place the shrimp mixture in a shallow baking dish and sprinkle the top with the Feta cheese. Bake the shrimp for 5 minutes or until the shrimp is cooked through and the cheese begins to melt. Serves 2–3

Time to Cook

One of the numerous reasons this is a great cookbook is that in most cases, when the lucky person you are serving consumes your food, they may think you spent your whole day in the kitchen. In reality, the majority of these recipes should take no more than an hour to prepare, and most of the recipes take less than an hour. The time to prepare refers to active time. For example, if you are making a flank steak recipe that requires marinating for 24 hours, but to prepare the marinade takes ten minutes, then the active time is 10 minutes, plus the time necessary to broil or grill the steak.

I have purposely not indicated on any recipe how long it takes to cook because no two people are alike in terms of how they approach following a recipe and what short cuts or extra time it may take to make a particular recipe.

What is important is to have FUN when you're cooking. I love to cook, so I'm going to enjoy myself no matter what. Here are examples of things I do to find even more joy in my cooking experiences:

- Pet Clyde
- Pour a glass of wine
- Listen to music
- Dance with Clyde
- Listen to a BOT (Book on Tape)

- Encourage my guests to join me. Everyone always wants to be in the kitchen anyway, so I relax and enjoy the camaraderie
- Hug and kiss Clyde

Halibut Fillets with Pecan Shallot Topping

Adapted from The Gourmet Cookbook (2004), Condé Nast Publications

INGREDIENTS

2 tbsp. extra virgin olive oil

½ cup finely chopped shallots

¼ cup chopped toasted pecans

1 tbsp. unsalted butter

1 tsp. grated lemon zest

1 tbsp. finely chopped fresh flat-leaf (Italian) parsley

¼ tsp. Herbamare® or salt

1 lb. halibut fillet, skinned

Herbamare® or salt and black pepper for sprinkling on fillets

PREPARATION

Heat one tbsp. of the olive oil in a small skillet over low heat. Add shallots and cook for approx. 3 minutes or until they are softened. Add the pecans and continue to cook for about another minute. Add butter and stir until melted. Remove skillet from heat and stir in lemon zest, parsley, and ¼ tsp. Herbamare®.

Heat the remaining tbsp. olive oil in a heavy skillet over moderately high heat until it is hot but not smoking. Sprinkle fish with Herbamare® and black pepper. Add fish to skillet and cook, turning once, until golden and just cooked through, which should take approx. 3–5 minutes per side, depending on the thickness of the fillets.

Spoon the topping evenly over each fish portion. Serves 2–3

Chinese-Style Shrimp

INGREDIENTS

1 tsp. salt

1 egg white

1 tbsp. cornstarch

1 lb. large (preferably jumbo) shrimp, shelled and deveined

4 tbsp. grapeseed oil

2 tbsp. chopped scallions (white part)

2 tbsp. finely chopped fresh gingerroot

2 tbsp. tomato ketchup

1 tsp. sugar

1 tbsp. red-wine vinegar

3 tbsp. chopped scallions (leaves – dark green part)

PREPARATION

Whisk together the salt, egg white, and cornstarch in a medium bowl. Add the shrimp and turn to coat well with the batter.

Heat the oil in a large non-stick heavy skillet over moderate heat until it is very hot. Add the scallions (white part), the gingerroot, and the ketchup and stir-fry for approx. 30 seconds. Pour in the shrimp and all of the batter, along with the sugar and the vinegar. Stir-fry, stirring frequently, for approx. 3 minutes, or until the shrimp is pink on all sides and just cooked through. Do not overcook!

Sprinkle generous amount of chopped scallion greens on top of each serving. Serves 2

What's the best day to begin a diet? Tomorrow!

Crunchy Shrimp with Toasted Couscous & Ginger-Orange Sauce

Sauce:

2 cups fresh orange juice

2 tbsp. chopped fresh cilantro leaves

4 tbsp. mayonnaise

3 tbsp. chicken broth

1 tbsp. grated fresh gingerroot

1 tbsp. fresh lime juice

1 tsp. ground cumin

½ tsp. salt

½ tsp. cayenne pepper

Couscous:

2 tbsp. butter

3 tbsp. sliced almonds

1 cup couscous (preferably whole wheat)

1½ cups chicken broth

½ cup fresh orange juice

½ tsp. salt

⅓ cup chopped scallions (white part only)

Shrimp:

1½ lbs. very large or jumbo shrimp, shelled and deveined

2 egg whites, lightly beaten

1 cup panko (Japanese breadcrumbs)

1 tsp. chopped fresh cilantro

½ tsp. grated fresh gingerroot

⅛ tsp. black pepper

2 tbsp. canola oil

PREPARATION

To prepare sauce, place the orange juice in a small saucepan and bring to a boil. Cook until reduced to ¾ cup. Remove from the heat and cool, then stir in the rest of the sauce ingredients and set aside.

For the couscous, melt the butter in a small skillet and sauté the almonds over moderate heat until they are lightly browned. Set aside. Place the couscous in a large nonstick skillet and cook over medium heat until toasted to a nice brown nutty color, stirring constantly. Add the chicken broth, orange juice and salt and bring to a boil. Remove from heat, cover and let stand for 5 minutes. Fluff the couscous with a fork and stir in the scallions, almonds and butter. Replace cover to keep warm.

To prepare the shrimp, combine the shrimp and beaten egg whites in a mixing bowl and toss to coat. On a plate combine the panko, cilantro, ginger and pepper.

Heat the oil in a large heavy non-stick skillet over medium heat until it is very hot, but not smoking. Dip the shrimp on both sides lightly in the panko mixture and add to skillet in a single layer. Cook for approx. 2 minutes (the bread coating should be browned and crispy). Turn the shrimp over and cook an additional 2–3 minutes, or until they are done. Do not overcook! If it is necessary to cook the shrimp in batches, when the first batch is removed from the skillet, put on a plate and cover with foil to keep warm.

To serve, place a generous helping of couscous on each serving plate, top with shrimp, and spoon sauce over the shrimp. Serves 4

Susan ("Flish")

When I first moved to D.C. I met Flish through a mutual friend who knew I was seeking a roommate. We discovered during our first meeting that we were both passionate about great food (cooking it as much as eating it), good wine, and travel. Certainly a solid foundation for building a relationship!

Flish lives in Florida and used to have her own catering business there. One of her most frequently requested dishes to prepare (no surprise!) was her: Churnchy Shrimp with Toasted Couscous & Ginger-Orange Sauce.

Alexandria, VA, 1989
Happy Together

Shrimp with Basil-Garlic Butter

Adapted from Gourmet magazine, Condé Nast Publications

INGREDIENTS

¾ lb. jumbo shrimp, shelled and deveined

2 tbsp. extra-virgin olive oil

3 large cloves garlic, finely chopped

⅓ cup dry vermouth

1 tbsp. fresh lemon juice

2 generous tbsp. chopped sun-dried tomatoes (packed in oil)

4 tbsp. unsalted butter

½ cup shredded fresh basil leaves

½ tsp. Herbamare® or salt

¼ tsp. black pepper

PREPARATION

Heat 1 tbsp. of the olive oil in a large non-stick heavy skillet until it is hot but not smoking. Sauté the shrimp for approx. 1 minute on each side; the shrimp will be pink and firm. Do not overcook! Remove shrimp from the skillet and set aside. Pour off the oil and any juices released from the shrimp and wipe skillet lightly with a paper towel.

Reduce heat to low and add to the skillet the remaining tbsp. of olive oil. Add the garlic and cook, stirring, for about ½ minute. Add the vermouth, lemon juice and chopped tomatoes. Increase heat to moderately high and cook the mixture until it is reduced to approx. ⅓ of the original amount. Note: You will have more success with this sauce if the ingredients (i.e. the vermouth, lemon juice, sun-dried tomatoes, and butter) are close to room temperature before adding. When the sauce is reduced, reduce heat to low, add the butter, basil leaves, Herbamare® and pepper and stir gently until the butter is melted. Return the shrimp to the skillet and cook briefly or just until the shrimp are heated through. Serves 2–3

Broiled Lemon Thyme Rockfish

INGREDIENTS

1 lb. rockfish fillets

Herbamare® or salt and black pepper (for sprinkling on fish)

¼ cup mayonnaise

2 tsp. grated lemon zest

1 tbsp. fresh lemon juice

1½ tbsp. finely chopped shallots

½ tsp. (generous) anchovy paste

1 tsp. chopped fresh thyme leaves

PREPARATION

Place fish skin side down on a lightly oiled broiler pan and sprinkle lightly with Herbamare® or salt and black pepper. Stir the remaining ingredients together and spoon evenly over top of the fish.

Preheat the broiler. Broil the fish 6–7 inches from the heat until just cooked through, which should take 8–10 minutes. Serves 2

Sue and I have reached a nice compromise about giving and taking – she gives me everything, and I take it.

Soup

Without question, soup is one of my favorite things to eat, and also something I love to make, as did my mother. I cherish the memories of Toni in her kitchen preparing a large kettle of soup. "Chicken Soup" has become practically a synonym for "comfort food." I have especially fond memories of my mother's Chicken Corn Soup. I don't have an actual recipe for this. Basically, she would place chicken breasts (including the bones and skin) in a large pot filled with water, add salt and pepper, and cook until the chicken was done. The chicken was then removed from the bones, skin and bones discarded, cut into pieces and returned to the pot. She would then add chopped fresh parsley, chopped onions, and uncooked corn, cut from the cob, and more salt and pepper. The soup then was left to simmer until the onions were softened and the corn was cooked crisp-tender. The key to the success of this soup was the incredible quality of York County silver queen corn, which is as sweet as candy. Toni would not make this soup unless corn was in peak season, purchased locally. My brother-in-law Larry still makes my mother's version of Chicken Corn Soup and does a fine job. He makes it for me sometimes if I'm really nice and don't beat him too badly at gin rummy.

There ain't nothing like the real thing.

Testimonial

After a decade of enjoying Sue Cassidy's cooking in D.C., I moved to the West Coast but stayed in touch with the best cook I had ever met. Recently my wife and I traveled back to the capital to visit friends. Along with the historic monuments and exhilarating energy of the city, I couldn't wait to once again experience Sue's cooking. A delicious dinner, the welcoming faces of Sue and her husband Pat, and the playful antics of their fuzzy cat Clyde made for a perfect evening.

As the best evenings often do, our dinner slipped by quickly but not the memory of Sue's great cooking. It was as delicious as I had remembered.

Congratulations to anybody who owns "Cooking With Clyde" as you will never be without recipes that are sure to impress even the most finicky of connoisseurs.

Greg Dunigan
Film Producer of "A Little Inside" (HBO)
Burbank, CA

Lamb Curry Soup

Adapted from Gourmet magazine, Condé Nast Publications

INGREDIENTS

Leg of lamb, sufficient to provide 3 cups of small (half inch) pieces, uncooked (1 to 1½ lbs.) – Note: Assure all fat is removed!

3 cups chicken broth

1 cup chopped onion

1 cup seeded and chopped tomatoes

4 tsp. curry powder

1 tbsp. ketchup

½ tsp. salt

¼ tsp. pepper

½ cup apple, cored, peeled and diced

¼ cup diced banana

¼ cup raisins

¼ cup brown rice (uncooked)

2 tbsp. butter

¼ cup flour

1 cup milk

PREPARATION

In a large saucepan or Dutch oven, combine the lamb with 3 cups of water. Bring the water to a boil, and boil for 5 minutes. Skim off as much of the froth as possible that rises to the surface. Reduce heat to medium-low, and add the chicken broth, onion, tomatoes, curry powder, ketchup, salt and pepper. Simmer the soup, covered, for 1 hour and 30 minutes. Remove cover and add the apple, banana, raisins and rice. Simmer for 5 minutes.

In a small skillet, melt the butter, then stir in the flour and cook the roux over low heat, stirring, for several minutes. Remove from the heat, and add approx. 1 cup of the soup. Whisk this mixture until it is smooth, and stir into the soup. Simmer the soup an additional ½ hour, uncovered, or until the rice is cooked. Stir in the milk. Simmer an additional 5 minutes and add salt to taste. Note: I add approx. 1 tsp. of salt. You may prefer more or less. Serves 4–6

Turkey Sausage Vegetable Soup

INGREDIENTS

1 tbsp. olive oil

1 to 1¼ lbs. Italian turkey sausage, hot/spicy

1 large white onion, chopped

5 large garlic cloves, finely chopped

½ lb. mushrooms, coarsely chopped (stems trimmed)

4 to 6 cups chicken broth

½ cup dry vermouth

1 cup brown rice, uncooked

1 14½ oz. can diced tomatoes, undrained

½ tsp. salt

½ tsp. pepper

1 generous tbsp. chopped fresh basil

1 large zucchini squash, diced

Parmesan cheese

PREPARATION

In a large pot heat the olive oil over moderate heat. Squeeze sausage meat out of casings and pinch off pieces about the size of a walnut. Place directly as you go into the heated oil and lightly brown (approx. 2 batches). When you finish with each batch, remove with a slotted spoon and set aside in a bowl.

Add the chopped onions to the pot and cook until translucent and softened. Add garlic and cook for about a minute. Then add mushrooms and cook for about 2 minutes. Add 4 cups of chicken broth, vermouth, rice, tomatoes, sausage, salt, pepper and basil and bring to a brisk simmer. Reduce heat to low and simmer until the rice is tender (about 45 minutes). If desired to make the rice cook faster, after about ½ hour of cooking without a lid, put a lid on the pot for about 10 minutes. Remove lid and add the diced zucchini. Cook for about 10 minutes. The zucchini should not be overcooked, meaning they should be soft but still bright green. If at this point the soup appears to be thicker than desired, add an additional 1–2 cups of chicken broth.

Top individual bowls with grated Parmesan cheese, or serve on the side. Serves 4

Velvet White Almond Gazpacho

(From the kitchen of Nathalie Cadot)

INGREDIENTS

3 thick slices of white bread, crusts removed (if not thick, use 4 slices of bread)

4 oz. skinned and blanched almonds

5 large garlic cloves

¾ cup extra virgin olive oil

¼ cup white wine vinegar

2 tsp. sea salt

2 cups water

Seeded green grapes (large) for garnish

PREPARATION

Soak bread in water for several minutes. Squeeze out the water and place the moistened bread in a food processor. Add the almonds and peeled garlic cloves and blend until smooth. With the motor running, add the olive oil in a slow stream. At this point the mixture should be extremely velvety and smooth, with no discernable lumps. Add the vinegar and salt and continue to process until these ingredients are incorporated completely. Add a small amount of the 2 cups of water and blend.

Remove the soup to a storage container and add the remainder of the 2 cups of water. Stir until the water is thoroughly combined.

Cover and chill for a couple of hours before serving. It is also fine to make this soup the day before and chill it overnight. There may be some separation, so stir well before serving. The soup should be removed from the refrigerator about 20 minutes before serving because if it is too cold it loses its perfume and taste.

Cut grapes in half and arrange, cut sides down, decoratively on the top of each soup serving bowl (3–4 grapes per serving). This soup is very filling, so if you are serving it as a first course, which Nathalie frequently does, exercise portion control.

Nathalie

A native of France, Nathalie now resides in Northern Virginia. French people have a wonderfully sensible approach regarding food: dining experiences are to be savored slowly, to relish not only the quality and flavors of the food, but to bask in the pleasure of your companions.

Nathalie should be writing her own cookbook since the meals she has prepared for me have always sent me to a new dimension. She has the ability to make anyone who is served a meal in her home feel as though a priceless gift has been bestowed.

Chère Nathalie

Tomato Paste

Often a recipe will call for a small amount of tomato paste, like one or two tbsp. There was a time when I was not aware that you could buy tomato paste in a tube instead of only in cans, thereby being able to use smaller amounts without having to deal with the tomato paste left over. Plus, the tomato paste I use (Amore®) is a much better quality than you would get in a can.

Amore® also makes a great Italian Pesto Paste, and I also always use Amore® Italian Anchovy Paste.

Cleveland-Style Chili

INGREDIENTS

3 tbsp. grapeseed oil

3 medium onions, chopped (should measure between 3–4 cups)

4 lbs. very lean ground beef

6 large garlic cloves, finely chopped

⅓ cup chili powder

2 tbsp. sweet (Hungarian-style) paprika

2 tsp. cumin

1 tsp. ground coriander

1 tsp. ground allspice

1 tsp. dried oregano

½ tsp. cayenne pepper

½ tsp. cinnamon

¼ tsp. ground cloves

¼ tsp. ground mace

2 ½ cups water

1 large bay leaf or 2 small bay leaves

1 28-oz. can crushed tomatoes, not drained

2 tbsp. red wine vinegar

2 tbsp. molasses

1 tsp. Herbamare® or salt

Accompaniment: grated Cheddar cheese

PREPARATION

In a large heavy kettle, heat the oil over moderate heat and cook the onions until they are softened. Add the beef and cook, stirring and breaking up the lumps, until the beef is no longer pink. Add the garlic, chili powder, paprika, cumin, coriander, allspice, oregano, cayenne, cinnamon, cloves, and the mace and cook the mixture, stirring, for one minute. Add 1½ cups of water, the bay leaf/leaves, crushed tomatoes, vinegar, and molasses and simmer the mixture, uncovered, stirring occasionally, for at least 2 hours. Add the remaining 1 cup of water as the chili is cooking, gradually, or to assure that the beef is <u>barely</u> covered. You may not find it necessary to add the entire extra cup. This chili should be very thick but soupy enough to be ladled. Discard the bay leaf/leaves and season with 1 tsp. of Herbamare® or salt.

Note: Traditionally called "Cincinnati-Style Chili," renamed because of my brother-in-law Kevin and his wife Ute who are rabid Cleveland Browns fans. Two of their pug doggies were named "Cleveland" and "Rocks" (you get the drift).

Chili Chez Sue Chef

Note: Go to a chili cook-off competition sometime and you'll see how many variations there are of this popular "soup." I was once a judge in a chili contest, and I was amazed what people came up with (most of the offerings extremely tasty). The bottom line is that many people who make chili think their recipe is the best. I wouldn't say mine is the best – just simply and modestly worthy of rapturous acclaim.

INGREDIENTS

2 tbsp. canola or grapeseed oil

1 lb. hot Italian sausage links in casings

2 large white onions, chopped

2 large green bell peppers, chopped

1½ lbs. round steak, cut into very small cubes

1 14½ to 15 oz. can stewed tomatoes (break into small pieces with spoon while cooking)

6 very large garlic cloves, finely chopped

1 28-oz. can tomato sauce

2 bay leaves

1 6-oz. can tomato paste

1 12-oz. bottle of beer (not dark beer)

3 tbsp. Mexican-style chili powder

2 tsp. ground cumin

1 tbsp. sugar

2 tsp. salt

PREPARATION

Heat 1 tbsp. of the oil in a large soup pot over moderate heat. Remove the casings from the sausage and with hands, break into small pieces and add to the pot. Sauté sausage until browned and all fat has been rendered. Line a large plate with paper towels, and turn sausage and grease onto the plate. There will be a small amount of grease remaining in the pot. To this grease, add the second tbsp. of oil. Add chopped onions and green peppers to the pot and cook until tender. Add round steak and cook, stirring occasionally, until the meat is no longer pink. Return sausage to pot.

Add all of the remaining ingredients and simmer over low heat, stirring occasionally, for 2 hours.

The chili is now ready to serve, and is delicious. However, if you make it the day before, and allow it to sit in the refrigerator overnight, it will be even better. Reheat and serve and let the raves begin. Serves 4–6

Lentil Spinach Soup

INGREDIENTS

1 lb. Italian turkey or chicken link sausage

1 tbsp. olive oil

1 large sweet yellow onion, chopped

5 cups chicken broth

1 cup dried lentils, rinsed

¼ tsp. red pepper flakes

12 oz. fresh spinach (baby leaves)

1 tsp. Herbamare® or salt

Parmesan cheese

PREPARATION

Slice sausage into ¼ inch rounds. Heat the olive oil in a large saucepan (or Dutch oven) over moderately high heat. Cook the sausage until lightly browned on both sides, remove with a slotted spoon and set aside. Add onion to pot and cook over moderate heat until softened, but not browned. Return the sausage to the pot and add chicken broth, lentils, and red pepper flakes. Bring to a boil. Reduce heat to low, cover and simmer for 25–30 minutes, or until lentils are tender. Make sure you do not overcook or lentils will be not just tender but mushy. Remove cover and stir in spinach and cook several minutes more, or until spinach has wilted and is tender. Stir in Herbamare® and cook for a few more minutes.

Serve Parmesan cheese on the side to be sprinkled on top of soup if desired. Serves 4

Cauliflower Cheddar Soup

INGREDIENTS

1 cup chopped shallots (or a combination of shallots and scallions, or all scallions (white part only)

2 tbsp. unsalted butter

1 small head of cauliflower, separated into flowerets

3 cups chicken broth

1 tsp. Herbamare® or salt

½ tsp. black pepper

1¼ cup sharp Cheddar cheese, grated

4 tbsp. finely chopped scallion greens

PREPARATION

In a heavy saucepan, melt the butter over low heat and cook the shallots/scallions, stirring, just until softened. Add the cauliflower and the broth and bring to a boil. Reduce heat to low and simmer, covered, for about 15 minutes, or until the cauliflower is tender.

Remove from heat and let sit a couple minutes. With an immersion blender, blend mixture until the cauliflower is puréed and mixed thoroughly with the broth. The soup should have a smooth, creamy appearance and texture. Next, stir in the Herbamare®, pepper, Cheddar and scallion greens. Return soup to heat and cook until the cheese has melted and the soup is hot. Serves 4

Santa Fe Corn Chowder *Adapted from Gourmet magazine, Condé Nast Publications*

INGREDIENTS

2 tbsp. sunflower oil

1 lb. hot & spicy sausage (I use chorizo – Spanish sausage)

1½ tbsp. butter

1 cup chopped onion

½ cup chopped celery

1 cup chopped red bell pepper

½ cup chopped green bell pepper

1 1-lb. bag frozen white sweet corn

1 bay leaf

1 tsp. dried thyme

6 cups chicken broth

1 large boiling potato, peeled and cut into ½ inch cubes

¼ cup milk

½ tsp. salt

¼ tsp. pepper

2 tbsp. chopped fresh cilantro

PREPARATION

Heat the oil in a large pot or kettle. Cut chorizo into small pieces and place directly in the pot. Cook, stirring occasionally, until fat is released and the sausage is well browned on all sides. Line a large plate with several paper towels. Turn the sausage onto the plate and let the excess grease drain onto the paper towels.

Add the butter to the pot (do not wipe the pot first). Add the onion, the celery, and the bell peppers and cook the vegetables, stirring occasionally, until they are softened. Add the corn, the bay leaf, and the thyme, along with the reserved cooked sausage, and cook the mixture, stirring, for several minutes. Add the broth and simmer the mixture, stirring occasionally, for 30 minutes. Add the potato and the milk and continue to simmer the soup, stirring occasionally, for another 30 minutes, or until the potatoes are very tender.

Discard the bay leaf, season the soup with salt and pepper, and stir in the chopped cilantro. Serves 8

Note: This soup is yummy the day you make it, but is even better the next day. I find this is the case with many soup recipes.

Chicken Tortilla Soup

INGREDIENTS

1 tbsp. extra-virgin olive oil

¾ cup chopped red onion

3 large garlic cloves, finely chopped

4–5 cups shredded chicken meat removed from a rotisserie roasted chicken (this is easiest done by hand – use white and dark meat combination)

1½ cups frozen whole-kernel corn (or a 1 lb.. bag)

½ cup dry white wine (or dry vermouth)

2 tbsp. chopped seeded jalapeño pepper

1 tsp. ground cumin

1 tsp. Worcestershire sauce

2 tsp. chili powder

2½ cups chicken broth (preferably organic free-range chicken broth)

1 large (28-oz.) can diced tomatoes, drained

2 cans (undiluted) cream of tomato soup (preferably Amy's® Cream of Tomato)

1 tbsp. fresh lime juice

Optional garnishes to serve on the side: Tortilla chips, sour cream, grated cheddar cheese

PREPARATION

Heat the olive oil in a large non-stick pot over medium heat. Add onion and sauté until softened. Stir in all remaining ingredients except for the lime juice and bring slowly to a boil. Reduce heat and simmer for one hour. Right before serving, stir in the lime juice and simmer for another couple minutes. Serves 6–8

Windham, NH, 2006
Mamma Mia, Karen

Karen

Karen now lives in North Carolina, but is originally a "Jersey Girl." Knowing Karen makes me understand what kind of woman Bruce Springstein had in mind when he sang that song.

Once I visited Karen in New Hampshire on a cold, blustery day. As with most of my friends, when we arrived at her home we headed directly to the kitchen, where I was overtaken by a heavenly aroma. I said, "I hope that's my lunch!" It was, and here is her recipe for Chicken Tortilla Soup.

Turkey Chili

INGREDIENTS

1 turkey breast with skin (big enough to yield 2 lbs. of turkey cubes, or approx. 2½ lbs.

¼ cup grapeseed oil

2 cups chopped sweet yellow onions

2½ tbsp. finely chopped garlic

1 tbsp. ground cumin

1 lb. ground turkey

⅔ cup medium barley

2 one-lb cans chickpeas, drained and rinsed

1 fresh jalapeño pepper, seeded and inner membranes removed, finely chopped (should equal approx. 3–4 tbsp.)

6½ cups chicken broth plus additional ½ cup to mix with cornstarch

1 tsp. dried marjoram

½ tsp. ground savory

1½ tbsp. cornstarch

1 tsp. Herbamare® or salt

Monterey Jack cheese for sprinkling on top (or shredded Mexican blend, e.g. Sharp Cheddar, Monterey Jack, Asadero and Queso Blanco cheeses)

PREPARATION

Preheat oven to 350 degrees. Generously sprinkle the turkey breast with salt and pepper. Roast the turkey until done; the time will vary depending on the size of the breast used. The turkey should feel springy to the touch, and the skin should be golden brown. Remove from the oven and set aside to cool enough so it can be handled.

In a large kettle or Dutch oven, heat the oil over moderate heat and cook the onions until softened. Add the garlic and cook one minute longer. Add the cumin and cook, stirring, for 5 minutes. Add the ground turkey and cook, breaking up into small pieces, until the turkey is cooked through and no longer pink.

While the ground turkey is cooking, remove the skin and bones from the roasted turkey breast and cut the meat into small cubes. If you use a breast that weighs about 2 ½ lbs., you can assume that after the bones and skin are removed, you will have approx. 2 lbs. of turkey meat remaining. Add the cubed turkey to the kettle along with the barley, chickpeas, chopped jalapeño pepper, 6 ½ cups of the chicken broth, marjoram, and savory and simmer the mixture, covered, stirring occasionally, for 45 minutes.

Dissolve the cornstarch in the remaining ½ cup of chicken broth and add to the chili. Continue to cook, uncovered, for an additional 15 minutes, stirring occasionally. Add the Herbamare®, stir to combine, and cook for an additional 5 minutes. Ladle chili into bowls, and top each serving generously with grated cheese. Serve additional cheese on the side. Serves 8–10

It's a new day – and I'm feline fine.

Eggplant Tomato Soup with Basil

INGREDIENTS

1 medium eggplant (approx. 1 lb.)

6 tbsp. extra-virgin olive oil

2 large shallots, finely chopped (approx. 1 cup)

2 large garlic cloves, finely chopped

1 tsp. dried oregano

1 large (28-oz.) can petite diced tomatoes, drained

1½ cups chicken broth

1 tsp. Herbamare® or salt

¼ tsp. black pepper

⅛ tsp. cayenne pepper

1 cup packed fresh basil leaves, rinsed and dried on paper towels

3 oz. crumbled goat cheese

PREPARATION

Place eggplant on a broiling pan lined with aluminum foil. Preheat broiler and put broiler pan with eggplant on the lower third of the oven. Broil until the eggplant is charred on all sides, and the inside is very soft. Remove from oven, put eggplant on a plate and allow it to cool until it is not too hot to be handled. At that point, peel off the skin (with a knife remove all eggplant from the skin that clings to it) and cut all of the cooked eggplant into very small pieces. The pieces will appear more like mush than defined pieces of eggplant.

Heat 3 tbsp. of the olive oil in a medium sized saucepan over moderately low heat and add the shallots, garlic and oregano. Sauté for several minutes, or until the shallots are tender. Add the eggplant, tomatoes, chicken broth, Herbamare®, pepper and cayenne. Simmer, partly covered, for 30 minutes.

Puree the basil in a mini food processor with the remaining 3 tbsp. of olive oil. Add the goat cheese to the processor and blend until combined and set aside.

When soup is spooned into serving bowls, place a good-sized dollop of the basil goat cheese mixture on the top of each serving. Serves 4–6

Sausage & White Bean Stew

Adapted from The Gourmet Cookbook *(2004), Condé Nast Publications*

INGREDIENTS

2 tbsp. extra-virgin olive oil

1 lb. sweet Italian sausage, broken into pieces

5 large garlic cloves, finely chopped

1 tsp. red pepper flakes

10–12 oz. fresh baby leaf spinach

2 15 to 16-oz. cans white beans (such as navy or great northern), drained and rinsed

3 cups chicken broth

2 tbsp. unsalted butter

½ cup finely grated Parmigiano-Reggiano cheese

2 cups chopped and seeded fresh tomatoes

2 tbsp. chopped fresh flat-leaf parsley

½ tsp. Kosher salt

Additional shaved or grated Parmigiano-Reggiano cheese for sprinkling on top

PREPARATION

Heat 1 tbsp. of the oil in a large saucepan or Dutch oven over moderately high heat until hot. Brown the sausage, stirring and breaking up pieces until they are small, until it is no longer pink. Remove sausage from the pot with a slotted spoon and drain on paper towels. Pour off all excess grease.

Add the second tbsp. of olive oil to the pot, reduce heat to moderately low. Add the garlic and red pepper flakes and cook, stirring, for approx. 1 minute. Add spinach and cook, stirring, until wilted. Add beans and cook for an additional minute. Return the drained sausage to the pot.

Add chicken broth and bring to a gentle boil. Stir in the butter, cheese, tomatoes, and parsley and cook, stirring, until the butter is melted and the stew is thoroughly heated. Add the salt.

Serve with additional cheese on the side for sprinkling on top of stew. Serves 4–6

Crabmeat Gumbo

INGREDIENTS

¼ lb. salt pork, cubed

¼ cup butter (4 tbsp., 2 of the tbsp. softened to room temperature)

¾ cup chopped onion

2 cups frozen okra, defrosted on a large plate lined with paper towels

1 28-oz. can petite diced tomatoes (undrained)

3 large cloves garlic, finely chopped

¼ lemon, very thinly sliced, remove seeds

1 bay leaf

3 cups boiling water

½ tsp. salt

¼ tsp. paprika

Several drops of Tabasco sauce

1 tsp. Worcestershire sauce

2 tbsp. flour

1 lb. lump crabmeat, picked over carefully to remove all shells

1 tsp. Herbamare® or salt

Brown rice to accompany, cooked according to package directions

PREPARATION

In a heavy pot, cook the salt pork over medium heat until fat has been rendered and the salt pork cubes are well browned. Remove the salt pork with a slotted spoon and place on paper towels to cool. To fat remaining in the pot add 2 tbsp. of the butter and the onions and cook until the onion is softened and transparent.

When the salt pork is cool enough to handle, remove completely any fat that remains on the cubes, and cut the meat that is left into very small pieces. Add to the pot.

Add the okra, tomatoes, garlic, lemon and bay leaf to the pot and bring to a boil. Add the boiling water, salt, paprika, Tabasco sauce and Worcestershire sauce. Lower the heat and simmer, partially covered, for one hour.

Blend the 2 tbsp. of softened butter with the flour until it forms a paste and stir this mixture, a little at a time, into the simmering vegetables. When thickened and smooth, stir in the crabmeat and the Herbamare®. Continue to heat until very hot and serve over cooked rice. Serves 4–6

Curried Lentil Soup with Tomatoes & Spinach
Adapted from The Gourmet Cookbook (2004), Condé Nast Publications

INGREDIENTS

¼ cup grapeseed oil

1 generous cup chopped onions

3 large garlic cloves, finely chopped

1 tbsp. finely chopped fresh gingerroot

1 tbsp. curry powder

1 tsp. ground cumin

1 cup lentils, rinsed well with cold water in a colander

3 cups chicken broth

2 cups water

1 generous cup chopped seeded fresh tomatoes

1 10-oz. package fresh baby leaf spinach

1½ tsp. Herbamare® or salt

½ tsp. black pepper

1 tbsp. fresh lemon juice

PREPARATION

Heat oil in a large heavy saucepan (or Dutch oven) over moderate heat; add onion and cook, stirring occasionally, until softened and lightly browned. Add the garlic and ginger and cook, stirring, for 1 minute. Add curry and cumin and cook, stirring, for 30 seconds. Add lentils, stock, water, and bring to a boil. Reduce heat and simmer, covered, until lentils are tender, 20–25 minutes.

Stir in tomatoes and spinach and simmer, uncovered, stirring occasionally, until the spinach is totally wilted and incorporated. Add Herbamare®, pepper and lemon juice. Serves 4

Turkey & White Bean Chili

INGREDIENTS

1 tbsp. extra-virgin olive oil

1 medium onion, rough chopped (to equal approx. 1¼ cups)

2 large garlic cloves, finely chopped

1 lb. ground turkey breast

1 tbsp. chili powder

1 tsp. ground cumin

1 15 to 15½ oz. can small white beans, rinsed and drained (e.g. cannelloni, white navy beans – I like Goya® Habichuelas Blancas)

1 14 to 15 oz. can diced tomatoes

1 cup chicken broth

¼ cup chopped fresh cilantro leaves

2 tsp. Herbamare® or salt

Grated cheese of choice to serve on the side (optional)

PREPARATION

Heat the oil in a large saucepan or Dutch oven over medium-high heat. Add the onion and cook, stirring occasionally, until softened. Add the garlic and cook for an additional minute.

Add the turkey and cook, breaking up the meat, until no pink pieces remain. Stir in the chili powder and cumin. Add the drained beans and the tomatoes with juice and chicken broth. Bring to a boil. Reduce heat to medium-low, cover, and cook until flavors blend, about 15–20 minutes. Remove cover and add cilantro and Herbamare®. Cook for an additional 10 minutes. Serves 4–6

Spicy Lamb & Lentil Soup with Cilantro Cream

INGREDIENTS

3 tbsp. butter

2 medium sweet yellow onions, chopped

1 cup chopped fresh flat-leaf (Italian) parsley

2 tbsp. chopped celery leaves

1 tbsp. black pepper

1 tsp. tumeric

1½ lbs. boneless lamb (all fat removed), cut into 1 inch cubes

2 tbsp. grapeseed oil

1 lb. spicy sausage, sliced ¼ inch thick (e.g. smoked Andouille)

1 28-oz. can crushed tomatoes

4 cups beef broth

3 cups water

2 cups lentils, rinsed well with cold water in a colander

½ cup fresh cilantro leaves, loosely packed

½ cup sour cream

1 tsp. salt

PREPARATION

In a large kettle/Dutch oven, melt the butter over moderate heat and add the onions, parsley, celery leaves, pepper and tumeric. Cook until the onions are tender. Add the lamb cubes, stir to combine with the onion mixture, and cook for another 10 minutes, stirring frequently.

Meanwhile, in a separate skillet, heat 2 tbsp. of grapeseed oil over moderately high heat. Add the sausage slices and cook, stirring frequently, until the sausage is nicely browned on both sides. Remove with a slotted spoon and put on paper towels to drain off any excess grease.

Add the sausage, tomatoes, beef broth, water and lentils to the kettle and bring to a boil. Reduce heat to low, cover with a lid, and cook for 1 hour.

Place cilantro, sour cream and salt in a mini-food processor and blend until well combined and the cilantro is chopped. Remove with a spatula and add mixture to the soup, stirring to combine thoroughly. Cook an additional 5–10 minutes. Serves 10

Lentil Soup with Brown Rice

INGREDIENTS

3 tbsp. extra-virgin olive oil

1¼ cup chopped onion

1¼ cup chopped celery

6 cloves garlic, minced (to equal at least 1 tbsp.)

7 cups chicken broth

½ cup long grain brown rice

2 large tomatoes, chopped to equal at least 2 cups

¾ cup dry brown lentils, rinsed in cold water in a colander

1 tbsp. chopped fresh thyme (or 1½ tsp. dried thyme)

1 tbsp. chopped fresh oregano (or 1½ tsp. dried oregano)

1 generous tbsp. fresh lemon juice

1½ tsp. Herbamare® or salt

¼ tsp. black pepper

Grated Italian cheese to serve on the side (e.g. Asiago, Padano Parmesan)

PREPARATION

Heat the olive oil in a large pot or Dutch oven over medium heat. Add the onion, celery and garlic; cook for approx. 10 minutes, or until tender, stirring occasionally. Stir in the broth and uncooked brown rice. Bring to boiling; reduce heat and simmer, uncovered, for 10 minutes. Stir in the tomato and lentils, increase heat and return to boiling; reduce heat again and cover. Simmer for approx. 30 minutes or until the rice and lentils are tender, but not mushy.

Stir in the thyme, oregano, lemon juice, Herbamare® and pepper and simmer for about 5 minutes. Top each individual serving with about a tbsp. of grated cheese and serve additional grated cheese on the side. Serves 6

Purée of Asparagus Soup with Fontina

INGREDIENTS

1 tbsp. extra-virgin olive oil

1 tbsp. butter

½ cup (generous) chopped shallots

1 large garlic clove, finely chopped

2 lbs. asparagus, tough ends removed, snapped in half

4 cups chicken broth

1½ cups Fontina cheese (or substitute other Italian cheese, e.g. Asiaga or Parmesan)

½ cup finely chopped Prosciutto ham (best done in a mini-food processor) *Note: If you want this to be a vegetarian soup, omit the Prosciutto*

½ tsp. dried chervil

½ tsp. Herbamare® or salt

¼ tsp. black pepper

Shaved Parmigiano Reggiano cheese for garnish

PREPARATION

Heat the oil and butter over medium heat in a large saucepan (or Dutch oven). Add the shallots and sauté for about five minutes, or until softened. Do not brown. Add the garlic and stir to combine with the shallots.

Add the asparagus and broth to the pan and bring to a simmer. Cook until the asparagus is just tender. Remove from the heat and pour mixture into a large bowl. Let cool for several minutes, and then carefully purée with a hand immersion blender until the asparagus is very smooth. Return the asparagus mixture to the saucepan and add the cheese and prosciutto (if using). Stir in chervil, Herbamare® and pepper. Gently reheat mixture. Spoon into serving bowls and garnish each serving with some shaved Parmigiano Reggiano. Serves 4

Spinach Soup with Couscous & Chickpeas

INGREDIENTS

2 tbsp. extra-virgin olive oil

4 large cloves garlic, finely chopped

½ cup chopped shallots

8 cups vegetable broth

½ cup couscous

2 cups canned chickpeas (garbanzo beans), rinsed thoroughly and well drained

2 6-oz. packages baby leaf spinach

1 cup chopped fresh flat-leaf parsley

3 tbsp. chopped scallions

1 tbsp. chopped fresh dill, or 1½ tsp. dried dill

1 tsp. salt

½ tsp. black pepper

Juice of one medium lemon

1 tbsp. unsalted butter

PREPARATION

Heat the oil in a large pot over medium heat. Add the garlic and shallots and cook for 2 minutes, stirring frequently. Pour in the vegetable broth and bring to a boil.

Stir in the couscous and chickpeas and cook for 10 minutes, stirring often. Add the spinach, parsley, half of the scallions, dill, salt and pepper. Cook the soup for 10 more minutes, stirring frequently.

Just before serving, stir in the lemon juice, butter, and remaining scallions. Serves 4–6

Clyde's Clips:

It has been said that one of the ways cats demonstrate how happy they are is by sleeping. I resemble that remark.

Tomato-Basil Soup

INGREDIENTS

4 tbsp. butter

2 tbsp. olive oil

1 medium sweet (e.g. Vidalia) onion, sliced very thinly

½ cup chopped shallots

2 large sprigs of fresh thyme

½ tsp. salt

¼ tsp. pepper

4 garlic cloves, finely chopped

2 to 2½ lbs. fresh, ripe tomatoes, seeded and chopped

3 tbsp. tomato paste

1½ cup chicken broth

6 tbsp. coarsely chopped fresh basil

½ cup milk (2% low-fat OK)

¼ cup Parmesan cheese

¼ tsp. salt

Pesto to accompany (see p. 165)

PREPARATION

Heat the butter in a large pot over moderate heat and add the olive oil, and then add the sliced onion, shallots, thyme sprigs, salt and pepper. Cook stirring occasionally, until the onion is wilted. Add the garlic and stir for about one minute.

Add the tomatoes and tomato paste, stir to blend, and simmer for approx. 10 minutes. Add the chicken broth and half (3 tbsp.) of the chopped basil. Reduce heat and simmer for 30 minutes.

Remove pot from heat and remove thyme sprigs from the soup. With a hand blender, process the soup until it is smooth, but do not be concerned about making it perfectly smooth. Return pot to the stove over low heat. Stir in the milk, remaining 3 tbsp. of basil, and the Parmesan cheese and cook for several more minutes. Add the remaining ¼ tsp. of salt.

Place soup in individual serving bowls and top each serving with a generous dollop of pesto. Serves 6

Vegetables

My mother almost always cooked with fresh vegetables, mostly because she felt the flavor was better, not because of the nutrition aspect. It is important to know that frozen vegetables may provide even more nutrients, because the "fresh" produce you just bought at the grocery store may not be as fresh as you think, since time has elapsed from harvesting to being sorted, packaged and shipped. But the truth remains that frozen foods rarely taste as good as fresh (especially locally grown produce); in addition, processing may change the consistency.

The most important factor for retaining the nutrients in vegetables is how you cook them. Boiling vegetables in water is the worst way to cook vegetables in terms of loss of nutrients. When vegetables are boiled, especially boiled for more than a very short period, many of the nutrients leave the vegetables and are retained in the water. The best way to cook vegetables, not just to retain the nutrients but for flavor, is to steam, roast or grill them, and to keep the cooking time to the minimum. (See p. 215)

Getting back to Toni, my mother made the best vegetables imaginable because of a very simple and always successful procedure. Here's what she did: Steam vegetables, and when cooked perfectly, set aside. Pour off boiling water from pan used to set the vegetable steamer in, return to the stove and over moderately high heat, brown a generous amount of butter until it is a deep nutty shade of brown. Return the vegetables to the pan with the butter, stir gently to coat evenly, add a little salt (and pepper if desired). My mother mostly used the steaming with brown butter preparation for green vegetables, often broccoli, asparagus, or green beans – Magnifico!

I eat, therefore I am.

Testimonial

Sue and I met through our mutual friend Sheila, who was my neighbor. Over 20 years of friendship we have shared many meals together. My favorite meals have always been the ones prepared by Sue. She cooks like she lives – with passion, color and a zest for all that is good in the world.

Sue's delicious dishes can put a smile on your face and make your taste buds do a flavor dance. Having read some of the other testimonials, I am particularly looking forward to trying Sue's ginger cream cookies (hint hint).

Congratulations to Sue and her buddy Clyde for introducing so many to their love of cooking and to each other.

Judy Deason
Director of Administration, King & Spalding
Washington, DC

Green Beans with Mushroom Butter

INGREDIENTS

4 tbsp. unsalted butter

1 cup finely chopped mushrooms

2 small garlic cloves, finely chopped

¾ tsp. salt

⅛ tsp. pepper

1 lb. French-style (thin) green beans, ends trimmed

PREPARATION

In a small skillet, melt butter and cook over moderate heat until a nutty brown color. Remove from heat. Add mushrooms, garlic, salt and pepper and stir to combine. Set aside.

In a steamer set over boiling water, steam the green beans, covered, until tender (approx. 5 minutes). Remove beans from the steamer and toss them gently with the mushroom butter, combining well. Serves 4

Peas with Fresh Mint & Onions

INGREDIENTS

2 tbsp. unsalted butter

1 cup coarsely chopped onions

1 10-oz. package frozen petit green peas

2 tbsp. finely chopped fresh mint leaves

½ tsp. Herbamare® or salt

⅛ tsp. white pepper

PREPARATION

Heat the butter in a 12-inch heavy skillet over moderate heat. Add the onions and cook, stirring occasionally, until soft. Add peas, mint, Herbamare® and pepper and cook, stirring, until the peas are heated through.

Note: Small (petit) peas will cook quickly even though added to the skillet still frozen. Do not overcook – peas should be heated through but not mushy. Serves 3–4

Cauliflower Cheddar Gratin

INGREDIENTS

1 small head cauliflower, cut into small florets

2 tbsp. unsalted butter

1 tbsp. flour

¾ cup milk

1 cup sharp Cheddar cheese, coarsely grated

¼ cup finely chopped scallion greens

½ tsp. salt

¼ tsp. black pepper

1 tbsp. cream style horseradish (whipped)

10 (2-inch square) whole grain saltine crackers

PREPARATION

Steam the cauliflower in a vegetable steamer until tender, but not overcooked or mushy. When done, place in a buttered medium-sized baking dish.

While cauliflower is cooking, melt 1 tbsp. butter in a heavy saucepan over moderately low heat and whisk in the flour. Cook roux over low heat, whisking, for 3 minutes. Add the milk slowly, whisking, and bring to a boil, continuing to whisk. Reduce heat and simmer the sauce, whisking occasionally, for about 5 minutes. Remove from the heat and add the cheese, scallion greens, salt and pepper, and whisk until the cheese is melted. Pour the sauce over the cauliflower and stir gently to combine.

Coarsely crumble crackers by hand into a small bowl. Melt remaining 1 tbsp. butter in a small saucepan, remove from heat and stir in the horseradish. Add saltine crumbs to saucepan and stir gently to coat evenly. Sprinkle crumb topping evenly over the cauliflower.

Preheat oven to 450 degrees. Bake gratin in middle of oven until the topping is golden brown, approx. 10 minutes. Serves 4

Goat Cheese Mashed Potatoes

INGREDIENTS

1½ lbs. small red-skinned potatoes

8 oz. crumbled mild goat cheese

4 tbsp. butter, softened to room temperature

1 tbsp. fresh lemon juice

½ tsp. dried thyme

1 tsp. Herbamare® or salt

¼ tsp. black pepper

PREPARATION

Place potatoes in a large pot and cover with salted cold water (the water should come to about one inch above the potatoes). Bring the water to a boil, reduce heat and simmer the potatoes until they are very tender. Test with a knife (the knife should slide into the potatoes with no resistance). This will take about 30–40 minutes. If you want to speed up the process, cover the pot with a lid while the potatoes are simmering. Drain potatoes in a colander.

Place potatoes in a large bowl and add the goat cheese and softened butter. Mix with a hand-held electric mixer until the cheese and butter are completely incorporated and the potatoes are thoroughly mashed. The potatoes will not be perfectly smooth because of the inclusion of the potato skins. Stir in the lemon juice, thyme, Herbamare® and pepper and spoon into an oven-proof casserole serving dish. If you are not ready to serve the potatoes right away, reheat in the casserole dish before serving for 10–15 minutes in a preheated 325 degree oven. Serves 6

Tomatoes Provençal

Another recipe from Toni. I have made one change: My mother prepared this recipe with bottled Italian dressing. I think it is much better using homemade dressing, and I typically use the "Versatile Vinaigrette" recipe that is also used in my "Mozzarella and Tomato Salad" recipe.

INGREDIENTS

3 medium tomatoes

3 tbsp. (approx.) Versatile Vinaigrette (see p. 157)

2½ tbsp. butter

1 cup soft fresh bread crumbs (preferably whole wheat bread)

1 tbsp. finely chopped fresh parsley

2 medium cloves garlic, minced

½ tsp. salt

¼ tsp. pepper

PREPARATION

Cut out stem ends from tomatoes, and cut a thin slice from the other end to allow the tomato half to sit levelly. Cut tomatoes in half crosswise and scoop out the majority of the seeds (don't remove any pulp) and place in a baking dish. Dribble approx. ½ tbsp. of the vinaigrette/salad dressing over each tomato half.

In a small saucepan, melt butter and remove from heat. Add bread crumbs, parsley, garlic, salt and pepper and combine well. Spoon bread crumb mixture evenly over the tomato halves.

Preheat oven to 425 degrees. Bake the tomatoes approx. 10 minutes, or until the tomatoes are softened and the topping is browned. Serves 3–6

Toni with her sister & best buddy
York, PA, 1985

Stuffed Potatoes with Red Peppers & Shallots

INGREDIENTS

1 large baking potato

Peanut oil

3 tbsp. butter

⅓ cup finely chopped shallots

⅓ cup finely diced sweet red pepper

2 tbsp. chopped fresh chives

½ tsp. salt

¼ tsp. pepper

¼ cup sour cream

¼ cup plain yogurt

Grated Parmesan cheese for sprinkling tops (approx. 2 tbsp.)

PREPARATION

Preheat oven to 400 degrees. Wash potato with cold water and dry, and lightly rub skin with peanut oil. Bake the potato in the middle of the oven directly on the rack for at least one hour, preferably 1½ hours. The skin should feel very hard and crisp to the touch.

While potato is baking, heat the butter in a medium sized skillet, and sauté shallots and red pepper until tender. Add chives and salt and pepper; remove from heat and set aside.

When potato is baked, remove from the oven and let sit for a minute or two until it can be more easily handled. Cut the potato in half lengthwise (be careful – hot steam will escape), and scoop potato pulp into a bowl with a spoon. Be careful not to break or pierce skins. Place empty potato skin halves in a shallow baking dish.

Add the sour cream and yogurt to the pulp and mix well until thoroughly combined and fluffy. Add the sautéed vegetable mixture next, and mix until well combined.

With a spoon, divide the mixture evenly among each potato half, mounding on top. Finish by sprinkling each potato with some grated Parmesan cheese. Return to preheated oven and bake for approx. 10 minutes or until the potatoes are very hot and the tops are lightly browned. Serves 2

Lemon-Glazed Carrots

INGREDIENTS

1 tbsp. sunflower oil

2 tbsp. butter

1 lb. carrots, sliced diagonally about ¼ inch thick

¾ tsp. salt

2 tbsp. light brown sugar

2 tsp. grated lemon rind

1 tbsp. lemon juice

PREPARATION

Heat the oil and 1 tbsp. of the butter in a heavy skillet. Add the carrots and sauté, stirring, until carrots are evenly coated and shiny, about 2 minutes.

Add ⅓ cup of boiling water and the salt; cover skillet with a lid and simmer until the carrots are barely tender. The time this takes depends on the thickness of the carrots. Add the brown sugar, lemon rind, lemon juice, and remaining 1 tbsp. butter. Stir well to combine and melt sugar; simmer uncovered until the extra liquid evaporates and the carrots are glazed. Serves 4–6

I turn over the remote when you break out the catnip.

Sweet Potato & Carrot Purée

INGREDIENTS

2–3 large sweet potatoes (1½ to 2 lbs.)

1 lb. baby carrots

1 tbsp. firmly packed dark brown sugar

6 tbsp. unsalted butter, softened

½ cup crème fraîche (a good brand is Vermont Butter & Cheese Company®)

½ tsp. nutmeg

1 tsp. salt

⅛ tsp. cayenne pepper

PREPARATION

Scrub potatoes and cut a small deep slit in the top of each. Place potatoes directly on the center rack of a preheated 400 degree oven and bake for at least an hour, or until the potatoes are extremely tender when pierced with a fork. Remove from the oven and cool until they can be handled.

While the potatoes are cooking, steam carrots in a vegetable steamer until they are very tender. Place in a large bowl. Scrape out the flesh of the sweet potatoes and add to the carrots along with the brown sugar, softened butter and crème fraiche. Beat with a hand mixer until the mixture is very smooth and not at all lumpy. If preferred, instead of a hand mixer use a food processor fitted with a steel blade.

Add the nutmeg, salt and cayenne and mix or process briefly to blend.

Reduce the oven temperature to 350 degrees. Place the purée in an ovenproof serving dish and cover with foil. Heat the dish about 15–20 minutes or until hot. Serves 6

Roasting Peppers

The flavor of roasted bell peppers is a wonderful enhancement to many recipes. There are a lot of varieties of bottled roasted peppers that are acceptable if you want to save time. However, I feel it is always worth the time it takes to roast your own peppers, and it is relatively easy. Here's what to do:

Rinse peppers and cut out the stem. Preheat broiler and place peppers in a single layer on a broiler pan lined with foil. Broil peppers approx. 8–10 inches from the heat, turning often, until the peppers are well blackened on all sides. If you have never done this before, there may be some concern that you are ruining the peppers by burning them as they become very black. Not to worry, this is what is supposed to happen.

When the peppers are very soft and black, remove from the oven and cool until they can be handled. With your hands, peel off the blackened skin. The pulp will have some blackened areas remaining after the skin is peeled off, which is the way it should be. Remove the seeds and membranes on the inside of the peppers and proceed as desired, e.g., cut into strips or chop.

Twice-Baked Potatoes with Cheese & Chiles

INGREDIENTS

1 large baking potato

Peanut oil

2 tbsp. diced canned mild green chili peppers

1½ tbsp. chopped black olives

3 tbsp. sour cream, plus additional for topping

½ tsp. Herbamare® or salt

¼ tsp. black pepper

¼ cup grated Cheddar cheese, plus extra for sprinkling on top

PREPARATION

Rinse and dry potato and rub all over lightly with peanut oil. Place potato on the middle rack of a 400 degree preheated oven and bake for at least an hour. The skin should feel crispy to the touch, and the potato is tender when pierced with a fork.

Let the potato cool slightly and cut in half lengthwise. With a spoon, scrape the potato into a bowl. Be careful to remove as much potato as possible without tearing the potato skins. Put the skins in a small shallow oven-proof baking dish and set aside.

Mash the potato pulp and stir in the diced chili peppers, chopped olives, and sour cream. Season with Herbamare® and pepper and stir in ¼ cup grated Cheddar cheese.

Divide the potato mixture equally among the shells, and sprinkle liberally with additional grated cheese. Bake again, still at 400 degrees, until the potatoes are hot and the cheese on top is melted and bubbling. Top each potato with a generous dollop of sour cream and serve. Serves 2

Green Beans with Brown Butter Sauce

INGREDIENTS

1 lb. fresh green beans (French style)

2 tbsp. butter

2 tbsp. flour

1 cup chicken broth

1 bay leaf

½ tsp. salt

¼ cup grated Parmesan cheese

PREPARATION

Steam green beans until tender, but still firm and set aside. While green beans are steaming, brown the butter in a heavy large saucepan over medium heat until it is a deep nutty brown color. Add the flour and whisk until combined and cook for a couple minutes. Then add chicken broth, bay leaf and salt and continue cooking and whisking until sauce is well combined and thickened.

Add the grated cheese and stir until melted. Remove bay leaf from pan. Put green beans in saucepan and with a large spoon stir gently until beans are evenly coated with the sauce. Serves 4–6

Note: French cut green beans are the ones that are slender and smaller than regular green beans. All the green bean recipes in this book call for this type of green bean, because they are generally much more tender and flavorful. However, they are also more expensive, but worth it.

Please leave me a message. My brain can't get to my body right now.

Steaming Vegetables

When water is heated to the boiling point it changes into steam, which is compressed so that it supplies heat and power. Vegetable steamers (the ones I've used) are metal, and typically unfold to provide a flat surface that is filled with holes on which you place the vegetables. The steamer has "feet" on the bottom that keep the steamer above the water, and has a handle in the middle for removing the steamer from the pan when the vegetables are cooked.

Here's what you do: Heat water in a pan large enough to hold your vegetable steamer and bring to the boiling point. Steam will begin to rise off the surface of the water. Place the steamer with vegetables on top in the pan over the water. Make sure that the amount of water does not reach the bottom of the steamer – there should be air space between the top surface of the water and the bottom of the steamer. Immediately place a lid on the pan, and reduce the heat to moderately low.

The tricky point from here is to assure that the vegetables are not overcooked. There is no set time because it depends on what you are cooking. It is important to remove the lid every couple of minutes and test the vegetables with a knife tip to assess when they are done, which means that they are beginning to get tender, but are still firm. A good rule of thumb is that steamed vegetables should not change color. It is especially easy to see if you've overcooked bright green vegetables, such as broccoli or green beans, because if you do, they turn an unattractive yellowish-green color. When steaming vegetables it is always better to err on the side of slightly undercooking them than to slightly overcook them.

Brussels Sprouts with Garlic & Pine Nuts

Think you don't like Brussels sprouts? Try this recipe and you may change your mind!

INGREDIENTS

2 tbsp. unsalted butter	1 tbsp. extra-virgin olive oil	2 tbsp. pine nuts
2 large garlic cloves, very thinly sliced	½ lb. Brussels sprouts, ends trimmed off and cut in half lengthwise	Salt and black pepper

PREPARATION

Melt the butter in a 10 inch heavy skillet over moderate heat. Add garlic and sauté, stirring, until pale golden. With a slotted spoon, transfer the garlic to a small dish and set aside.

Reduce heat to moderately low, and add the olive oil to the skillet. Arrange sprouts cut side down in the skillet in one layer. Cook uncovered without turning until sprouts are tender and undersides are a deep golden brown, about 15 minutes. Note: If you wish the sprouts to be more tender (but take care not to overcook) cover the sprouts during the last 5 minutes of cooking. Transfer the cooked sprouts to a plate and set aside.

Add the pine nuts to the skillet and cook, stirring, until they are golden brown. Stir in the garlic and sprouts. Sprinkle with salt and pepper and stir gently to combine all ingredients. Serves 2–3

Locally Grown Produce

Buying ingredients from local farmers and choosing organic foods are two good ways to take responsibility about the environment. When you cook your own food instead of buying fast or prepackaged food, you can have more control about putting locally raised food on your table.

I have noticed a recent trend in the food stores I frequent regarding local produce. Food produced locally is boldly marked as such, as if to say, "Good for us – look what we have to offer you!" If a food store you patronize does not offer local produce, consider telling the owner or manager that you would like to have the option to purchase more locally grown produce.

I'll relate an incident that occurred recently. I was in a food store on a mission to purchase some decent tomatoes. Most of the tomatoes available were anemic looking, and felt hard as a rock. Lo and behold, I came across a table laden with gorgeous looking tomatoes, with a big sign that proclaimed "Locally Grown!"

In the check-out line, the woman behind me was enviously eyeing my locally grown tomatoes. She proclaimed the tomatoes she was about to buy bore no resemblance to my beauties. I said, "Well, clearly you didn't select your tomatoes from the locally grown section." Without further ado, she exited the line, and retreated to the produce section to exchange her tomatoes for the clearly better option available. I had a huge smile on my face as I left the store, feeling a small but important victory had been won.

I have no intention of writing a political treatise here, or heralding a call to action. If I had the knowledge and writing skills of Barbara Kingsolver, I would have written "Animal, Vegetable, Miracle," a book that changed my life.

Peas & Cucumbers with Dill

INGREDIENTS

½ lb. cucumbers, preferably seedless

2 tbsp. unsalted butter

½ tsp. salt

⅛ tsp. black pepper

2 cups shelled fresh green peas or 2 cups of frozen peas (not thawed)

2 tbsp. water

1 tbsp. dried dill

2 tsp. fresh lemon juice

PREPARATION

Peel cucumbers and remove seeds if seedless cucumbers were not used. Quarter the cucumbers lengthwise and cut into ½ inch pieces. Heat the butter in a 12-inch heavy skillet over moderately high heat until the foam subsides. Add the cucumbers, salt and pepper and cook, stirring, for approx. 5 minutes. Add the peas and water, cover and simmer for an additional 5 minutes.

Remove the lid and stir in the dill and lemon juice. Serves 4

Wilted Spinach with Garlic

INGREDIENTS

1 tbsp. extra-virgin olive oil

1 tbsp. butter

3 cloves garlic, cut into very thin slivers or slices

12 to 16 oz. of fresh baby leaf spinach

½ tsp. salt

¼ tsp. black pepper

2 tbsp. toasted pine nuts (optional – but recommended)

PREPARATION

Heat the olive oil and butter in a large sauce pan (Dutch oven) over medium heat. Add garlic and sauté for 2 minutes, or until the garlic just begins to turn a golden color. Add the spinach, in batches if necessary, and toss (I use a plastic pasta fork) until all of the spinach is just wilted. Stir in the salt, pepper and pine nuts (if using) and serve.

Note: If you do not buy spinach that is in bags and pre-washed, and if you rinse the spinach, assure that as much moisture as possible is removed before cooking (a salad spinner is effective for this purpose). Serves 2–3

Baked Belgian Endive with Walnuts

INGREDIENTS

4 large Belgian endives (approx. 1 to 1 ¼ lbs.)

3 tbsp. extra-virgin olive oil

Herbamare® or salt and black pepper

3 tbsp. (generous) toasted coarsely chopped walnuts

½ cup shaved Parmigiano Reggiano cheese

PREPARATION

Preheat oven to 350 degrees. Trim endives by cutting off a small amount of the bottom (the bottoms should still be intact), and then quarter lengthwise. Place endives in a baking dish large enough to hold them in a single layer. Pour olive oil over and toss with fingers to coat evenly. Sprinkle endives generously with Herbamare® and pepper. Cover the baking dish with foil and bake in the middle of the oven for approx. 40 minutes, or until very tender.

Sprinkle the endives evenly with the walnuts and cheese and bake, uncovered, for about 10 more minutes, or until the cheese is melted. Serves 3–4

Sour Cream Mashed Potatoes

INGREDIENTS

4 medium or 3 large potatoes, peeled

4 tbsp. butter

⅓ cup (generous) minced onion

1 cup sour cream

2 tsp. Herbamare® or salt

1 can French fried onion pieces for sprinkling on top (_Optional_) Note: If you decide to include the onions, buy a high quality brand that is not made with hydrogenated (or partly hydrogenated) oil

PREPARATION

Place potatoes in large pot and add enough cold water to completely cover potatoes. Bring water to a boil and simmer, uncovered, until potatoes are very tender when tested with a fork. Remove potatoes from pot and place in a large bowl.

While potatoes are cooking, melt 2 tbsp. butter in a small saucepan and add onions. Sauté until the onions are translucent and softened. Put the onions in the bowl with the cooked potatoes along with the remaining 2 tbsp. butter, sour cream and the Herbamare®. Beat with a hand-held electric mixer until the potatoes are very fluffy and smooth.

Place in an oven-proof casserole dish and sprinkle top liberally with the French-fried onion pieces, if using. Bake at 350 degrees for 10–15 minutes, or until just heated through. Serves 6

Green Beans Oriental

Toni made this dish a lot for company; she liked the fact that it can be made ahead. A lot of green bean casseroles call for frozen or canned green beans, but of course my mom made this with fresh beans, which makes a big difference.

INGREDIENTS

¾ lb. fresh "French cut" green beans

2½ cups fresh bean sprouts

1 small onion, chopped fine

1 8-oz. can sliced water chestnuts

½ lb. fresh mushrooms, sliced thin

1½ cups grated sharp cheddar cheese

Cream Sauce:

3 tbsp. butter

1 tbsp. flour

1 cup milk

½ tsp. Herbamare® or salt

¼ tsp. black pepper

PREPARATION

For the cream sauce: Melt butter in a small saucepan over medium heat and whisk in the flour. Cook for a few minutes and whisk in the milk. Continue to cook until the sauce has thickened. Stir in the Herbamare® or salt and pepper. Set aside.

Steam the green beans until just tender. Place half of the beans on the bottom of a large casserole dish (I use a round one – 9 inches in diameter and 3 ½ inches deep). Sprinkle the beans with Herbamare® or salt and pepper. Cover the beans with half of the bean sprouts, half of the chopped onion, half of the water chestnuts, half of the mushrooms, and half of the cheese. Cover with half of the cream sauce.

Repeat layers with the remaining beans (sprinkled with Herbamare® or salt and pepper), bean sprouts, onions, water chestnuts, mushrooms and cheese. Top with remaining cream sauce.

Preheat the oven to 375 degrees and bake the casserole for approx. 45 minutes, or until the casserole is extremely hot and bubbly.

Note: If you make this ahead, refrigerate covered until ready to cook, and then bring to room temperature before baking. Serves 6

Sue says, "Carpe Diem" – I say Z-Z-Z-Z's the day.

Orange Butternut Squash

INGREDIENTS

1¼ to 1½ lbs. butternut squash, peeled and cut into large chunks

2 tbsp. butter, softened

1 fresh orange

1 generous tbsp. grated orange rind from orange

¾ tsp. salt

2 tbsp. maple syrup (good quality - pure)

PREPARATION

Steam the squash covered in a vegetable steamer until soft and tender but not mushy.

Remove from steamer, place squash in a serving bowl and add the butter. Mash the squash with an electric immersion blender until very smooth.

While the squash is cooking, grate the orange rind, then cut off the remaining rind from the orange. Cut the orange pulp segments into small pieces, removing all seeds. Some orange juice will be released when you are doing this. Keep as much juice as possible.

When the squash has been puréed, stir the rind, the orange segments with juice, salt and maple syrup into the squash mixture. Serves 4

Asparagus Gratin

Adapted from Gourmet magazine, Condé Nast Publications

INGREDIENTS

1 lb. asparagus, tough ends removed and cut diagonally into 2 inch pieces

1 tbsp. mascarpone cheese

1 tbsp. finely grated Parmigiano Reggiano cheese

½ tsp. salt

1 tbsp. extra-virgin olive oil

1 tbsp. butter

¼ cup chopped shallots

½ cup fresh bread cubes (fresh bread cut into pieces approx. ½ inch in size)

2 tbsp. pine nuts

⅛ tsp. black pepper

¼ cup finely grated Parmigiano-Reggiano cheese

PREPARATION

Butter a shallow ceramic flameproof baking dish. Steam the asparagus until tender, and place in baking dish. Toss asparagus with the mascarpone cheese, 1 tbsp. of the Parmigiano-Reggiano cheese, and ¼ tsp. of the salt. Set aside.

While the asparagus is steaming, heat the oil and the butter in a heavy skillet over moderate heat and add shallots, stirring, until pale golden and softened, about 3 minutes. Add the bread cubes and pine nuts and continue to cook, stirring, until nuts and bread have begun to brown in spots. Remove skillet from heat and add the remaining ¼ tsp. salt, the black pepper, and ¼ cup Parmigiano-Reggiano cheese. Stir to combine well.

Preheat the broiler. Sprinkle the bread crumb mixture evenly over the steamed asparagus and broil approx. 7 inches from the heat until the topping is golden brown. Be watchful that the topping browns and does not burn. Serves 3–4

Sue's Tips: I was making this recipe one evening and simply ran out of steam (and time). So I stopped right after paragraph #1 above (in other words, I omitted making the topping). The asparagus is delicious with or without the topping. However, the topping is heavenly, so when making this recipe, I almost always take the extra steps to include it.

Ginger Carrots

INGREDIENTS

1½ lbs. baby carrots, trimmed

Juice from one very large orange (should measure at least ⅓ cup)

¼ cup honey

3 tbsp. unsalted butter

1 generous tbsp. grated orange rind

1 tsp. ground ginger

½ tsp. Herbamare® or salt

2 tbsp. minced crystallized ginger

PREPARATION

In a saucepan combine the carrots, orange juice, honey, butter, orange rind, ground ginger, and Herbamare®. Add enough cold water to not completely cover the carrots, but so that the bottoms of the carrots are slightly submerged. Bring to a boil and simmer the carrots, covered, for approx. 10 minutes, or until the carrots are just tender. Add the crystallized ginger and cook, uncovered, shaking the pan occasionally, over moderately high heat until the liquid is almost completely reduced and the carrots are glazed evenly. Serves 6

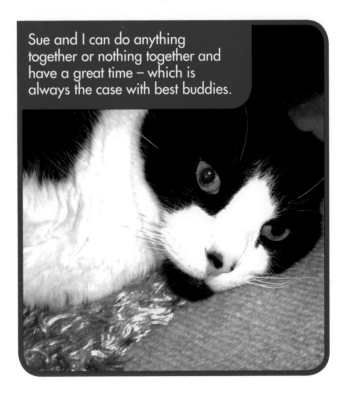

Sue and I can do anything together or nothing together and have a great time – which is always the case with best buddies.

Green Beans with Almonds

INGREDIENTS

½ lb. French cut (thin) green beans

2 tbsp. butter

2 tbsp. sliced almonds

1 tbsp. lemon juice

1 tsp. Dijon-style mustard

Herbamare® or salt

PREPARATION

Cook green beans in a vegetable steamer over boiling water until just tender. Remove steamer from pan and pour off water. To pan, add butter and almonds. Cook over moderate heat until both the almonds and the butter are a nutty golden brown color. Reduce heat to low and add the lemon juice and mustard; stir until combined.

Return green beans to pan and sprinkle with Herbamare®. Stir gently until beans are evenly coated with the sauce and warmed. Serves 2–3

Never feel guilty about anything. What's done is done. Move on and find another piece of furniture to destroy.

Zucchini with Pecan Brown Butter

INGREDIENTS

2 tbsp. butter

¼ cup chopped pecans

1 lb. zucchini (or 2 large zucchini)

¾ tsp. Herbamare® or salt

¼ tsp. black pepper

PREPARATION

Melt the butter in a large heavy skillet over moderate heat, and add the pecans and cook, stirring occasionally, until both the pecans and the butter are browned.

While the pecans are cooking, cut the zucchini in half lengthwise, and then cut each zucchini half lengthwise into thirds. Next cut the zucchini horizontally so that the pieces are about ½ inch wide.

When the butter and pecans are browned, add the zucchini to the skillet along with the Herbamare® and pepper and cook, stirring frequently, until the squash is just tender, which will take approx. 10–15 minutes. Serves 4

Asparagus with Caesar Dressing

INGREDIENTS

1 tsp. crushed garlic

1 tbsp. Dijon mustard

1 tbsp. fresh lemon juice

2 tbsp. extra-virgin olive oil

1 lb. fresh asparagus, tough ends removed

¼ cup shaved Parmigiano Reggiano cheese

PREPARATION

In a small bowl, whisk together the garlic, mustard, lemon juice and olive oil until well combined. Set aside.

Steam the asparagus just until tender. Place cooked asparagus on a serving dish. Spoon the dressing over the asparagus. Sprinkle with the cheese. Serve warm or at room temperature. Serves 4

Potato-Tomato Gratin *Adapted from Gourmet magazine, Condé Nast Publications*

INGREDIENTS

1½ lbs. yellow-skinned potatoes (Yukon Gold is a good choice)

¼ cup milk

5 tbsp. unsalted butter

½ cup Kalamata olives, pitted if available (measure olives whole, and then chop)

4 large scallions, white part chopped to equal about 2 tbsp.)

1 tsp. Herbamare® or salt

½ tsp. black pepper

1 large garlic clove, minced

1½ cups fresh bread crumbs

¼ cup chopped fresh flat-leaf parsley leaves

⅓ cup grated Parmesan cheese

½ tsp. Herbamare® or salt

¼ tsp. black pepper

4 medium ripe tomatoes (vine-ripened is a good choice), cut into ¼ inch slices

PREPARATION

In a large heavy pot/kettle cover the potatoes with salted cold water by 2 inches and bring to a low boil. Simmer the potatoes until very tender, which should take 30–45 minutes. Drain in a colander and place in a large bowl.

Heat the milk with 3 tbsp. of the butter in a small saucepan until the butter is melted and set aside.

Mash the potatoes (unpeeled) with either a potato masher or a hand electric mixer. The potatoes should have more of a "smashed" than a "mashed" texture, meaning that there should be lumps and they should not be perfectly smooth. Gently fold in the heated milk, olives, scallions, 1 tsp. of Herbamare®, and ½ tsp. pepper.

Make the bread crumb mixture: In a non-stick skillet melt the remaining 2 tbsp. of butter over moderate heat, add the garlic and stir for about 30 seconds. Add the bread crumbs and cook, stirring, until golden. Remove from the heat and stir in the parsley, Parmesan, ½ tsp. Herbamare® and ¼ tsp. pepper and set aside.

Preheat oven to 400 degrees and butter a 2-quart gratin dish. Spread the potatoes in the gratin dish and top with the sliced tomatoes, overlapping them to completely cover the potatoes. Sprinkle the crumb mixture over the tomatoes and bake casserole in the middle of the oven until the top is golden brown and the tomatoes are tender, about 25 minutes. Serves 4–6

Sautéed Cherry Tomatoes with Garlic & Herbs

INGREDIENTS

1 tbsp. extra-virgin olive oil

1 pint cherry tomatoes, rinsed, dried, stems removed

½ tsp. Herbamare® or salt

¼ tsp. black pepper

3 tbsp. coarsely chopped fresh basil leaves

¼ cup thinly sliced scallions

2 tbsp. chopped fresh flat-leaf parsley

3 cloves minced garlic, or enough to equal 1½ to 2 tsp. minced garlic

1 tbsp. unsalted butter

PREPARATION

Heat the olive oil in a large skillet over medium heat. Add the tomatoes, Herbamare® and pepper and sauté, tossing occasionally, until some of the tomato skins begin to split, which should take approx. 5 minutes.

Stir in the basil, scallions, parsley and garlic and cook, stirring occasionally, for 2 minutes. Reduce the heat to low and add the butter. Continue to cook stirring gently, just until the butter is melted and the tomatoes are coated. Serve immediately. Serves 2–3

Broccoli with Brown Butter & Capers

INGREDIENTS

1 lb. fresh broccoli

3 tbsp. unsalted butter

2 tbsp. chopped capers

1 generous tbsp. chopped fresh flat-leaf parsley

¼ tsp. Herbamare® or salt

⅛ tsp. black pepper

PREPARATION

Cut stalks from broccoli and trim fibrous parts, then cut florets with whatever stems remain into florets that are approx. 1 to 1½ inches wide. Steam broccoli over boiling water, covered, until tender, approx. 6 minutes. Be careful to not overcook! Broccoli should be cooked just until tender, not soft/mushy.

Melt the butter in a small saucepan over moderate heat. Stir in the capers and cook, stirring occasionally, until the butter is a deep golden brown color. Remove from the heat and stir in the parsley, salt and pepper.

Toss the broccoli with the caper butter and serve hot. Serves 2–3

Broiled Tomatoes with Pesto

INGREDIENTS

2 large ripe tomatoes, cored and sliced in half horizontally

Herbamare® or salt for sprinkling on tomatoes

2 large garlic cloves

½ cup coarsely chopped basil

⅛ tsp. salt

Couple pinches of black pepper

2 tbsp. extra-virgin olive oil

¼ cup (generous) grated Parmesan cheese

2 tbsp. (generous) toasted pine nuts

PREPARATION

Place the tomato halves on a shallow broiler-proof baking dish and sprinkle tomatoes generously with Herbamare®. Place all remaining ingredients in a mini-food processor and process until pesto is finely chopped and all ingredients are well combined.

Place equal amounts of the pesto on the tomato halves. Preheat broiler and broil the tomatoes 6 to 8 inches from the heat until lightly browned, which should take approx. 5–10 minutes. Serves 2–4

Indian Carrots with Chutney

Adapted from Gourmet magazine, Condé Nast Publications

INGREDIENTS

⅓ cup slivered blanched almonds, toasted

¼ cup toasted sesame seeds

¾ lb. baby carrots, sliced in half lengthwise

4 tbsp. butter

½ tsp. curry powder

½ tsp. ground cumin

½ tsp. tumeric

1 apple, peeled, cored and diced

¼ cup golden raisins

¼ cup mango chutney

PREPARATION

Place the almonds and the sesame seeds in one layer in a shallow baking dish (pie plate is good) and toast in a preheated 350 degree oven, stirring occasionally, for about 10 minutes, or until they are golden.

Meanwhile, steam the carrots over boiling water, covered, in a vegetable steamer until just tender and set aside. In a large saucepan melt the butter over moderately low heat and stir in the curry powder, cumin, tumeric, toasted almonds, toasted sesame seeds, diced apple, raisins, chutney, and carrots. Cook the mixture until just heated through. Serves 4

Audrey

Audrey Hodtwalker Cassidy, my beloved mother-in-law, was a farm gal from Nebraska. Fond memories of Audrey include sitting in her kitchen in Gettysburg, Pa., sipping scotch and sodas together, laughing like schoolgirls.

The first time I spent Thanksgiving Day with the Cassidy family, Audrey made a side dish everyone raved about. I make this dish every year in her memory as a traditional part of our Thanksgiving meal. I know she would be delighted that I am now sharing with you her recipe for:

Spinach Soufflé

INGREDIENTS

2 16-oz. packages chopped frozen spinach, thawed

¼ lb. (8 tbsp.) melted butter

2 lbs. small curd cottage cheese (low-fat is preferable – 1% fat content)

½ lb. Kraft® Velveeta cheese, cut into small chunks

1 tsp. dry mustard

½ cup chopped shallots (The one change made was adding the shallots – I feel confident she would have approved!)

4 beaten eggs

PREPARATION

When the spinach is completely thawed, with hands, squeeze out as much excess water as possible. Place spinach in a large bowl and add the rest of the ingredients, except for the beaten eggs. When the spinach mixture is well combined, add the eggs and stir gently until all of the eggs are incorporated into the spinach mixture.

Preheat oven to 450 degrees. Turn the spinach mixture into a soufflé or other casserole-style baking dish. Bake 45 minutes to an hour, or until a knife inserted in the casserole comes out clean. Serves 6–8

Audrey with Sister Lee
Lincoln, NE, 1984

Creamed Squash with Cheese Au Gratin

INGREDIENTS

1 lb. yellow squash (approx. 4 medium squash)

1½ tbsp. butter

⅓ cup chopped shallots

2 tbsp. butter, softened

Sharp cheddar cheese, cut into small cubes (approx. ½ inch) to equal ¾ cup

¼ cup crème fraîche

2 tbsp. dry white wine

1 tsp. Herbamare® or salt

½ tsp. black pepper

½ cup fresh bread crumbs

¼ cup (generous) Parmesan cheese

PREPARATION

Trim ends off of the squash and then cut each squash into six pieces horizontally. Steam the squash in a vegetable steamer, covered, until very tender, but not mushy and drain in a colander.

While the squash is steaming, put ½ tbsp. of butter in a small saucepan and sauté the shallots until they are slightly softened. Set aside.

Place the drained squash in a large bowl and add the 2 tbsp. softened butter and mash the squash using either a potato masher or an immersion blender (my preference) until the butter is blended and the squash is puréed with no lumps remaining. Gently stir in the cheddar cheese cubes, crème fraîche, white wine, sautéed shallots, Herbamare®, and pepper until all ingredients are well combined. Pour squash mixture into a gratin dish, or a quiche dish.

Melt the remaining tbsp. butter (I do this in the same skillet used to cook the shallots) and cool slightly. Place the bread crumbs and Parmesan in a small bowl and stir in the melted butter. Sprinkle the crumbs evenly over the squash.

Preheat oven to 350 degrees and bake the squash for approx. 25–30 minutes, or until it is bubbling and the top is golden. Allow to sit for 5–10 minutes before serving. Serves 4

Corn Pudding

(Another recipe from the kitchen of Toni, my magical mother, who made simple recipes that made you hopeful seconds would be offered)

INGREDIENTS

4 tbsp. butter

1 cup chopped onions

2½ cups canned cream-style corn

3 tbsp. flour

2 tbsp. sugar, preferably organic

½ tsp. salt

¼ tsp. black pepper

4 eggs

1 cup buttermilk (low-fat OK, or regular whole milk)

Nutmeg and cinnamon for sprinkling

PREPARATION

Melt the butter in a small skillet and sauté the onions for 5–10 minutes over low heat, until they are opaque and softened. Transfer the onions with butter to a bowl and add the corn, flour, sugar, salt and pepper and mix until well combined.

Add the eggs and buttermilk and continue to stir until eggs and buttermilk are completely incorporated into the corn mixture.

Preheat oven to 350 degrees. Put the corn mixture in a soufflé style baking dish. Sprinkle the top generously with nutmeg and cinnamon. Bake uncovered for 2 ¼ hours, or until the pudding is set and nicely browned on top. Serves 6

Summer 1980, York, PA

Roasted Red Potatoes with Lemon

INGREDIENTS

3 lbs. small red potatoes, quartered

2 tbsp. butter

2 tbsp. extra-virgin olive oil

2 tbsp. fresh lemon juice

½ tsp. fresh thyme leaves, chopped, or 1 tsp. dried thyme

1 tbsp. grated lemon peel

2 tbsp. minced fresh parsley

PREPARATION

Preheat oven to 375 degrees. Butter a large shallow oven-safe casserole dish. Add potatoes. (Note: If potatoes are medium sized, cut into quarters, and then cut each quarter piece in half) and season generously with salt and pepper.

Melt butter with olive oil in small saucepan; add lemon juice and stir. Pour over potatoes and toss well with a spoon. Make sure that butter mixture is distributed as evenly as possible over potatoes. Sprinkle with thyme. Bake for 1 hour. Stir potatoes a couple times during this period.

Remove from oven and add grated lemon peel; toss to coat evenly. Return casserole to oven and continue baking until potatoes are tender and a very deep golden brown, approx. 20 minutes. During last 5 minutes of baking, sprinkle potatoes with minced parsley and stir to coat evenly. Serves 4–6

Twice-Baked Potatoes with Parmesan

Toni's version of twice-baked (stuffed) potatoes is still my favorite. This recipe is also very rich, so half a potato per person is the right amount. Ti amo, mamma mia!

INGREDIENTS

2 medium-sized russet (baking) potatoes

Peanut oil for rubbing the potatoes

3 tbsp. butter, softened to room temperature

4 tbsp. sour cream

4 tbsp. grated Parmesan cheese

2 tbsp. minced fresh chives

½ tsp. salt

½ tsp. pepper

PREPARATION

Preheat the oven to 400 degrees. Rinse potatoes well, dry and rub all over with peanut oil. Bake the potatoes directly on the rack in the middle of the oven for 1½ hours. The shells should be very hard and crisp.

While the potatoes are baking, in a medium sized bowl combine well the remaining ingredients and set aside. When the potatoes are done, remove from oven and place on a cutting board. Allow to cool for a few minutes until they are easier to handle, and with a very sharp knife, halve the potatoes lengthwise. Be careful, because the insides will be very hot and steam will escape.

Scoop out the insides of the potatoes carefully, leaving the shells as thin as possible, and add potato to the bowl with the other ingredients. Place the shells on a shallow baking dish. With a large spoon, combine the potato mixture well. Do not try to make the mixture perfectly smooth; it is preferable if it is well combined, but slightly lumpy looking. Spoon the mixture evenly into the potato skins, return to the oven and cook for an additional 10–15 minutes, or until the tops are lightly browned. Serves 4

A day without laughter...was a rare occurrence in Toni's Life | York Country Club, '80s

Mushrooms Parmesan
(Fungi alla Parmigiana)

INGREDIENTS

12 mushrooms (1½ to 2 inches in diameter)

3 tbsp. extra-virgin olive oil

1 tbsp. butter

¼ cup chopped shallots

1 large garlic clove

⅓ cup fine fresh bread crumbs (preferably whole wheat)

¼ cup grated Parmesan cheese

1 tbsp. chopped parsley

½ tsp. salt

⅛ tsp. dried oregano

PREPARATION

Clean mushrooms and remove stems. Chop stems into small pieces and set aside. Pour 2 of the 3 tbsp. of olive oil in a shallow baking dish and spread to coat the bottom evenly. Place the mushroom caps open-end up in the dish in a single layer.

Heat the remaining tbsp. of olive oil with the butter in a medium skillet over low heat. Add the chopped mushroom stems, shallots and garlic. Cook slowly until the shallots and mushroom stems are softened and remove from heat.

In a mini-food processor pulse enough bread to measure ⅓ cup. Add the cheese, parsley, salt and oregano to the processor and pulse just until combined. Add this mixture to the skillet and combine gently with the shallot mixture.

Preheat oven to 400 degrees. Divide the stuffing mixture among the mushroom caps evenly, pressing lightly on the stuffing. Bake for 15–20 minutes, or until the mushrooms are tender and the tops are browned.

Note: I like to serve these as a side dish, or as an appetizer, or sometimes just by themselves for my lunch.

Onion & Potato Gratin

INGREDIENTS

4 tbsp. unsalted butter

2 large sweet yellow onions, sliced thinly (should equal 5–6 cups)

½ tsp. salt

¼ tsp. black pepper

1 lb. baking potatoes, peeled and cut into thin (⅛-inch) slices

Additional salt and pepper for sprinkling on potatoes

1 cup half and half

¼ cup (generous) grated Parmigiano Reggiano cheese

¼ cup (generous) grated Gruyère cheese

PREPARATION

Heat the butter in a large heavy skillet over moderate heat. Add the onions, salt and pepper and cook, stirring occasionally, until the onions are very soft and golden. Spoon half of the onions into a gratin dish, spread evenly on the bottom, and top with the sliced potatoes. Sprinkle the potatoes generously with salt and pepper, and top the potatoes with the remaining cooked onions.

Preheat oven to 400 degrees. Pour the half and half over the potato/onion mixture, and then sprinkle the mixture with the two cheeses. Bake the gratin in the preheated oven for 35–40 minutes, or until it is bubbling and a deep golden brown on top. Serves 4

I like to think "inside" the box.

Braised Belgian Endive Gratin

INGREDIENTS

4 Belgian endives (approx. 1 lb. total)

1 tbsp. fresh lemon juice

2 tbsp. unsalted butter, cut into small pieces

¼ tsp. salt

1 tsp. sugar, preferably organic

⅓ cup chicken broth

⅓ cup grated Gruyère cheese

¼ cup panko (Japanese dry bread flakes – a good choice is Sushi Chef® - Baycliff Co.)

PREPARATION

Trim the ends of the endives, but leave the root ends intact, and halve lengthwise. Place the endives cut sides down in a large heavy cooking pot. Add lemon juice, butter pieces, salt, sugar and chicken broth. Cover the pot with a buttered round of wax paper, the buttered side down, top with a lid, and bring to a boil. Reduce heat and simmer, covered, for 20 to 30 minutes, or until the endives are very tender.

Lightly butter a broiler-proof rectangular gratin dish, or other flameproof shallow baking dish, that is big enough to hold the endives in one layer. With a slotted spoon transfer endives to the baking dish, cut sides down. Stir the cheese and bread crumbs together in a small bowl, and sprinkle evenly over endives.

Preheat broiler and broil about 6 inches from the heat until the topping is golden brown, which should take approx. 3–5 minutes. Serves 4

Eggplant Gratin *(Another very easy and yummy recipe from la cucina of mamma mia Toni)*

INGREDIENTS

1 1-lb eggplant, cut into ½ inch slices

Salt for sprinkling on the eggplant

Mayonnaise (approx. ½ cup)

½ cup finely grated Parmesan cheese

½ cup fresh bread crumbs (preferably whole wheat) – use mini-food processor

PREPARATION

Place eggplant slices in a single layer on paper towels and sprinkle with salt. Let eggplant sit for 1 hour, then with more paper towels, blot out the moisture (beads of water will have gathered on the top of the eggplant slices). Note: This is an important step because this procedure removes the bitterness from the eggplant.

Preheat oven to 425 degrees. With a knife, spread both sides of each eggplant slice lightly with mayonnaise. Combine the bread crumbs and cheese on a plate with a fork. Dip each eggplant slice in this mixture on both sides, and place slices on a greased cookie or baking sheet.

Bake the eggplant slices for 15 minutes. Turn over with a spatula and bake for an additional 5–10 minutes, or until eggplant is a deep golden brown on both sides. Serves 2–3

Ciao! Benvenuti alla mia cucina! (Hello, and welcome to my kitchen!)

Sweet Potato Casserole with Pecan Topping

This recipe is a combination of Toni's & my mother-in-law Audrey's recipes for Sweet Potato Casserole, plus my own adaptations – every recipe offers a chance for creativity!

INGREDIENTS

2 lbs. sweet potatoes

½ stick (4 tbsp.) unsalted butter, softened in a large bowl to room temperature

½ cup firmly packed dark brown sugar

2 large eggs

½ cup milk

⅛ tsp. salt

½ tsp. vanilla extract

½ tsp. almond extract

⅛ tsp. ground ginger

⅛ tsp. allspice

¼ tsp. nutmeg

¼ tsp. cinnamon

Topping:

½ cup chopped pecans

2 tbsp. firmly packed dark brown sugar

¼ tsp. cinnamon

PREPARATION

To cook sweet potatoes: In a large saucepan cover the potatoes with cold water (the water should come to about an inch above the potatoes). Bring the water to a boil over moderate heat, and cook the potatoes for 45 minutes, or until they are very tender when tested with a fork. Drain the potatoes in a colander and let them cool until they can be handled, and peel them. Place the potatoes in the bowl containing the softened butter.

With an electric mixer beat the potatoes with the butter until smooth. Add the sugar and beat until the sugar is incorporated. Beat in the eggs, one at a time, until combined. Beat in the milk, salt, extracts and spices, beating until the mixture is well combined.

Preheat the oven to 400 degrees. Butter a casserole dish (I like to use a soufflé dish) and pour the potato mixture into it. Bake in the preheated oven for 30 minutes.

While the potatoes are cooking, make the topping by mixing together all topping ingredients in a small bowl. After the potatoes have baked for ½ hour, remove from the oven, sprinkle the topping evenly over the potatoes, return to the oven and bake for an additional 10 minutes. Serves 5–6

Sue's Tips:

Basil has quite an impressive history. The Greeks regarded basil as their royal herb, and in India, basil was considered to be a sacred herb.

Grab a handful of fresh basil and inhale the aroma. Or get some basil "essential oil" and apply topically. Basil has been known to refresh a fatigued mind and to restore mental clarity and alertness.

Basil also has been known to be an aphrodisiac. Maybe I should have mentioned this attribute first…

Removing Asparagus Stems

When you are trimming asparagus (removing the tough ends) do not cut them off with a knife. To assure that you are removing all of the tough and fibrous portion, here's what you do: Hold each asparagus stalk individually in the middle. With the other hand, break off the end at the point where it breaks off easily. If there is resistance, it means that portion of the asparagus stalk is tough. Keep moving up the stalk until it breaks naturally and easily. Sometimes you will be amazed how much of the asparagus is broken off, and as a result be distressed because you feel as though you are wasting a lot of it. Do not fret, because all you are doing is removing the portion that is not tender nor flavorful and should not be eaten.

Sautéed Zucchini Squash with Tomatoes

INGREDIENTS

2 medium large zucchini squash

1½ tbsp. butter

1 cup chopped fresh tomatoes

2 cloves garlic, finely chopped

½ tsp. salt

½ tsp. dried basil

PREPARATION

Trim ends from zucchini and slice approx. ¼ inch thick. Melt butter over low heat in large skillet. Add zucchini and sauté over low heat until softened but not mushy.

While squash is cooking chop tomatoes to measure one cup and chop garlic. When squash is softened, add tomatoes, garlic, salt and basil to skillet, stirring gently until well combined. Continue cooking for approx. 5 additional minutes, or until tomatoes are softened, but still hold their shape. Serves 2

Asparagus Italian Style

INGREDIENTS

1 lb. asparagus

4 tbsp. extra-virgin olive oil, warmed

2 tbsp. chopped capers

2 tbsp. chopped fresh parsley

4 tbsp. grated Parmesan cheese

4 tbsp. finely chopped Prosciutto ham (best if done in a mini-food processor)

PREPARATION

Steam asparagus until tender but not overcooked. Place equal amount on 4 small plates.

Cook olive oil over very low heat in a small saucepan until just warmed, not hot. Stir in the capers and parsley and spoon an equal amount over each serving of asparagus. Top each serving with equal amount of the Parmesan cheese and Prosciutto ham. Serves 4

Notes: